KIMBELL MASTERPIECE SERIES

Poussin's *Sacrament of Ordination*

HISTORY, FAITH, AND THE SACRED LANDSCAPE

JONATHAN W. UNGLAUB

Kimbell Art Museum
Fort Worth

DISTRIBUTED BY
Yale University Press
New Haven and London

KIMBELL MASTERPIECE SERIES

Published by the Kimbell Art Museum, Fort Worth
Distributed by Yale University Press, New Haven and London

Kimbell Art Museum
3333 Camp Bowie Boulevard
Fort Worth, Texas 76107-2792
www.kimbellart.org

Yale University Press
302 Temple Street
P.O. Box 209040
New Haven, Connecticut 06520-9040
www.yalebooks.com/art

Produced by the Publications Department of the Kimbell Art Museum
Megan Smyth, Manager of Publications
With thanks to Robert LaPrelle, Judy Mahan, and Mark Marr

Designed by Tom Dawson

Printed in Canada by Friesens

ISBN 978-0-300-19591-0
Library of Congress Control Number: 2013950111

FRONT COVER AND FRONTISPIECE: Nicolas Poussin (French, 1594–1665, active in Italy), *The Sacrament of Ordination (Christ Presenting the Keys to Saint Peter)* (details), c. 1636–40. Oil on canvas, 37¾ x 47⅞ in. (95.9 x 121.6 cm). Kimbell Art Museum, Fort Worth

BACK COVER: Nicolas Poussin (French, 1594–1665, active in Italy), *Self-Portrait*, 1650. Oil on canvas, 38⅝ x 29⅛ in. (98 x 74 cm). Musée du Louvre, Paris

Contents

Introduction   2

"Pupil of His Museum and of His House": Poussin
   and Cassiano dal Pozzo   5

"Seven Sacrosanct Treasures": The Two Series
   of Sacraments   17

Staging the Ordination: Papal Supremacy and the
   Sistine Chapel   35

Peter, Paul, and the Early Church   49

Paul and the Dal Pozzo *Ordination*   55

The Sacred Landscape and the Apostolic Mission   65

Epilogue   79

Acknowledgments   85

Notes   86

Bibliography   94

Photograph Credits   102

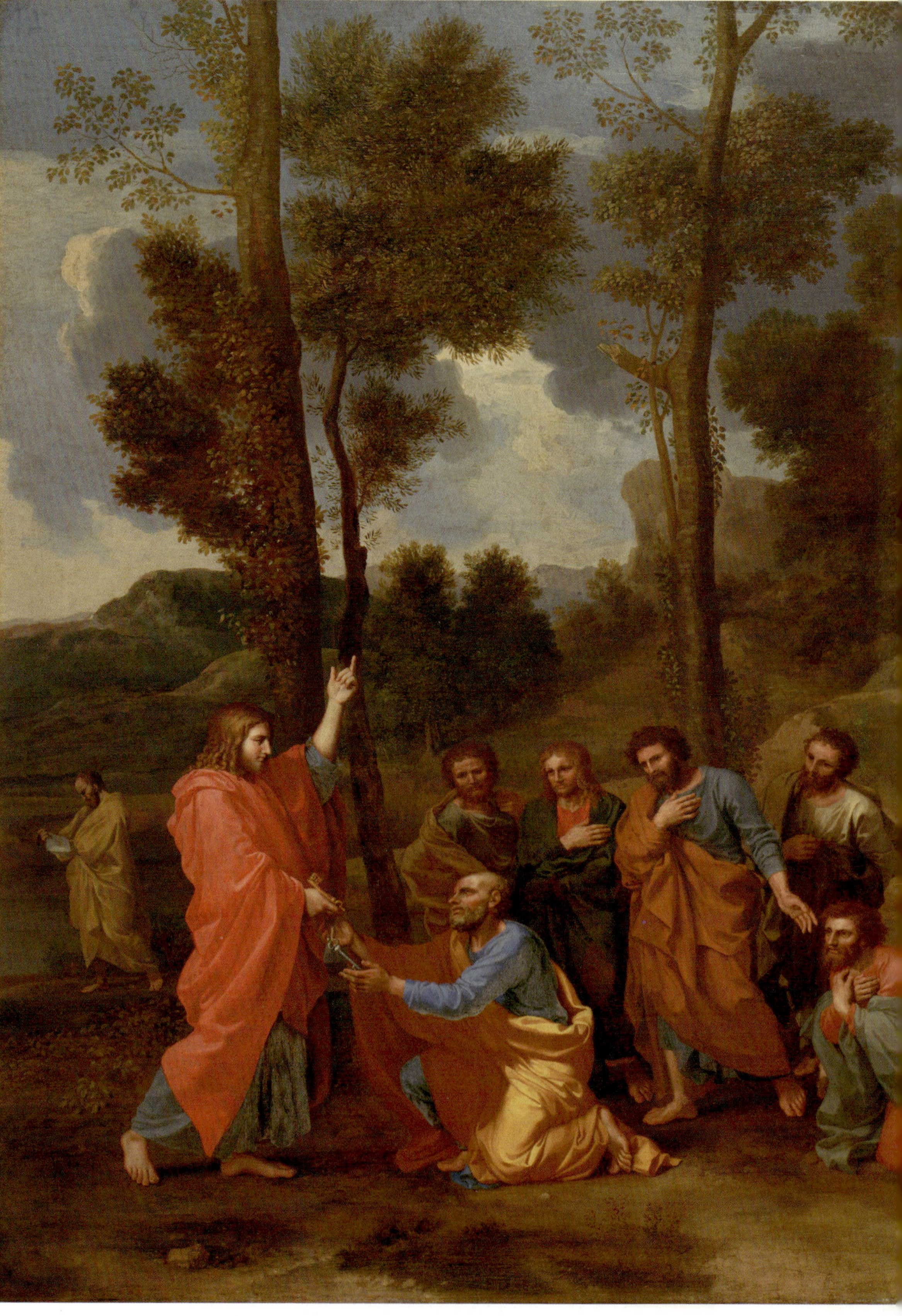

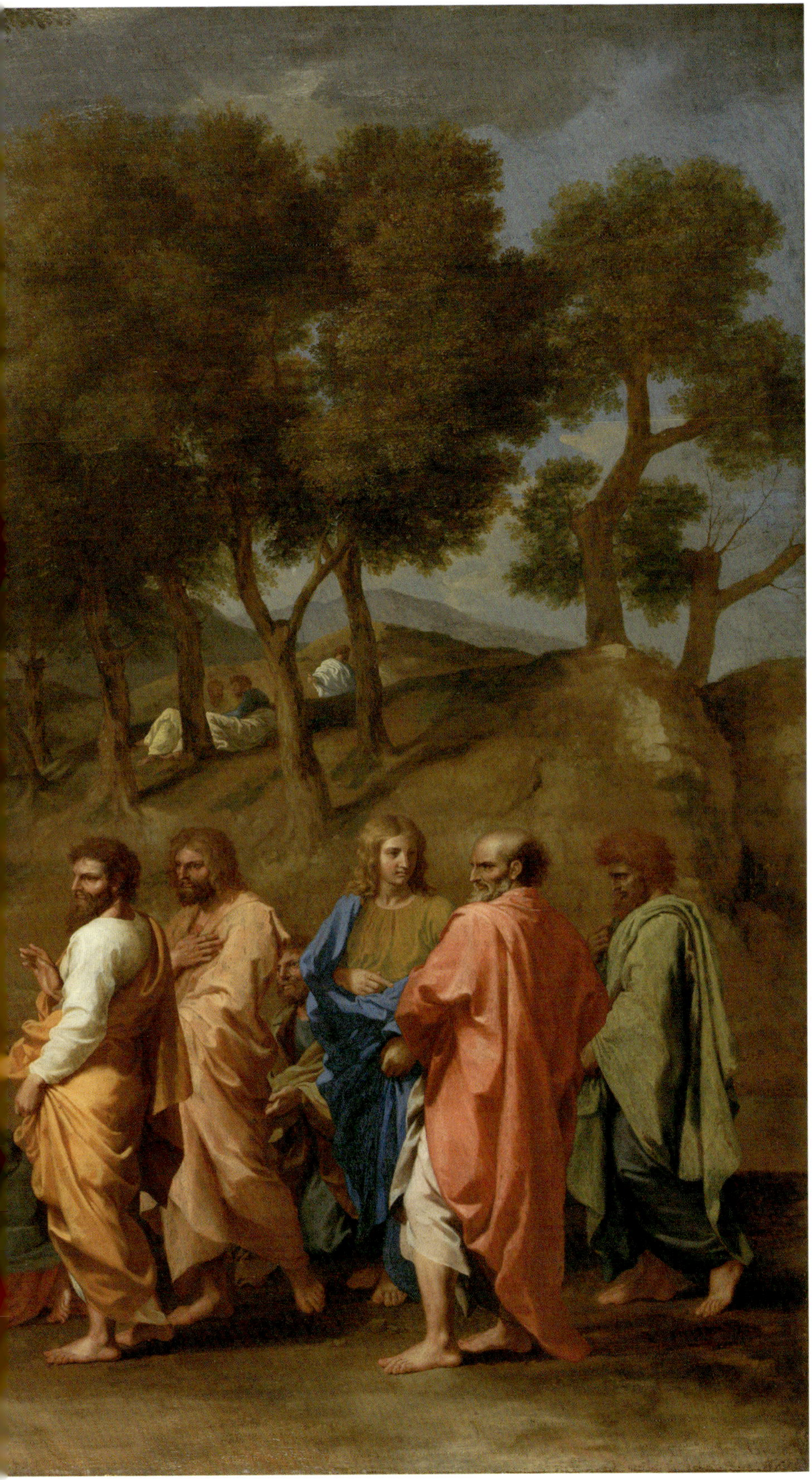

Fig. 1. Nicolas Poussin (French, 1594–1665, active in Italy), *The Sacrament of Ordination (Christ Presenting the Keys to Saint Peter),* c. 1636–40. Oil on canvas, 37¾ x 47⅞ in. (95.9 x 121.6 cm). Kimbell Art Museum, Fort Worth

Introduction

NICOLAS POUSSIN (1594–1665) IS BEST KNOWN AS THE FOUNDER OF FRENCH CLASSICISM, though he actually spent almost his entire career in Rome. While his works incorporated some of the dynamic visual rhetoric of the nascent Roman baroque style, Poussin primarily looked to the past, to the High Renaissance masters Titian, Leonardo da Vinci, and Raphael, and revered, above all else, Greek and Roman antiquity. He so thoroughly absorbed classical art and was so steeped in ancient history, myth, and topography that his paintings seem like re-creations from that era. He applied this knowledge not only to the illustration of exemplary classical and biblical tales, but also to a new, ambitious conception of landscape. Nature, restructured through an innate sense of rational order, imbued historical, religious, and mythological themes with a universal resonance.

Simply scanning *The Sacrament of Ordination* (fig. 1), acquired by the Kimbell Art Museum in 2011, one can readily discern the rigor and harmony of Poussin's art. Before the commanding figure of Jesus, the artist arranges the apostles into a frieze across the foreground with a rhythmic variation in pose, orientation, and movement. All the figures are dressed in appropriate ancient garments and exhibit clearly delineated gestures and expressions as they venerate the Lord and his designated successor, Peter. Far from being a mere backdrop, the hills and trees reanimate the foreground ensemble. Two slender but lofty trunks punctuate the encounter between Christ and the genuflecting Saint Peter, as well as the related, secondary grouping of a slightly bowed disciple grasping his breast in reverence and extending his hand to an even more humbly prostrate companion. Above the rocky knoll to the right is a grove of less imposing trees that recede in parallel rows, like the subtly animated figures before them. The way Poussin achieves balance and order while avoiding rigidity is a defining feature of his classicism. His *Self-Portrait* of a few years later, made for his long-time friend and patron Paul Fréart de Chantelou (1609–1694), exemplifies this sense of prevailing logic (fig. 2). As the artist pivots his head, the horizontals and verticals of the framed canvases arrayed behind him subtly align with his eyes, hairline, head, and left flank, embedding his form in the matrix. On one of the canvases, a female allegory of painting converges

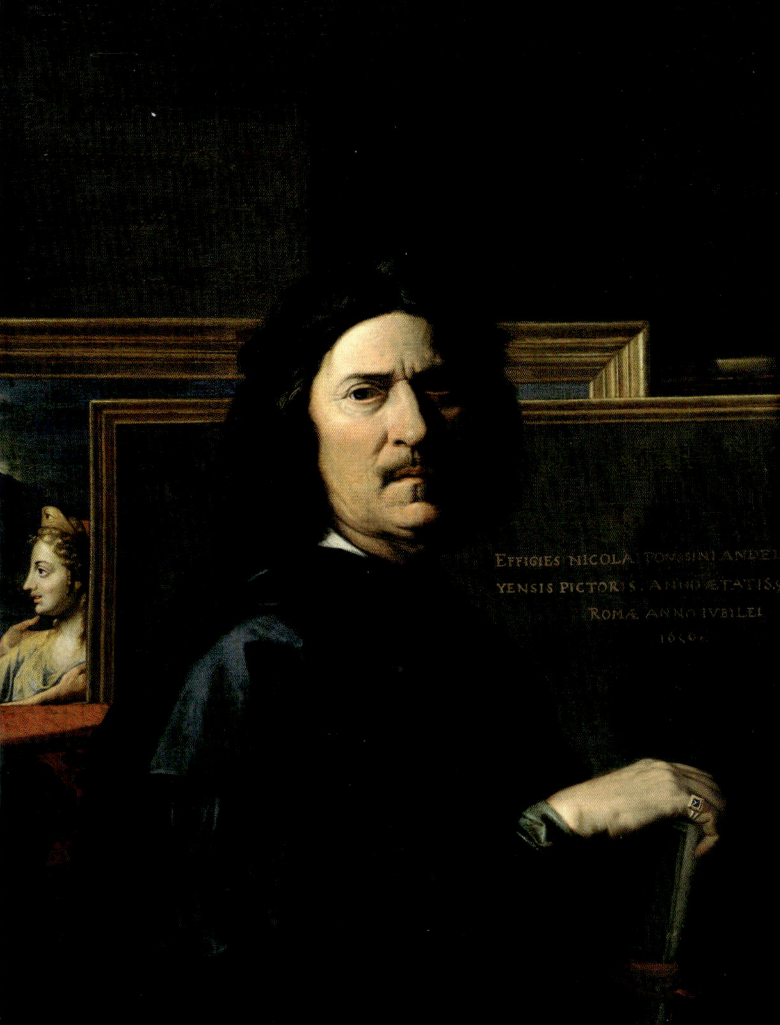

Fig. 2. Nicolas Poussin (French, 1594–1665, active in Italy), *Self-Portrait*, 1650. Oil on canvas, 38⅜ x 29⅛ in. (98 x 74 cm). Musée du Louvre, Paris

with a pair of embracing arms, a motif Poussin's biographer Giovanni Pietro Bellori identified as "friendship and the love of painting."[1] With the intimacy of Poussin and Chantelou's relationship distilled to an emblem, one can almost read in Poussin's gaze what he had earlier written to the friend he fixes therein: "My nature compels me to seek out and love things that are well ordered and flee confusion."[2] Yet Poussin's fundamental understanding of painting as an intellectual endeavor, grounded in the study of classical culture, owed much more to an earlier friendship with the patron who commissioned the *Ordination*: Cassiano dal Pozzo (1588–1657).

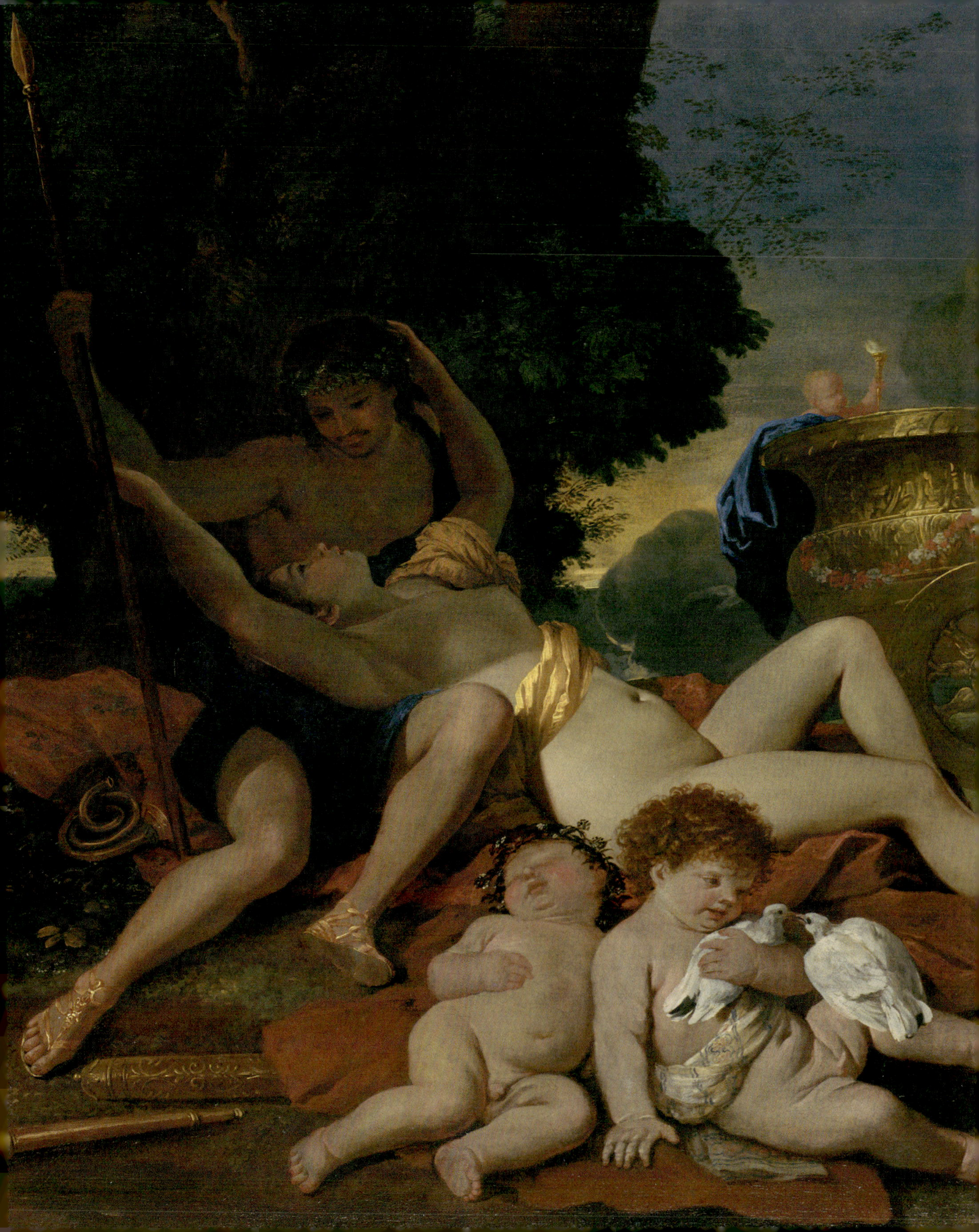

"Pupil of His Museum and of His House": Poussin and Cassiano dal Pozzo

POUSSIN WAS BORN IN 1594 IN THE TOWN LES ANDELYS IN NORMANDY.[3] AS A YOUTH, HE enrolled in the Jesuit Latin school at Rouen, where he gained a solid literary education. Though he associated with a few artists, he was never formally apprenticed and learned much from studying engravings after the Renaissance masters and antiquities. Transferring to Paris in the later 1610s, Poussin gained entry to the court of the Queen Regent, Marie de' Médicis. There, he attracted the attention of the famous court poet Giambattista Marino (1569–1625). Although Marino only commissioned a handful of drawings from Poussin, his belief in the mutually expressive aims of painting and poetry had a profound influence on the young artist.[4] As Marino departed France, he encouraged his new friend to travel to Rome; Poussin accepted, following in 1624.

Rome was the European art capital, attracting legions of foreign artists who came to study or settle. It was also the diplomatic center of Catholic Europe. Embassies supplied a rotating aristocratic clientele exploiting stints in Rome to build collections back home. The unique nature of the papal court catapulted a different family into prominence upon the election of each new pope, and every fleeting dynasty scrambled to leave its mark on Rome through conspicuous art patronage. This cyclical largesse seemed particularly auspicious with the elevation of Maffeo Barberini to the papacy as Urban VIII in 1623, and indeed he and his family did patronize art on an unprecedented scale.[5] Few could have foreseen, however, this enlightened man of letters submitting to the entrenched factions within the Counter-Reformation Church, which ultimately resulted in the infamous heresy trial of Galileo.[6] The inquisition would even censure Marino's poetry, but only after his death in 1625.[7] By then, Marino had introduced Poussin to Cardinal Francesco Barberini (1597–1679), the pope's nephew, and to the cardinal's secretary, Cassiano dal Pozzo, both of whom would become significant patrons of the painter. The fruits of their support would have to wait, however, as the cardinal departed on official missions to France later that year and to Spain in the following year, with Dal Pozzo as their chronicler.[8]

Nicolas Poussin, *Venus and Adonis*, detail of fig. 3

Marino is reported to have informed Cardinal Barberini that the young French artist had "the fury of the devil in him," signifying both poetic furor and personal intensity.[9] Such passion infuses Poussin's earliest works, especially mythological scenes like the Kimbell's *Venus and Adonis* (fig. 3), where the mythic lovers from Ovid's *Metamorphoses* embrace with the frank sensuality of Marino's licentious verse.[10] Yet poignancy tempers the overt carnality, as the tryst will be their last. In the distance, cupids ready the swan-hitched chariot for the goddess's departure, and the hound awaits the boar hunt that will seal Adonis's fate. Under the influence of Venetian masters like Titian, richly applied pigment morphs into yielding flesh, caressing shadows, and glimmering atmosphere; the painterly surface itself pulses and radiates desire.

Fig. 3. Nicolas Poussin (French, 1594–1665, active in Italy), *Venus and Adonis*, c. 1628–29. Oil on canvas, 38¾ x 53 in. (98.5 x 134.6 cm). Kimbell Art Museum, Fort Worth

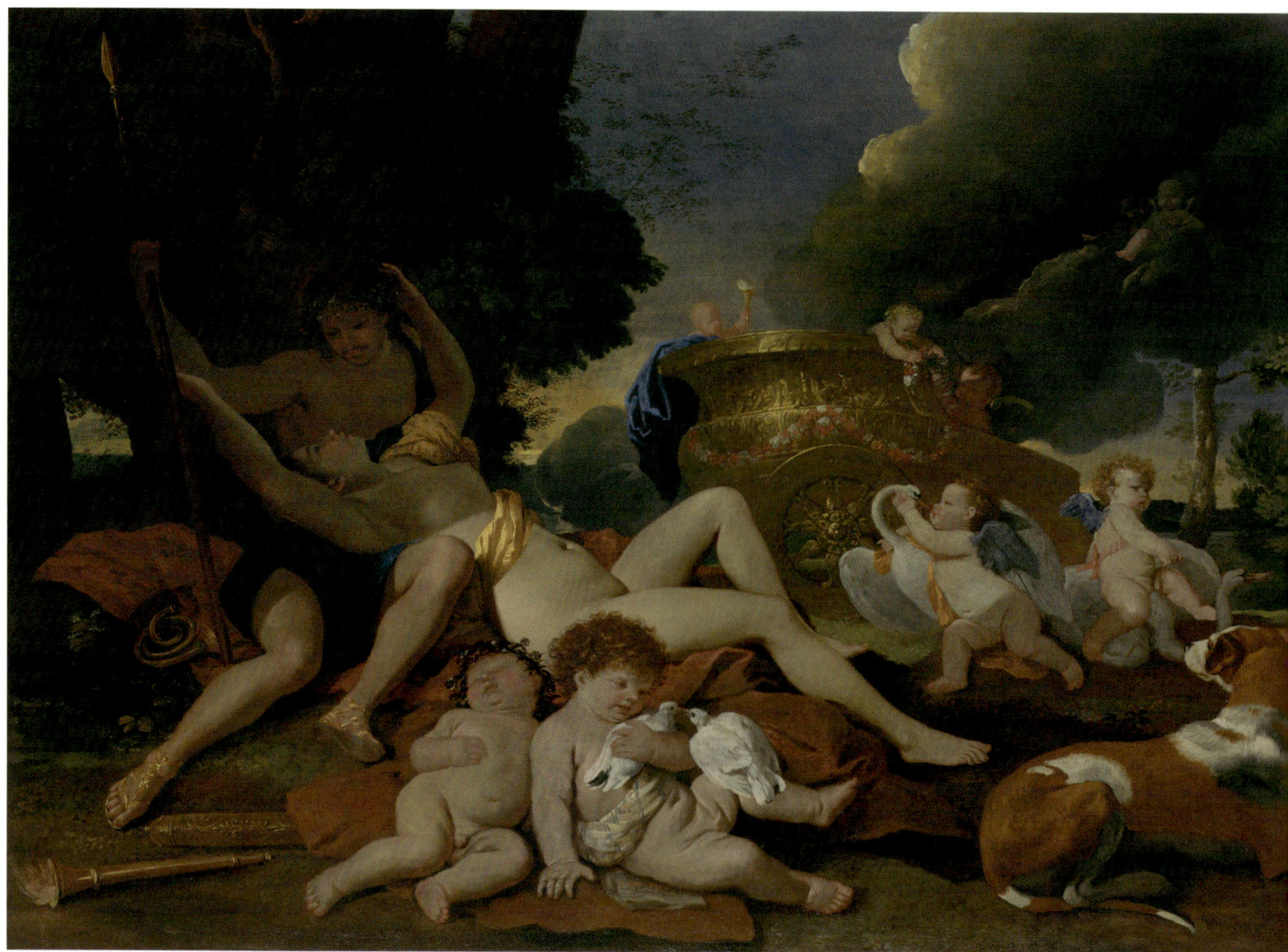

The later inventories of Cassiano dal Pozzo's collection indicate that he owned, and perhaps commissioned, the *Venus and Adonis*.[11] Ironically, Poussin's earliest surviving letter to Dal Pozzo apologizes for being unable to greet him in person owing to a serious infirmity, which contemporary sources reveal to have been a disease originating in just such venereal embraces: "mal di francia," as syphilis was dubbed in Italy.[12] Letters from Cassiano to a Bolognese physician seeking medications for an afflicted "painter friend" document his devotion to Poussin.[13] Yet medical assistance was the least of Dal Pozzo's contributions to Poussin's development. He would provide enduring patronage and, just as importantly, tutelage in various fields of learning essential to the painter's style.

One of the most enlightened patrons in seventeenth-century Rome, Cassiano dal Pozzo was born in Turin in 1588 (fig. 4).[14] As a youth, he moved to Pisa, where his uncle Carl Antonio

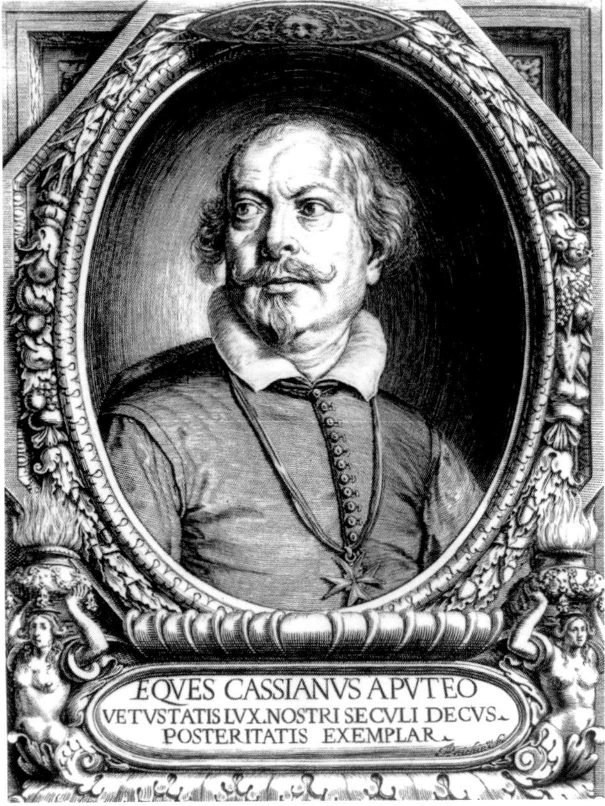

Fig. 4. Pietro Anichini (Italian, active 17th century), *Cassiano dal Pozzo*, 1664, engraving. After Jan van den Hoecke, from Carlo Roberto Dati's *Delle Lodi del Commendatore Cassiano dal Pozzo*

dal Pozzo was archbishop, and studied at its renowned university. Groomed for a legal career in the papal *curia*, Cassiano devoted himself almost entirely to intellectual pursuits upon arriving in Rome in 1612. As a central participant in the "Republic of Letters," an epistolary network among European intellectuals, he promoted the empirical study of nature and antiquity. He also gained membership into the preeminent early scientific society, the Accademia dei Lincei, which had sponsored Galileo. Dal Pozzo's numerous correspondents sought both his scholarly opinion and access to Barberini patronage, which he was in a position to broker after being appointed to Cardinal Francesco's household in 1623 and becoming his personal secretary in 1629.[15]

Dal Pozzo's most important scholarly pursuit was an ambitious two-pronged graphic campaign to record systematically the wonders of the natural world and the vestiges of ancient Rome's artistic and material culture. This enterprise, resulting in dozens of bound folios containing thousands of high-quality drawings by teams of artists, was collectively known as the Museo Cartaceo, or Paper Museum. Though it contained many drawings after well-known antiquities, including the Column of Trajan and the Ara Pacis, the full purview of the Paper Museum extended to all types of ancient Roman artifacts—funerary sculptures, sarcophagus reliefs, mosaics and wall paintings, decorative

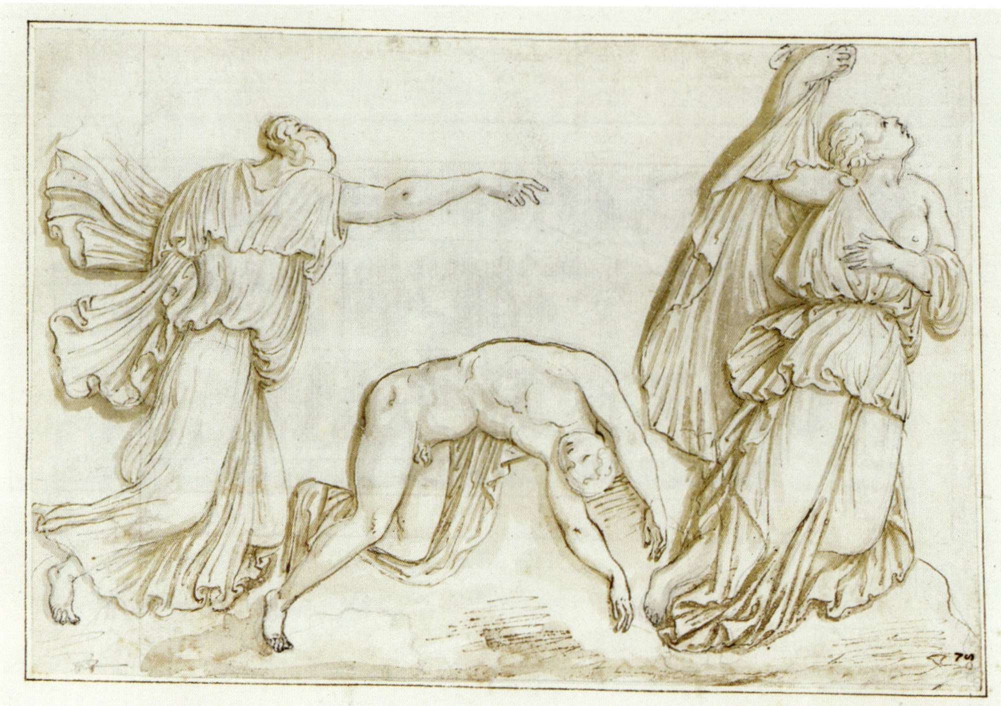

Fig. 5. *Studies after a Niobid Relief*, from the Museo Cartaceo of Cassiano dal Pozzo, 17th century, pen and wash. The Royal Collection, Windsor Castle

and household objects, cult figures and ritual paraphernalia, inscriptions, architectural ruins, and reconstructions of ancient buildings. The collection was truly archaeological in the modern sense, in that the paramount criterion was an object's documentary evidence of ancient Roman custom, costume, and ceremony rather than solely its artistic quality.[16]

Several of Poussin's own studies after the antique may derive directly from the Museo Cartaceo (fig. 5), especially those sheets that compile motifs from several sources.[17] Such consultation accounts for the antiquarian exactitude of Roman costume and paraphernalia in his paintings. Dal Pozzo was quick to realize that Poussin was blessed with a powerful intellect that made him an ideal beneficiary not only of the Museo Cartaceo, but also of his extensive library and the even greater resources of the Barberini library. Cassiano would later enlist Poussin in scholarly and art-theoretical projects based on manuscripts in these collections. Poussin confided to his friend and eventual biographer, the antiquarian and art theorist Giovanni Pietro Bellori, that he "was the pupil of his museum and of his house."[18]

Dal Pozzo's palace, located on the Via dei Chiavari, housed the Museo Cartaceo, his library, and his burgeoning collections of antiquities, natural curiosities, and art, featuring several of the Tuscan and French artists favored by the Barberini, including Pietro da Cortona, Valentin de Boulogne, and Simon Vouet. With the sustained acquisition of some two dozen Poussins over the next two decades, the Dal Pozzo collection became one of the most significant in Rome.[19] Nonetheless, it was a commission from Cardinal Barberini for a painting of *The Death of Germanicus* that provided Poussin with his first opportunity to showcase the antiquarian knowledge that he had mastered with the help of Dal Pozzo. The work illustrates the vigil of the great Roman general Germanicus and the oath among his faithful legions to avenge his death, which was likely orchestrated by the Emperor Tiberius (fig. 6). Poussin's immersion in ancient Roman culture is everywhere apparent—in the costumes, armor, sandals, and standards. Moreover, the composition itself aptly derives from a sarcophagus relief of the death of Meleager, mourned by his beloved Atalanta.[20]

Fig. 6. Nicolas Poussin (French, 1594–1665, active in Italy), *The Death of Germanicus*, c. 1627–28. Oil on canvas, 58¼ x 78 in. (148 x 198 cm). Minneapolis Institute of Arts

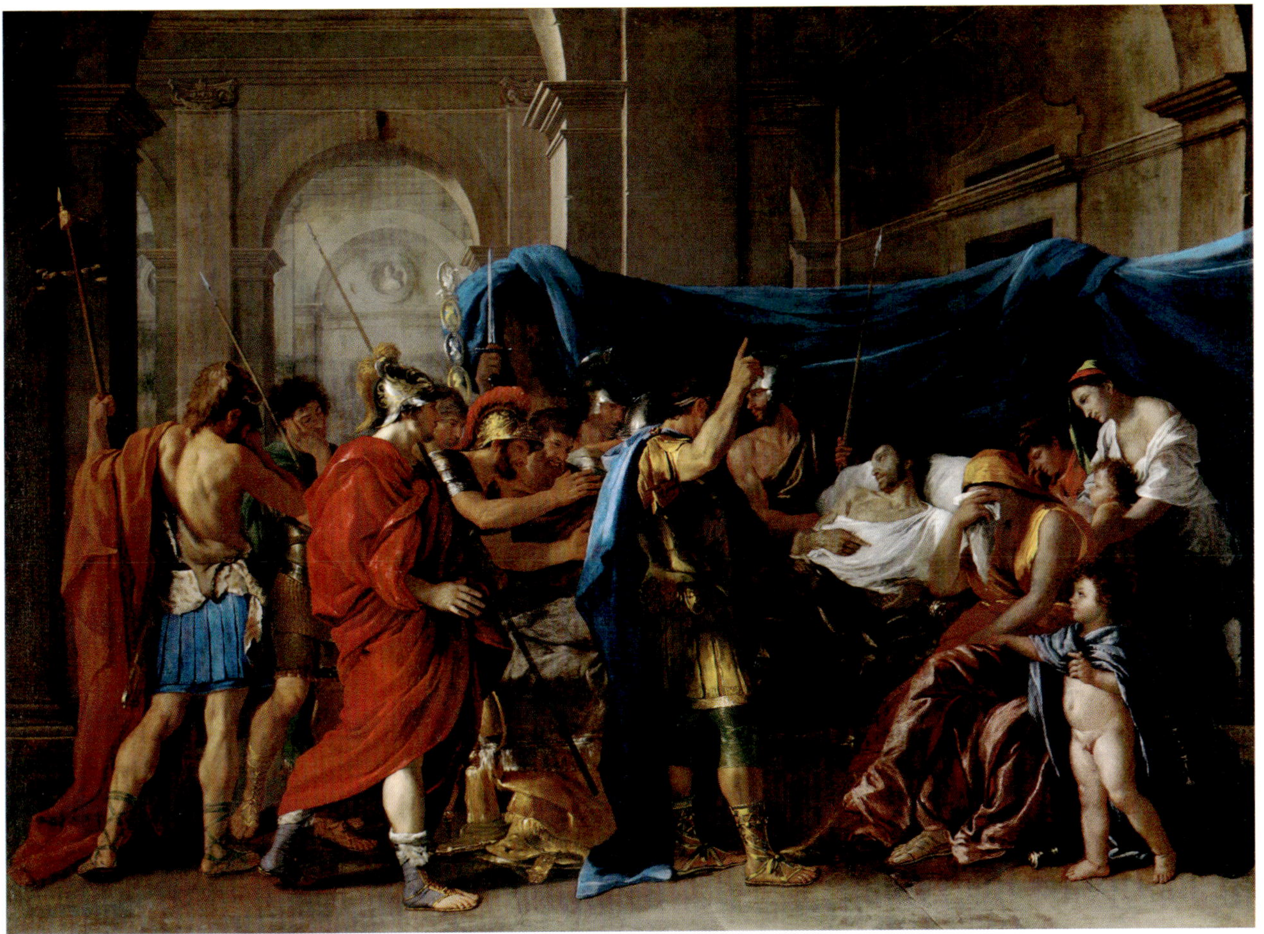

The *Germanicus* exhibits another legacy of classical culture: Poussin consciously emulates the compact, causal dramatic structure of ancient tragedy, pivoting on a reversal that afflicts its noble but flawed hero. He depicts a crescendo of emotion, from the visible consternation of the soldiers to the bereaved expressions of the family members, while Germanicus's wife, Agrippina, veils her face to express ineffable grief—a trope originating in the legendary ancient painting of the *Sacrifice of Iphigenia* by Timanthes. Conforming to the Roman historian Tacitus's account, Poussin shows the expiring general bemoaning his fate as an invincible warrior felled through the dastardly deception of poisoning. Scanning the range of emotions from desolation to defiance, one could hardly imagine a more vivid enactment of Germanicus's charge: "Strangers will bewail Germanicus: you will avenge him— if you loved me and not my fortune."[21] As Charles Dempsey has shown, *The Death of Germanicus* pioneered a new pictorial type later known as the "tableau," wherein the self-contained format of a gallery picture showcases a single, unified, dramatic event. What sets Poussin apart from his predecessors is his commitment to representing the full scope of the depicted subject, structured in an internally coherent and complete way.[22]

For all the classical rigor of *The Death of Germanicus*, Poussin's technique itself is somewhat the opposite: painterly, luminous, and expressive—Venetian in essence. The success of the picture

Fig. 7. Nicolas Poussin (French, 1594–1665, active in Italy), *Diana and Endymion*, c. 1630. Oil on canvas, 48 x 66½ in. (121.9 x 168.9 cm). Detroit Institute of Arts. Founders Society Purchase, General Membership Fund

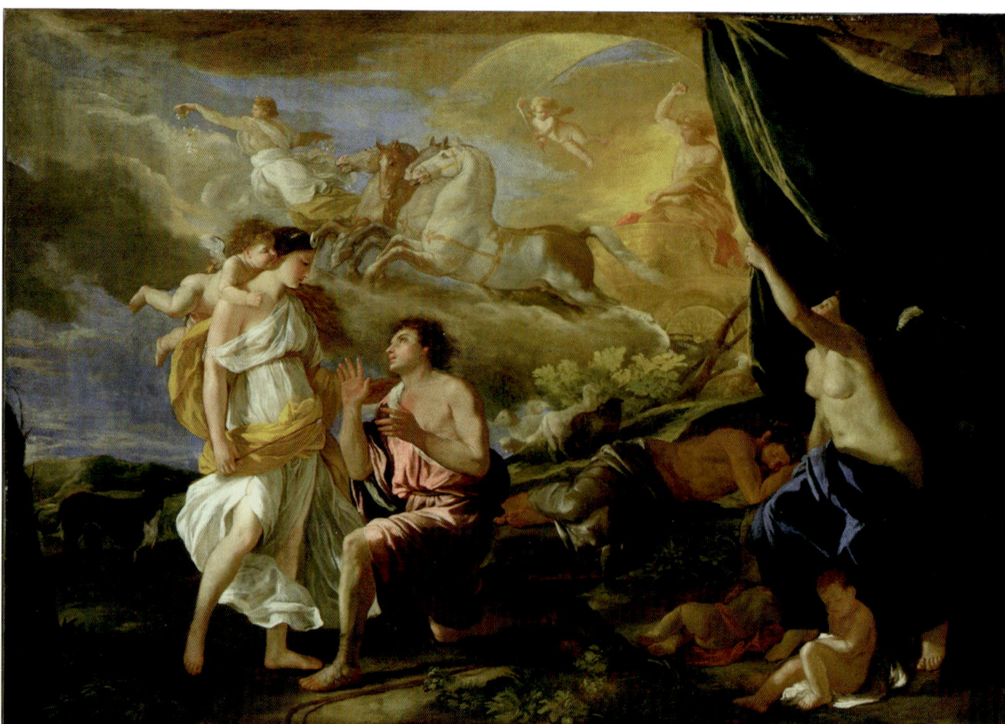

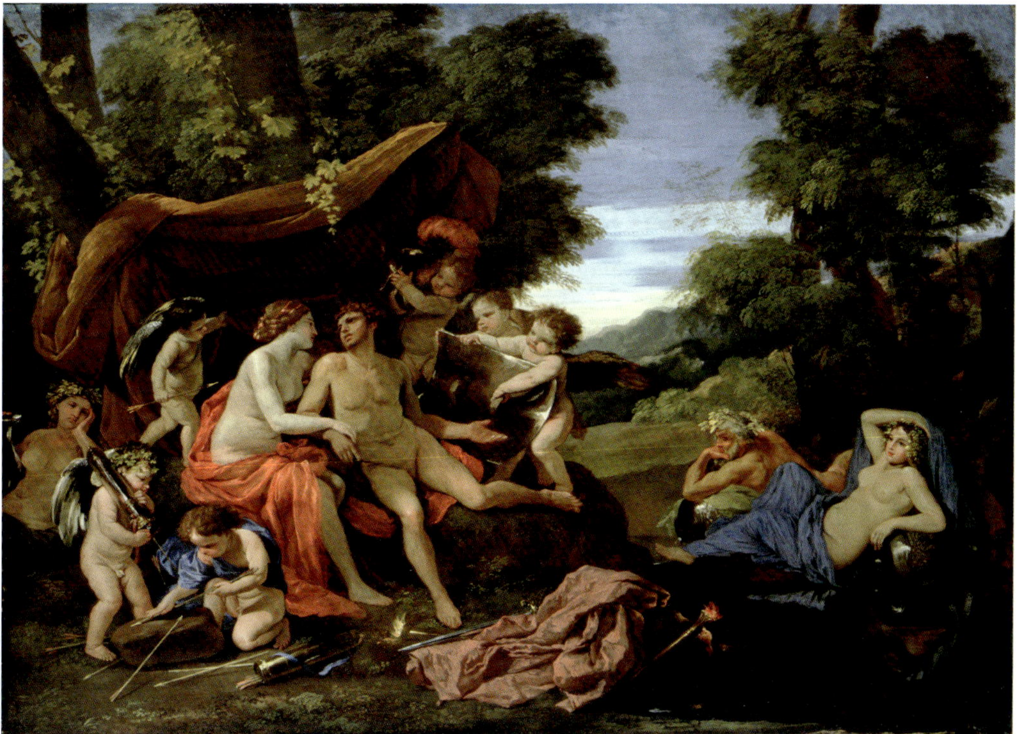

Fig. 8. Nicolas Poussin (French, 1594–1665, active in Italy), *Mars and Venus*, c. 1628. Oil on canvas, 61 x 84⅛ in. (154.9 x 213.7 cm). Museum of Fine Arts, Boston. Augustus Hemenway Fund and Arthur William Wheelright Fund

with its patron secured Poussin the most coveted of commissions—an altarpiece in the recently completed Saint Peter's Basilica, *The Martyrdom of Saint Erasmus*. Although reasonably well received, the altarpiece failed to generate many other lucrative public commissions for Poussin.[23] Instead, he focused on smaller-scale pictures—often Bacchic scenes or amorous myths drawn from Ovid's *Metamorphoses*—for private clients. Despite the erotic subject matter, Poussin often flaunted convention to emphasize the deferral or impossibility of sensual fulfillment. In *Diana and Endymion*, Poussin avoids the nocturnal tryst between the lunar goddess and mortal lover—eternally slumbering to preserve his youth and beauty—and instead poignantly captures their last mutual gaze (fig. 7). The impossible embrace between the imploring shepherd and the ravishing, but chaste, deity mimes that of Mary Magdalene confronting the resurrected Christ, who warns her not to touch him ("Noli me tangere"). Night draws back the curtains, as Apollo's streaking chariot signals the eternity of daily cycles lost to consciousness.[24]

In another of his mythological paintings, *Mars and Venus*, Poussin conceives of the goddess as the embodiment of natural generation—as described in the Roman philosopher Lucretius's didactic poem *De rerum natura*—who conquers a decidedly androgynous and emasculated god of war with the "ever-living wound of love" (fig. 8). As the most ambitious of Poussin's early works for Cassiano dal Pozzo, there is an acknowledgement here of the mortal consequence of venereal domination,

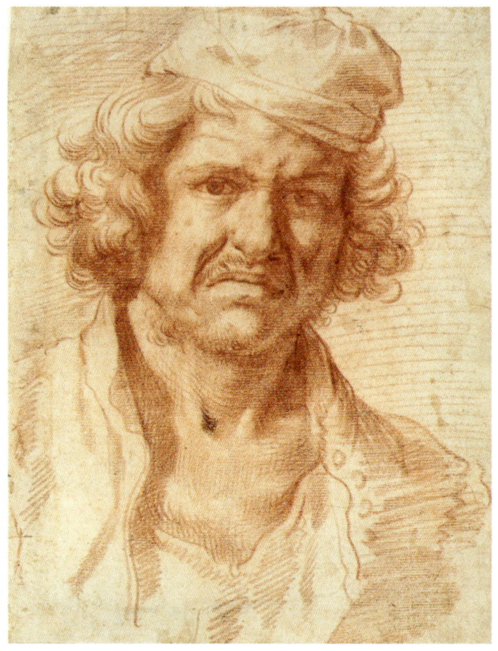

Fig. 9. Nicolas Poussin (French, 1594–1665, active in Italy), *Self-Portrait*, c. 1630. Red chalk, 10⅛ x 7¾ in. (25.6 x 19.7 cm). British Museum, London

Fig. 10. Nicolas Poussin (French, 1594–1665, active in Italy), *The Realm of Flora*, 1630–31. Oil on canvas, 51⅝ x 71¼ in. (131 x 181 cm). Gemäldegalerie Alte Meister, Staatliche Kunstsammlungen, Dresden

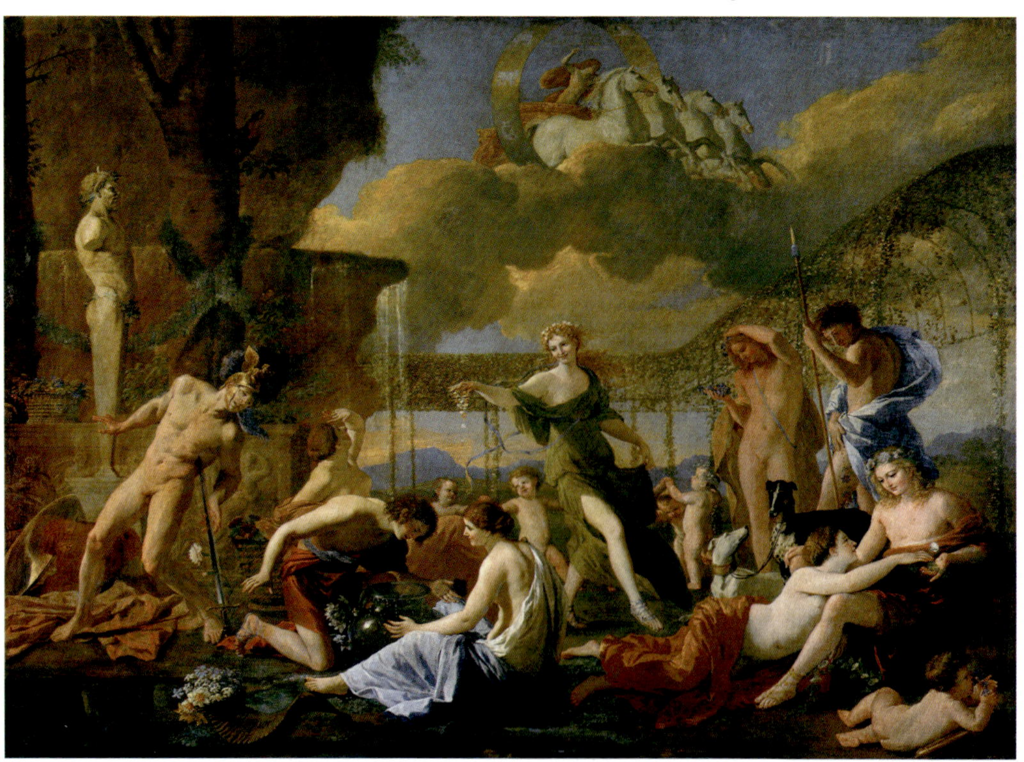

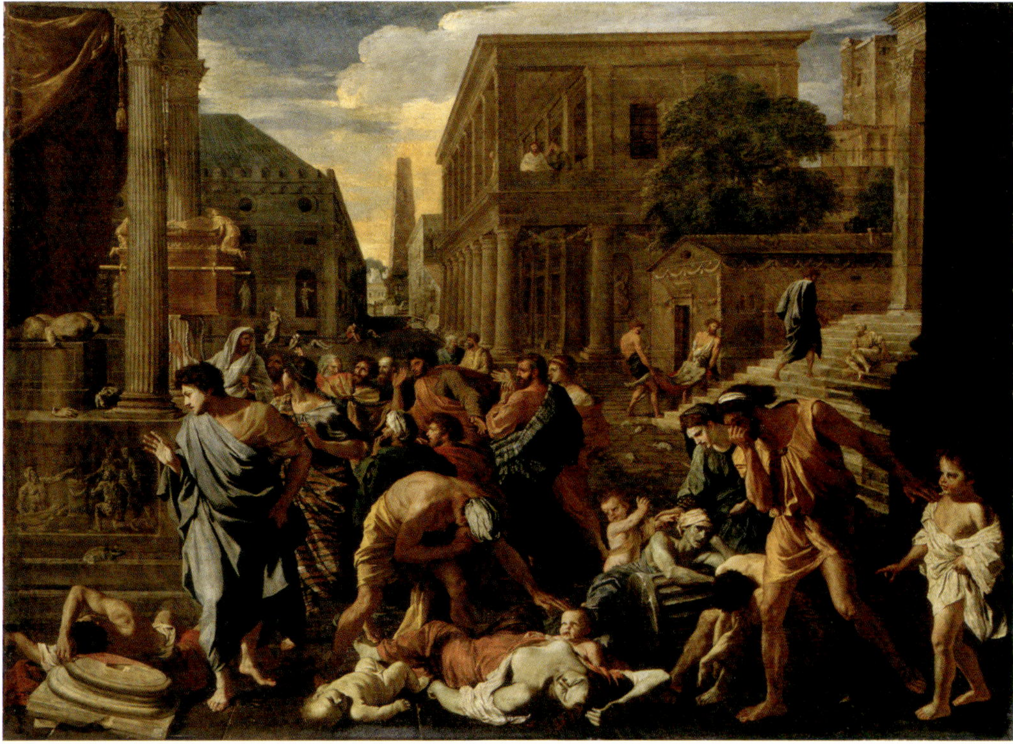

Fig. 11. Nicolas Poussin (French, 1594–1665, active in Italy), *The Plague at Ashdod*, 1630. Oil on canvas, 58¼ x 78 in. (148 x 198 cm). Musée du Louvre, Paris

sublimated into an ideal of beauty and artistic fecundity.[25] This is the message of a self-portrait in chalk that likely dates to about 1629, during Poussin's most severe bout with syphilis (fig. 9).[26] The rugged, weary countenance also conveys melancholy, the temperament most conducive to artistic inspiration.

The theme of amorous deferral and loss present in many of Poussin's paintings from the 1630s culminates in *The Realm of Flora*—a garden ensemble of Ovidian lovers whose tragic demise resulted in floral transformations (fig. 10). These love-death themes are the legacy of Marino and his followers but may also have had personal relevance.[27] After a nearly fatal bout of syphilis-related infirmities, Poussin was nursed back to health by the Dughet family, from whom he gained a wife, Anne-Marie, two brothers—his secretary and engraver, Jean, and the landscape painter, Gaspard—and an outlook of domestic tranquility that nurtured artistic efflorescence.[28]

In the painting produced in tandem with *The Realm of Flora*, *The Plague at Ashdod*, Poussin attains a level of unity and cohesion that would come to define his approach to pictorial narrative (fig. 11).[29] After the Philistines pillaged the Ark of the Covenant and installed it in the Temple of Dagon, God punished the desecrators by toppling the temple's idol and unleashing a pestilence that decimated the population of Ashdod. Poussin stages the story within distinct spaces of the pictorial

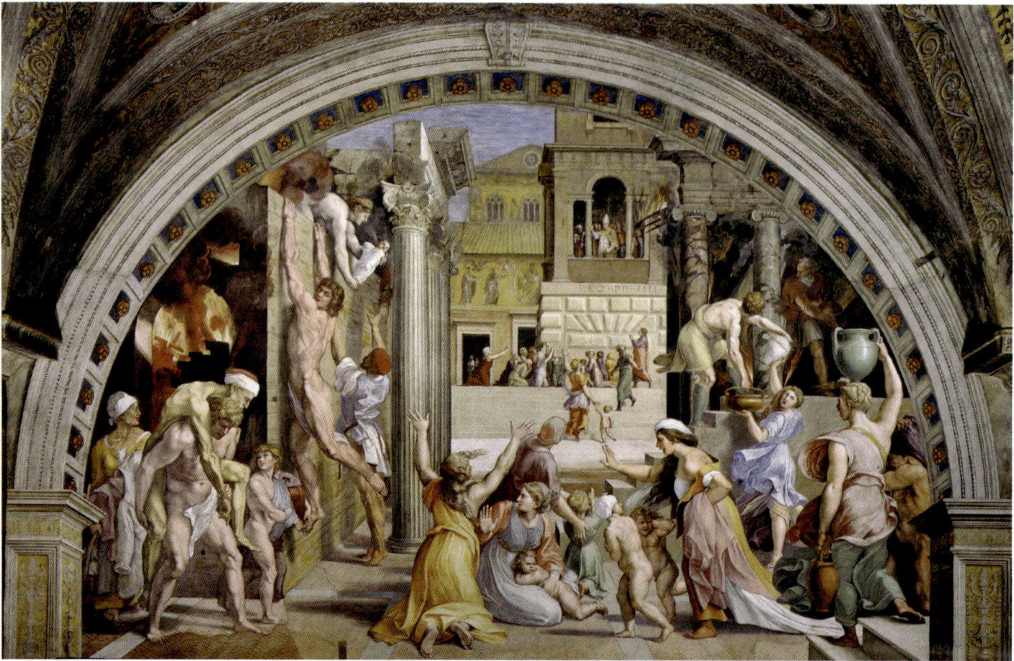

Fig. 12. Raphael (Italian, 1483–1520), *The Fire in the Borgo*, c. 1514. Fresco, 194⅞ x 286⅝ in. (495 x 728 cm). "Stanza dell' Incendio," Vatican Museums, Vatican City

field. In the middle ground, the Philistines react in horror to the sudden destruction of their god. The larger consequence of divine punition unfolds across the foreground, as figures respond in terror and desolation to the effects of the plague. Poussin encapsulates horror in the detail of the dead mother whose orphaned infant desperately attempts to nurse. The motif had precedents in an ancient painting of a siege by Timanthes and in Raphael's engraving *The Plague of the Phrygians*. Poussin reinvents convention by modeling the mother's sprawling cadaver on two ancient statues that deal with divine punishment: the *Dying Amazon* and the *Laocoön*. Only the charitable acts of alms and burial in the far distance counteract the ethically corrosive effects of idolatry.[30]

Poussin situates the complex drama in an imposing perspectival cityscape, conforming to the generic scenography that the ancient architectural theorist Vitruvius recommends for tragedy. In doing so, Poussin follows the example of Raphael, who devised a similarly grand architectural set for his fresco *The Fire in the Borgo* (fig. 12). Within this unified space, Raphael distills the conflagration into distinct figural episodes of flight, fire fighting, and desperate entreaty, which resolve in the papal benediction in the middle ground that will miraculously extinguish the flames. The arrangement of the complex drama within the tragic stage set correlates conceptually to the plot structure formulated in Aristotle's *Poetics*, in which actions build toward a climactic reversal: the divine punishment of idolatrous despoilers or papal salvation from disaster.[31] In the case of *Ashdod*, the cathartic effect of tragedy was highly relevant, as the bubonic plague itself descended the Italian peninsula in 1630–31, sparing, but nonetheless terrifying, Rome.[32]

Following *The Plague at Ashdod*, Poussin increasingly specialized in tableaux featuring narratives from history, the Bible, and classical literature. He aimed to achieve the richest and clearest exposition of a subject, constructing the pictorial field as an ample stage set defined by grand architecture or imposing landscape elements, as the story required. Within this space, he would strategically place distinct groups of figures, modest in scale but monumental in conception, whose highly calibrated gestures and expressions enact the full scope of the unfolding drama, anticipating or responding to an instance of climax or reversal.[33] While Raphael's works offered compositional paradigms, the vigorous movement of individual figures increasingly responded to the theoretical principles of Leonardo da Vinci. Dal Pozzo, who was overseeing the long-awaited publication of Da Vinci's *Trattato della pittura* (Treatise on Painting), enlisted Poussin to design illustrations for the precepts on bodily motion. Though the project would only reach fruition in 1651, Poussin's study of Leonardo in the 1630s helped imbue his relatively small-scale figures with their capacity for intense dramatic action.[34]

Increasingly, Poussin's paintings found their way back to Paris, establishing his reputation in his homeland. One of his two versions of *The Rape of the Sabines* was painted for Duc Emanuele de Crequis, the French ambassador to the Holy See.[35] Upon his death, the picture entered the collection of the first minister to Louis XIII, Cardinal de Richelieu, arguably the most powerful man in Europe and an influential arbiter of taste and culture.[36] Soon after, Richelieu commissioned from Poussin a series of Bacchanals depicting the triumphs of the sylvan gods Bacchus, Pan, and Silenus to adorn his new château. In *The Triumph of Pan*, Poussin imposes a rigorous compositional matrix, punctuated by the rhythmic pattern of Titianesque trees, upon the manic choreography of satyrs, fauns, and Bacchantes inspired by engravings after Raphael and Giulio Romano (fig. 13). As the lush Venetian palette of the earlier *Venus and Adonis* and *Diana and Endymion* yields to the lapidary classicism of late Raphael, these wanton figures exude no more sensuousness than the exquisitely rendered vases, masks, and thyrsi that litter the foreground. As such, the Richelieu Bacchanals epitomized the antiquarian spirit of the Museo Cartaceo.[37]

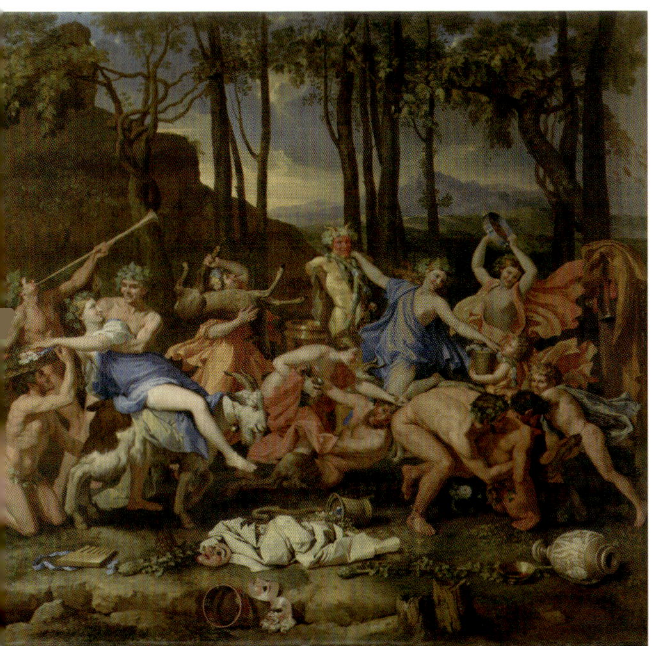

Fig. 13. Nicolas Poussin (French, 1594–1665, active in Italy), *The Triumph of Pan*, 1635–36. Oil on canvas, 53½ x 57½ in. (135.9 x 146 cm). The National Gallery, London. Bought with contributions from the National Heritage Memorial Fund and The Art Fund, 1982

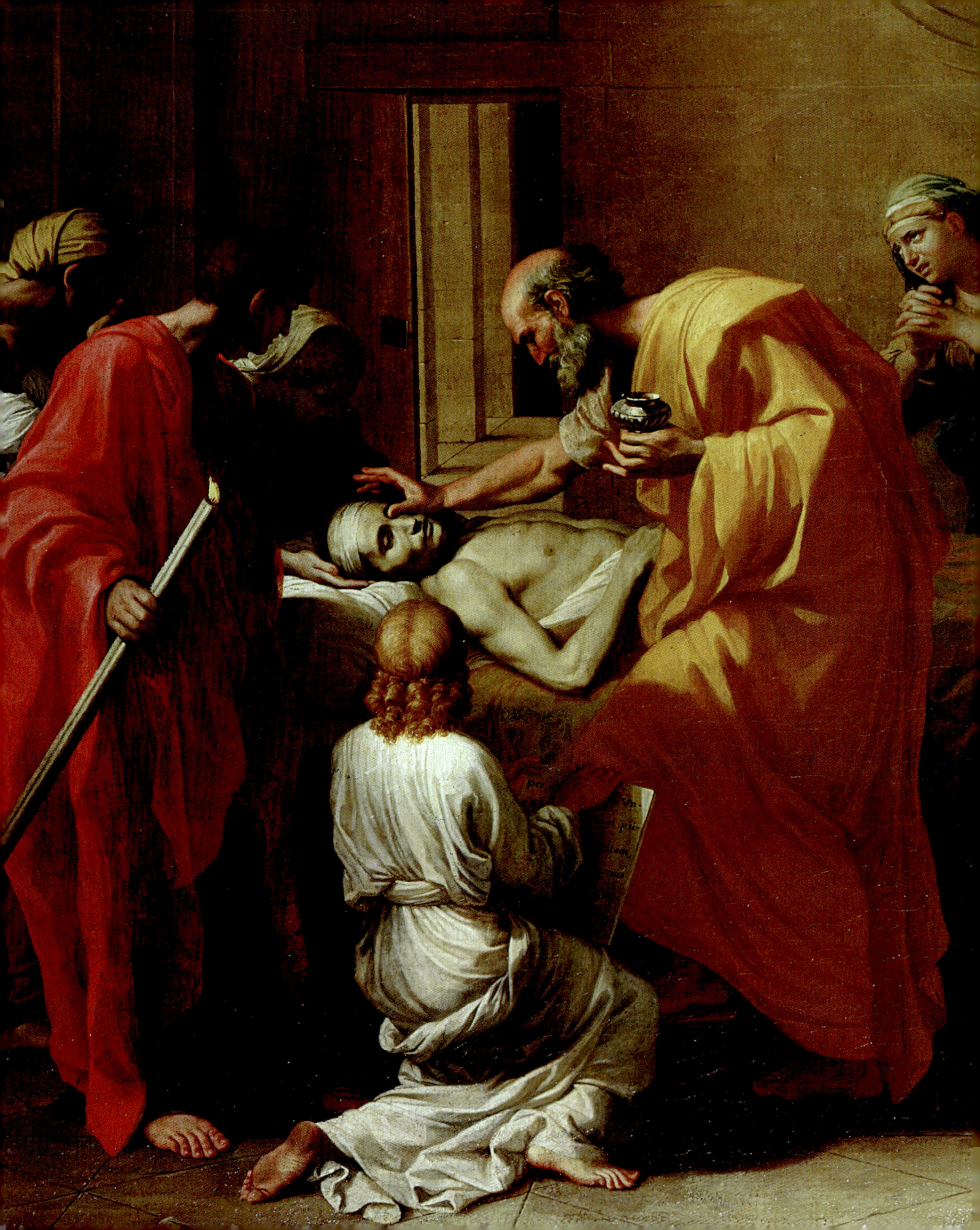

"Seven Sacrosanct Treasures": The Two Series of Sacraments

As Poussin finished the Bacchanals around 1636, Cassiano dal Pozzo offered the artist his most ambitious commission to date: paintings of the seven sacraments, each depicting either the foundation event of a sacrament or its practice in late antiquity—a theme corresponding to the collector's fascination with all facets of ancient Roman life. Cassiano had witnessed Poussin's stylistic transformation toward a crisp, Raphaelesque, classicizing idiom, with animated figures demonstrating the painter's studies of Leonardo's *Treatise*.[38] This grand style, what Poussin would later term a "maniera magnifica," after the most elevated form of rhetoric, was ideally suited to these lofty religious themes.[39] Poussin's rhetorical mastery and antiquarian knowledge were essential not only for appealing to the patron's interests but also for promoting the dictates of the Counter-Reformation Church.

The Protestant Reformation, which had been underway since the early sixteenth century, had denounced papal authority and contested several doctrines concerning the dispensation of salvation, including the validity of the seven sacraments. Beginning with Martin Luther, the reformers claimed that the sacraments, apart from baptism and the Eucharist, did not fully embody God's grace as revealed through Christ's actions and bequeathed to the faithful in the Gospel. Instead, penance, confirmation, ordination, matrimony, and extreme unction, while in some cases originating in biblical events, were human institutions that empowered the priesthood, rather than rituals of direct communion with God's absolving grace.[40] The most radical reformers, such as Ulrich Zwingli and John Calvin, denounced the veneration of images as inherently idolatrous and advocated their removal—even iconoclastic destruction—as impediments, rather than instruments, of true faith.[41] The decrees of the Council of Trent, issued in 1563, declared such stances anathema. Concurrently, Catholic historians aimed to demonstrate the authenticity of contested beliefs and practices in the early centuries of the church, before the establishment of Christianity as an official state religion. Foremost among these historians was Cesare Baronio, whose *Annales Ecclesiastici*, a massive, multivolume, year-by-year chronicle of church history, mines the writings of the church fathers and probes countless documents

Nicolas Poussin, *The Sacrament of Extreme Unction*, from *The Seven Sacraments for Cassiano dal Pozzo*, detail of fig. 19

in defense of hallowed ritual and doctrine. Significantly, Baronio's evidence also encompassed artifacts, visual monuments, coins, and archaeological vestiges of daily practices among early Christians.[42] Some of the most important evidence of this kind emerged from the newly excavated catacombs, the vast subterranean network of cemeteries beyond the walls of ancient Rome where Christians not only buried their dead but also held services and celebrations. While the remains of early martyrs ranked as the most spectacular finds, the catacombs yielded irrefutable evidence of late Roman rituals, costumes, and furnishings—including devotional images adorning walls, vaults, and sarcophagi.[43] Such discoveries bolstered treatises defending sacred imagery by archbishops Gabriele Paleotti and Federico Borromeo by tracing the proper use of religious pictures—the veneration of the prototype not the physical object—to the earliest eras of the church.[44] In these endeavors, the doctrinal aims of Counter-Reformation history and Cassiano dal Pozzo's archaeological interests intermeshed.

Several scholars in Dal Pozzo's immediate orbit produced learned studies on the doctrines and practices of the early church in the wake of Baronio, but more relevant for Poussin's visual conception of the *Sacraments* were Cassiano's contributions to paleo-Christian archaeology and the documentation of Rome's early Christian monuments.[45] These included his involvement with Cardinal Barberini in funding the publication of *Roma sotterranea* by Antonio Bosio (1575–1629), the pioneer explorer, surveyor, and chronicler of the Roman catacombs. Bosio's *magnum opus*

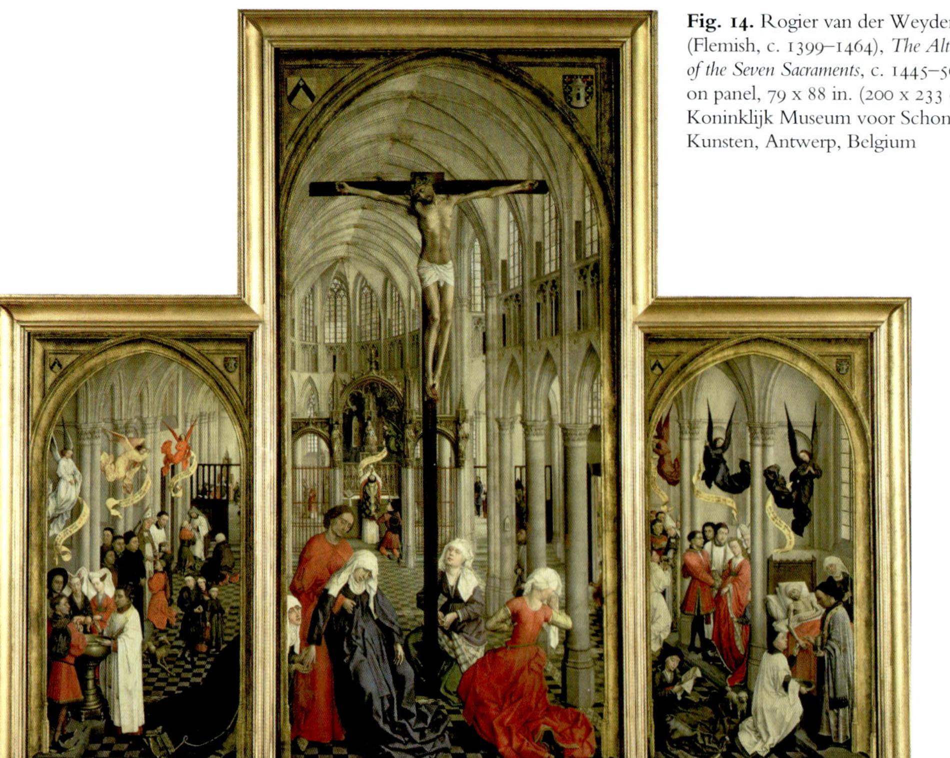

Fig. 14. Rogier van der Weyden (Flemish, c. 1399–1464), *The Altarpiece of the Seven Sacraments*, c. 1445–50. Oil on panel, 79 x 88 in. (200 x 233 cm). Koninklijk Museum voor Schone Kunsten, Antwerp, Belgium

exhaustively maps and describes the catacombs and documents the extraordinary artifacts found therein, especially wall paintings and sarcophagi. Dal Pozzo's Museo Cartaceo features dozens of studies of early Christian artworks and artifacts, several of which may have served as templates for the engraved illustrations in Bosio's published text.[46] Others related to Antonio Eclissi's concurrent documentation of the surviving, and vulnerable, decorations of the oldest Christian sanctuaries in Rome.[47] *Roma sotterranea* was extraordinary in its archaeological rigor, but it also served a propagandistic purpose in the Counter-Reformation climate. With physical artifacts, it was possible to establish the practice of the sacraments and the veneration of images among the earliest adherents of the Church and thereby uphold their legitimacy. Giovanni Severano, who edited Bosio's posthumous text, underscores how the work "manifests to the world great and precious treasures, such as the objects that are contained in the holy cemeteries:

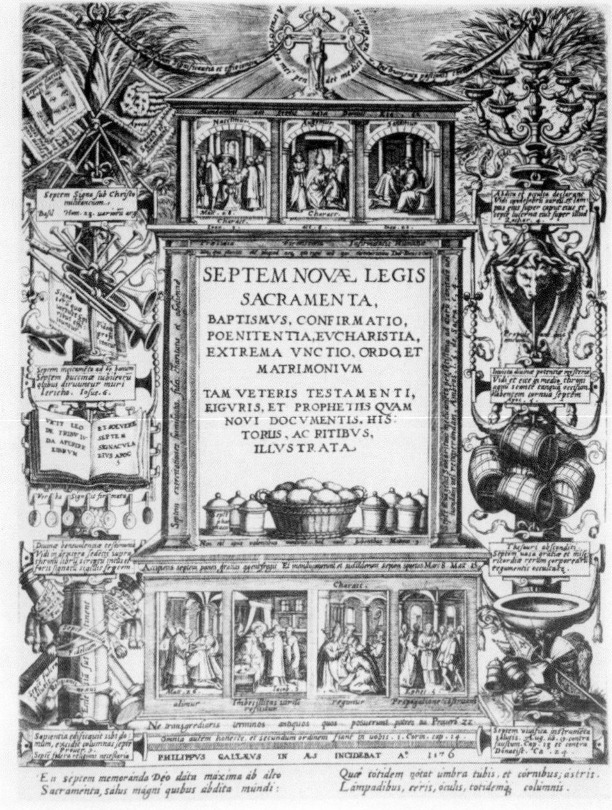

Fig. 15. Philips Galle (Flemish, 1537–1612), *Frontispiece* to *Septem novae legis Sacramenta*, 1576. Engraving, 10 x 7½ in. (25.5 x 18.9 cm). Graphische Sammlung Albertina, Vienna

ideas and images that truly portray the fledgling Church, as if from life. They [the catacombs] . . . are arsenals where one takes hold of the arms to fight against the heretics, and particularly against the iconoclasts, those who impugn sacred images, of which the catacombs abound."[48]

Poussin and Dal Pozzo conceived the *Sacraments* cycle as a similar arsenal of images that would underscore the historical legitimacy and antiquity of the holy rites. The very rarity of the subject in an Italian, and especially post-Reformation, context indicated the urgency of its message, as enhanced by the new visual evidence of early Christian archaeology. In a less doctrinally contentious era, Rogier van der Weyden painted an altarpiece that did portray the contemporary ministering of six of the sacraments in separate chapels of a grand Gothic interior (fig. 14). As the priest celebrates the Eucharist before the high altar, the foreground Crucifixion demonstrates the reenactment of Christ's bodily sacrifice through transubstantiation. Apart from this altarpiece and the more recent didactic engravings of Philips Galle (fig. 15), representations of the seven sacraments were exceedingly rare and outmoded.[49] The idea of an ensemble of individual cabinet pictures each illustrating one of the sacraments, in a completely secular context for a private patron, was absolutely unprecedented.

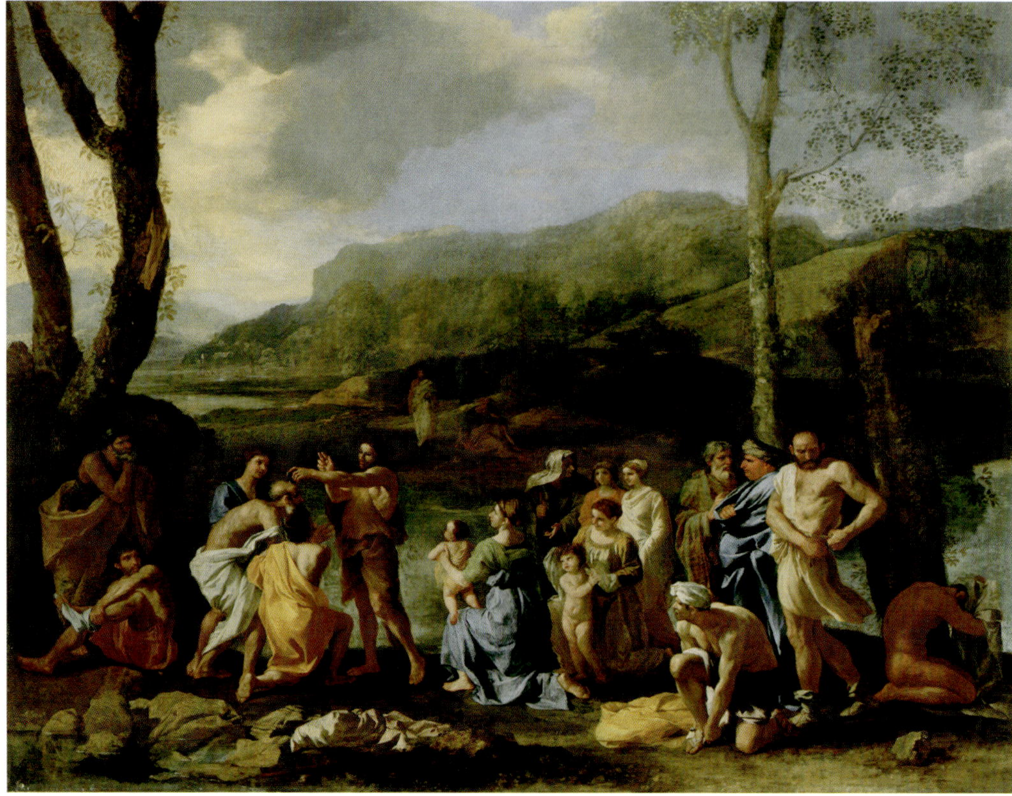

Fig. 16. Nicolas Poussin (French, 1594–1665, active in Italy), *Saint John Baptizing in the River Jordan*, c. 1635. Oil on canvas, 37¹³⁄₁₆ x 47¹³⁄₁₆ in. (96 x 121.4 cm). The J. Paul Getty Museum, Los Angeles

Echoing Severano, Carlo Roberto Dati, one of Dal Pozzo's closest associates and an expert on ancient painting, notes how Poussin's pictures animate hallowed events, hailing the commission as "the seven marvels of the French brush, in which are expressed in life the seven sacrosanct treasures left by the Savior of the World to the Catholic Church."[50]

Poussin depicts the foundation event of each sacrament as described in the Bible, or the administering of the ritual at the time of the early church, as a lived dramatic experience. Galle's engravings, with their comprehensive illustration of each sacrament both in contemporary liturgical practice and its Old and New Testament prototypes, accompanied by a compendium of scriptural passages, clearly demonstrate the urgency in advocating their validity in the Counter-Reformation climate.[51] While the prints offered a convenient summa of raw material, Poussin had to select a subject conducive to the unified field of the tableau, its coherent dramatic staging, and the exemplary emotive expression of those receiving the Lord's grace through engaging in the rite.

Whereas *Ordination* and *Confirmation* will receive extended analysis in subsequent chapters, let us briefly consider the other *Sacraments*.[52] Baptism, of course, presents no doctrinal issues; it is a ritual manifestation of God's grace that Christ received directly and that all factions of Christianity acknowledge. Even before embarking on the *Sacraments* proper, Poussin had painted a baptism scene for Dal Pozzo: *Saint John Baptizing in the River Jordan*, with Christ approaching the river from the distance (fig. 16).[53] Arranged in a frieze across the foreground, adherents of all types undress and otherwise prepare for baptism by the charismatic preacher; behind them, an exquisite landscape with a meandering river and distant bluffs unfolds. The figural groupings and landscape setting and design anticipate the Kimbell *Ordination*, which is among the first of the *Sacraments* painted. Perhaps owing to Dal Pozzo's possession of a baptism scene, Poussin held off painting the actual *Sacrament of Baptism* until the very last (fig. 17). In 1640, before that painting was completed, Poussin was summoned to France to serve as court painter to King Louis XIII and Cardinal Richelieu. Finished in Paris, this canvas, which is somewhat larger and altogether more solemn than the earlier baptism scene, hones in on the instance of God's acknowledgment of his Son upon receiving the ritual

Fig. 17. Nicolas Poussin (French, 1594–1665, active in Italy), *The Sacrament of Baptism*, from *The Seven Sacraments for Cassiano dal Pozzo*, c. 1641–42. Oil on canvas, 37⅝ x 47⅝ in. (95.5 x 121 cm). National Gallery of Art, Washington D.C. Samuel H. Kress Collection

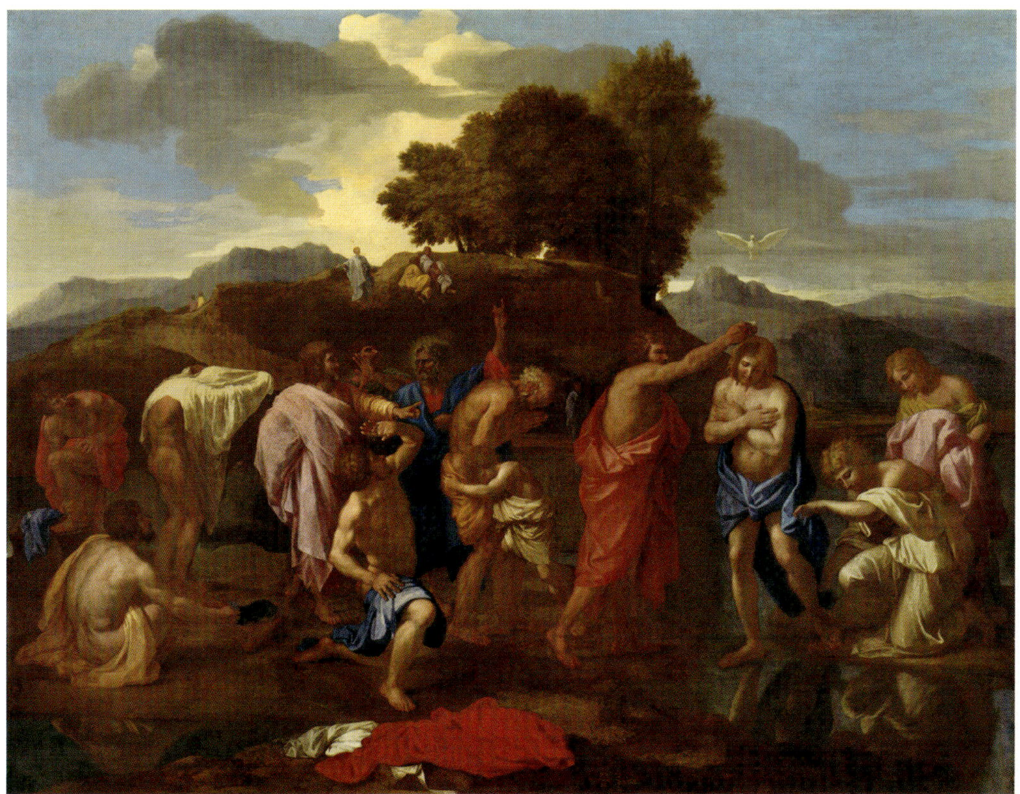

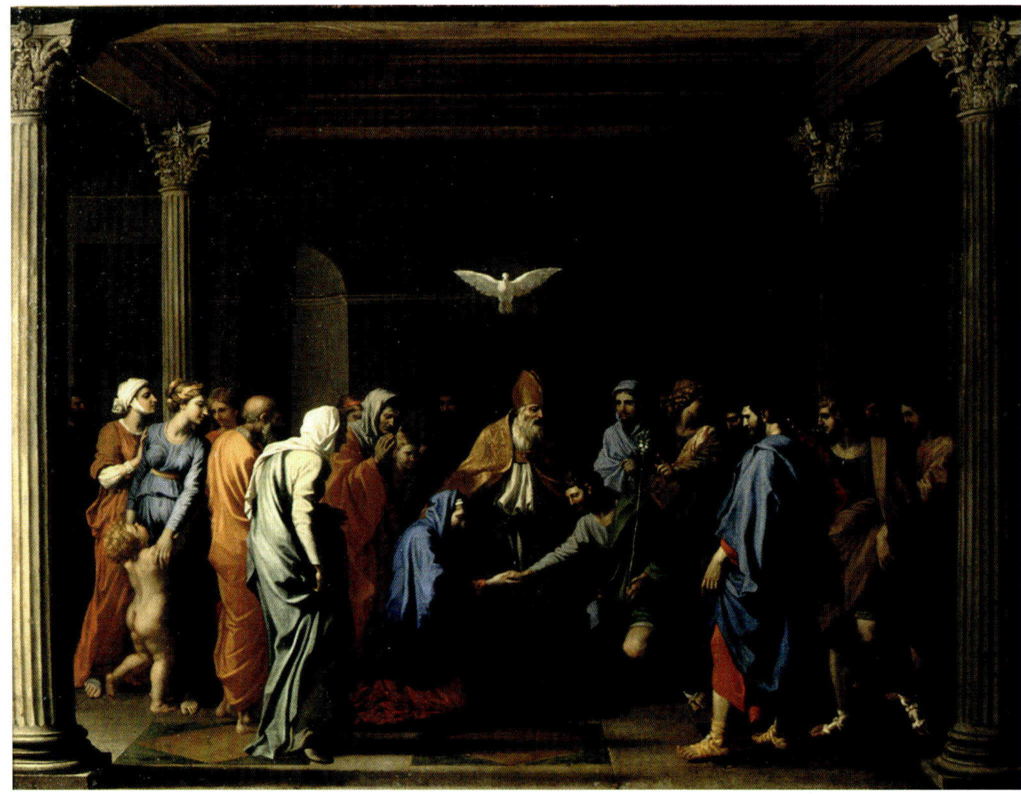

Fig. 18. Nicolas Poussin (French, 1594–1665, active in Italy), *The Sacrament of Marriage*, from *The Seven Sacraments for Cassiano dal Pozzo*, c. 1636–1640. Oil on canvas, 37¾ x 47⅝ in. (95.4 x 121 cm). The Duke of Rutland's Poussin Settlement, Belvoir Castle, Leicestershire, England

cleansing: "The heaven was opened and the Holy Ghost descended in a bodily shape like a dove upon him, and a voice came from Heaven, which said: 'Thou art my beloved Son. In thee I am well pleased.' " (Luke 3:21–22). Robed figures in the center gesticulate in reaction to God's pronouncement, an implicit portrayal of thunderous sound.[54] While the figures and composition conform to a number of Renaissance models, the positioning of Christ and John the Baptist astride the river, their alignment with the dove hovering between parting clouds, and the kneeling angels holding the robe all correlate to a newly unearthed paradigm for the sacramental event found in the catacombs and reproduced in Bosio.[55]

The two *Sacraments* set in day-lit interiors—*Marriage* and *Extreme Unction*—offer contrasting moods. In *Marriage*, Poussin depicts the earliest possible event, the marriage of the Virgin Mary to Saint Joseph, even though the post-Tridentine Church promoted Christ's miracles at the wedding feast at Cana as the biblical prototype for the sacrament (fig. 18). However, church fathers such as Augustine viewed the marriage of Joseph and Mary as an ideal relationship of loyalty, dedication, and child rearing, lacking only the conjugal relations between bride and groom, given the perpetual virginity of Mary.[56] As such, the episode exemplifies the two blessed states of matrimony and celibacy. Poussin expresses the harmonious union through the symmetry of the witnesses and the refined classicism of the four-columned hall.

Extreme unction has no precise scriptural basis in the New Testament, although James 5:14–15 does mention church elders anointing the sick and administering last rites. To lend the scene requisite venerability, Poussin situates *Extreme Unction* (fig. 19) in an ancient domestic interior, reworking *The Death of Germanicus*. Poussin likewise choreographs a dramatic climax: frantic efforts to cure—signaled by the apothecary and his assistant behind the bed and the exiting maidservant—yield to the solemn ritual of the priest and his acolyte anointing the dying man, as varied states of prayer and grieving are unleashed.[57]

The *Sacraments* that most thoroughly expound the archaeological expertise of painter and patron are *Penance* and *Eucharist*. Poussin arranges each scene around a triclinium, or ancient

Fig. 19. Nicolas Poussin (French, 1594–1665, active in Italy), *The Sacrament of Extreme Unction*, from *The Seven Sacraments for Cassiano dal Pozzo*, c. 1636–40. Oil on canvas, 37⅝ x 47⅝ in. (95.5 x 121 cm). The Fitzwilliam Museum, University of Cambridge

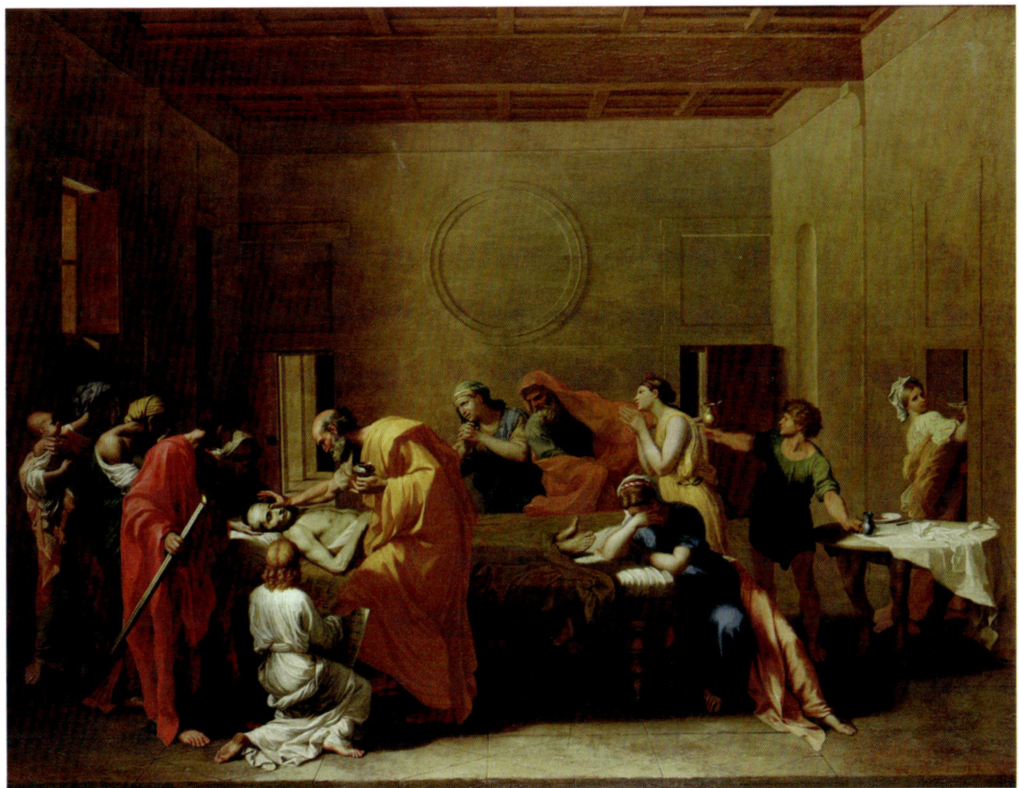

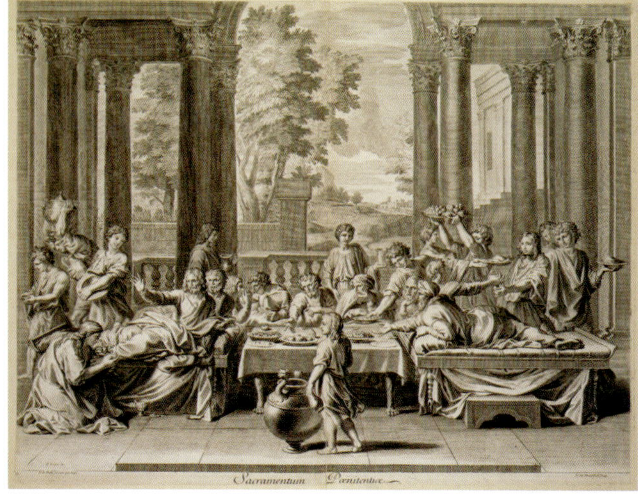

Fig. 20. Louis de Chatillon (French, 1639–1734), *Sacramentum Poenitentiae*, c. 1695–1711, engraving. After Nicolas Poussin's original painting of c. 1636–40, *The Sacrament of Penance*, from *The Seven Sacraments for Cassiano dal Pozzo*. The Getty Research Institute, Los Angeles

banqueting couch. Treatises devoted to this type of furnishing proliferated in the late sixteenth century, including *De Triclinio* (1588), authored by the Spanish Jesuit Pedro Chacón, a pioneer, like Bosio, of catacomb exploration, and *De Arte Gymnastica* (1569, 1601), by Giovanni Mercuriale. These texts helped clarify certain scriptural passages, such as Luke 7:38, which, in describing the Feast in the House of Simon the Pharisee, states that a sinful woman, generally viewed as Mary Magdalene, stood behind Christ to anoint and wash his feet with her tears while he was at the table.[58] Poussin adapted this arrangement to his painting of the scene, the prototype for the

sacrament of penance. Though the Dal Pozzo *Penance* was destroyed in a fire in 1816, copies and engravings record that Poussin situated the triclinium in a garden loggia (fig. 20). Poussin further consulted the Museo Cartaceo, which included copies of drawings by Pirro Ligorio of a triclinium constructed from three couches joined at the corners (fig. 21).[59] The painter also copied a banqueting scene from a catacomb fresco engraved in Bosio's *Roma sotterranea* depicting a crescent-shaped couch (fig. 22).[60]

The *Eucharist* is even more redolent of Poussin and Cassiano's intellectual kinship in re-creating the foundational event, the Last Supper (fig. 23). The arrangement of Christ and the apostles reclining upon the dining couches not only provided an archaeologically correct setting but also accounted for the position of John, specified in his Gospel (13.23–25) as "close to the breast of Jesus."[61] The painter

Fig. 21. *Study after Pirro Ligorio of a Roman Triclinium*, from the Museo Cartaceo of Cassiano dal Pozzo, 17th century, pen and wash. The Royal Collection, Windsor Castle

here adapts the triclinium to accommodate the figures along a horizontal, in keeping with traditional representations of the Last Supper, especially those of Leonardo da Vinci and Frans Pourbus.[62] Leonardo's legacy is also evident in the illumination through three distinct light sources; the sophisticated shadow projections evince Poussin's studies of the manuscripts on light and shade by Matteo Zaccolini, which were believed to record Leonardo's lost writings on optics. This work, like Leonardo's *Trattato*, was being prepared for publication with Cassiano's

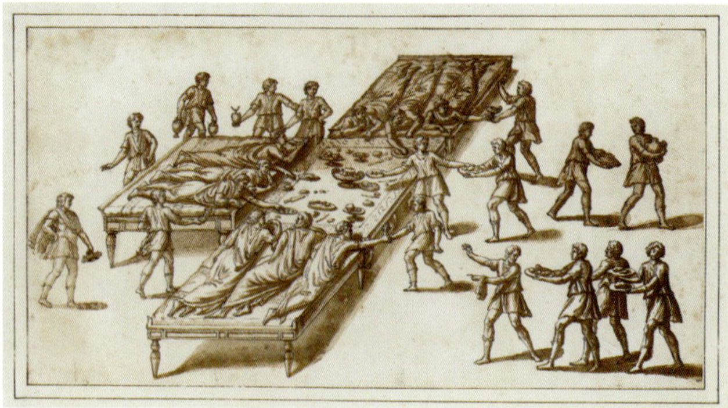

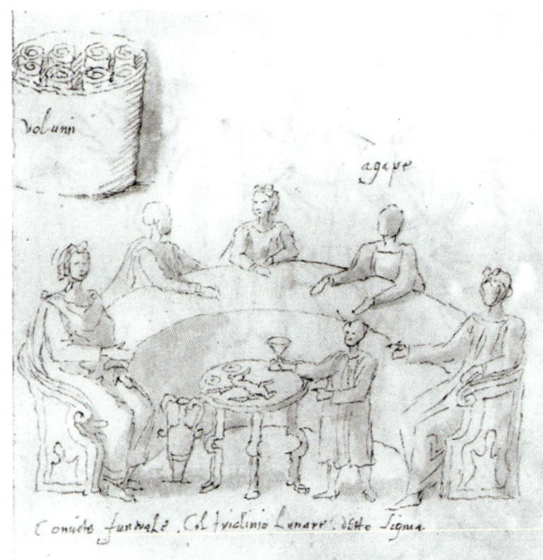

Fig. 22. Nicolas Poussin (French, 1594–1665, active in Italy), *Studies of a Banqueting Scene from the Catacomb of Saints Peter and Marcellinus and Volunni from the Catacomb of Saint Callixtus*, c. 1645. Pen, brown ink, and brown wash, 5½ x 4¾ in. (14 x 12 cm). After plate 391 and plate 221 of Bosio's *Roma sotterranea*. The State Hermitage Museum, Saint Petersburg

Fig. 23. Nicolas Poussin (French, 1594–1665, active in Italy), *The Sacrament of the Eucharist*, from *The Seven Sacraments for Cassiano dal Pozzo*, c. 1636–1640. Oil on canvas, 37⅛ x 47⅝ in. (95.5 x 121 cm). The Duke of Rutland's Poussin Settlement, Belvoir Castle, Leicestershire, England

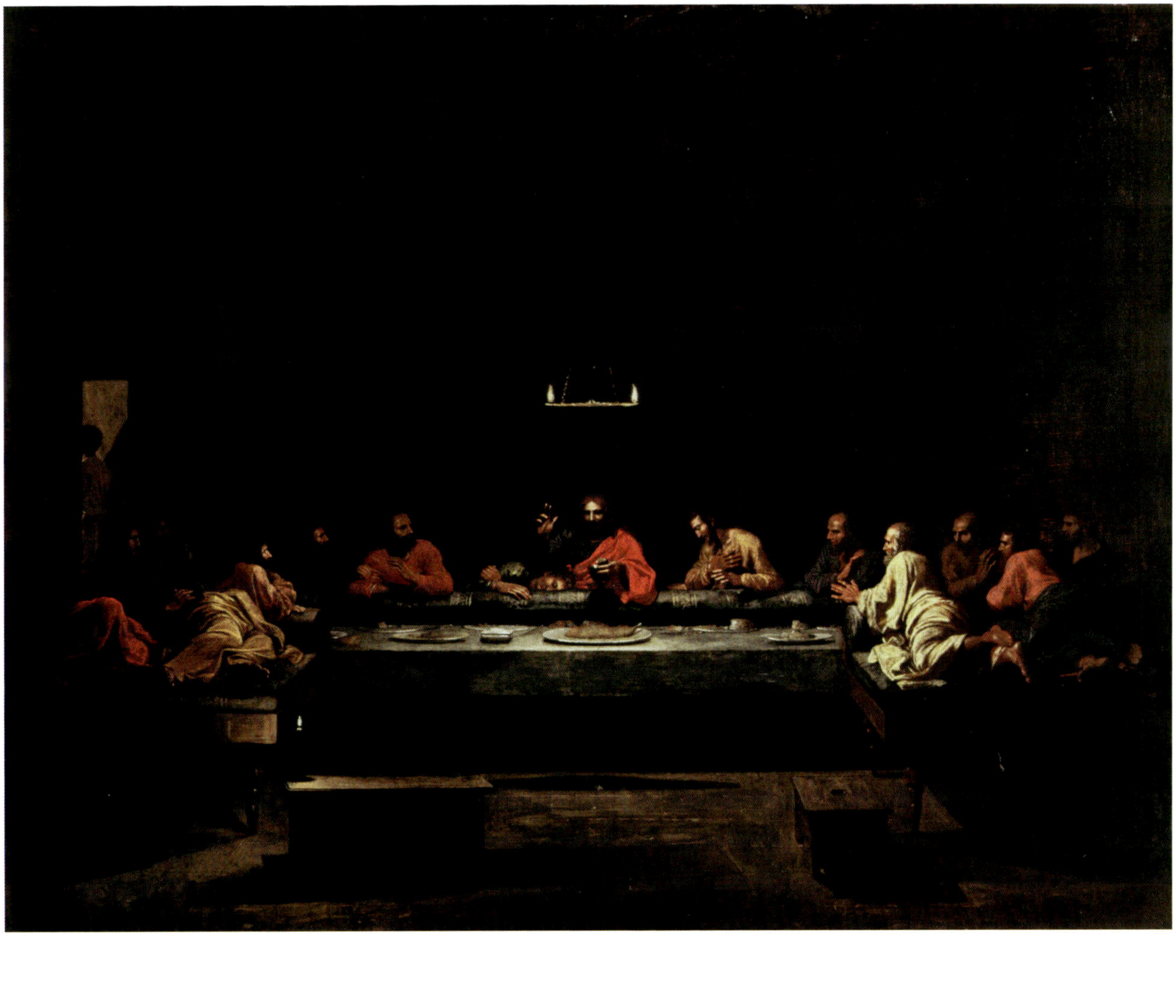

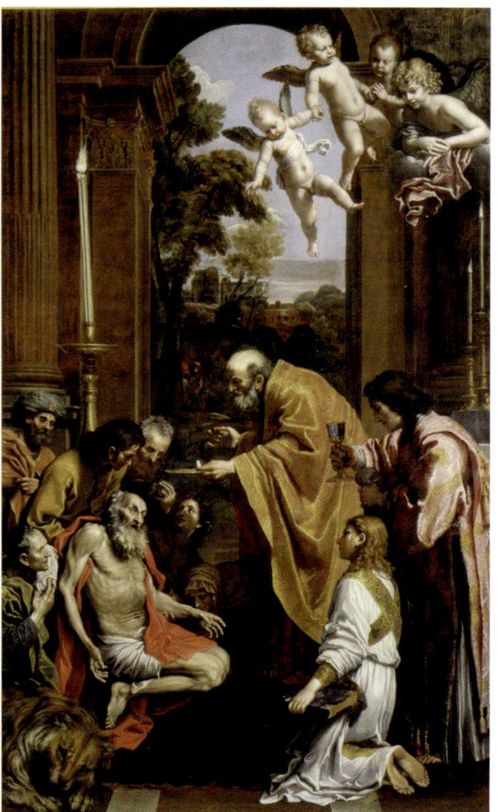

Fig. 24. Domenichino (Italian, 1581–1641), *Last Communion of Saint Jerome*, 1614. Oil on canvas, 165 x 100¾ in. (419 x 256 cm). Pinacoteca, Vatican Museums, Vatican City

support.[63] Thus the *Eucharist* attests not only to the antiquarian researches but also to the advanced art-theoretical scholarship that flourished under Dal Pozzo's auspices.

Once completed, the *Sacraments* were the highlight of the Dal Pozzo palace and dominated the "stanza dei Sagramenti," in the company of additional pictures by Poussin.[64] Among the first foreign visitors to see the newly installed paintings—with the exception of the delayed *Baptism*—were the brothers Fréart, cousins of François Sublet de Noyers, the director of royal works to Louis XIII. One, Roland Fréart de Chambray, would oversee the publication of Leonardo's *Treatise*, with Poussin's illustrations, in Paris and emerge as major art theorist. The other, Paul Fréart de Chantelou, was primarily a collector and amateur of painting. He had already commissioned one of Poussin's most ambitious works to date, *The Israelites Gathering Manna*. The Fréarts had not come to Rome in 1640 merely to pay homage to Poussin, however; under the

orders of Cardinal Richelieu, they invited the artist to serve as *premier peintre dui Roi*. To Richelieu, Poussin represented a native cultural triumph that belonged in France.[65] Beginning in 1639, letters from Sublet had offered Poussin the most propitious terms for his repatriation. To avoid further delay, Sublet dispatched the Fréart brothers to fetch the reluctant painter, and he accompanied them back to Paris at the end of 1640.[66] Upon his arrival at court, Poussin received every honor and privilege from the king and cardinal. Louis XIII even proclaimed: "Now Vouet has met his match." This comment would prove Poussin's undoing. Simon Vouet had been the leading painter in Paris since his return in 1627 from a lengthy sojourn in Rome and responded to Poussin's presence with malicious charges against his most important projects, including the decoration of the *grand galerie* of the Louvre. In a famous letter to Sublet, an exasperated Poussin laments the cabals against his plans and explains how viewing a work of art requires the exercise of rational judgment.[67] Besieged and misunderstood, Poussin returned to Rome at the first chance, in the summer of 1642. The deaths of Richelieu later that year and Louis XIII early the next accorded Poussin the unexpected circumstances to remain in Rome, where he forfeited courtly preferment for a far more valuable tranquility of spirit.[68]

While in Paris, Poussin sent letters to Cassiano with updates on the *Baptism* and complaints that remaining in Paris would turn him into a bungler with no knowledge of the antique.[69] In one letter, the artist divulges that Chantelou had "put it into the head" of Sublet de Noyers to request copies be made of Cassiano's *Sacraments*, initially for tapestry cartoons.[70] Cassiano protested of the difficulty of arranging for copyists, initially offering colored drawings, but ultimately acceded to the royal request to provide copies. Poussin expressed his relief that some other painter would execute the task, "since I know simply how to innovate and not to copy the things already made once by me."[71]

Dal Pozzo was even less accommodating when it became evident, after Poussin's return to Rome, that the copies were destined for a rival amateur, Chantelou. After attempting to enlist several copyists, Poussin soon realized that it would prove impossible to find a professional adequate to his standards, since "the crafty know

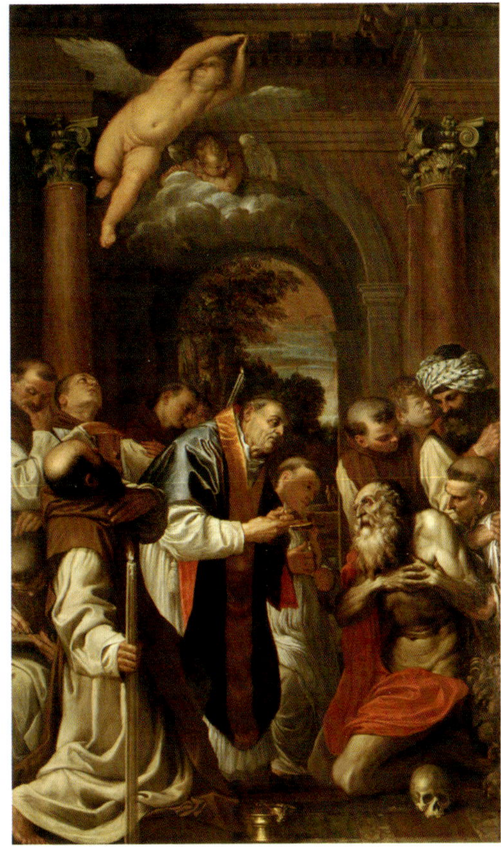

Fig. 25. Agostino Carracci (Italian, 1557–1602), *Last Communion of Saint Jerome*, 1592. Oil on canvas, 148 x 88¼ in. (376 x 224 cm). Pinacoteca Nazionale, Bologna

well how to take advantage of poorly made copies to discredit" the originals.[72] Poussin finally resolved to paint a new series, featuring "a different disposition" that would make "them worth more than copies." Poussin pledged to dedicate "all of my studies and all the force of my talent such as it is" to the series.[73]

Many letters from Poussin to Chantelou document his progress on the new series. As Poussin reports, Cassiano visited the painter's studio when the first picture, *Extreme Unction*, was blocked in enough to perceive the final result: "Although he put on a good face . . . he was astonished to see, with the same subject, a disposition so diverse and the actions of the figures all contrary to his."[74] Poussin's sentiments in this missive would eventually crystallize into his theoretical precept, recorded by Bellori: "Novelty in painting does not consist primarily in a subject that has never been seen, but in good and novel arrangement and expression, and in this way the subject that was commonplace and stale becomes singular and new."[75] Poussin also cites a controversial example of pictorial novelty, Domenichino's *Last Communion of Saint Jerome* (fig. 24). A few years earlier, rivals had charged Domenichino with plagiarizing from an altarpiece depicting the same subject by Agostino Carracci in Bologna (fig. 25). Despite common subject matter and compositional parallels, Domenichino's

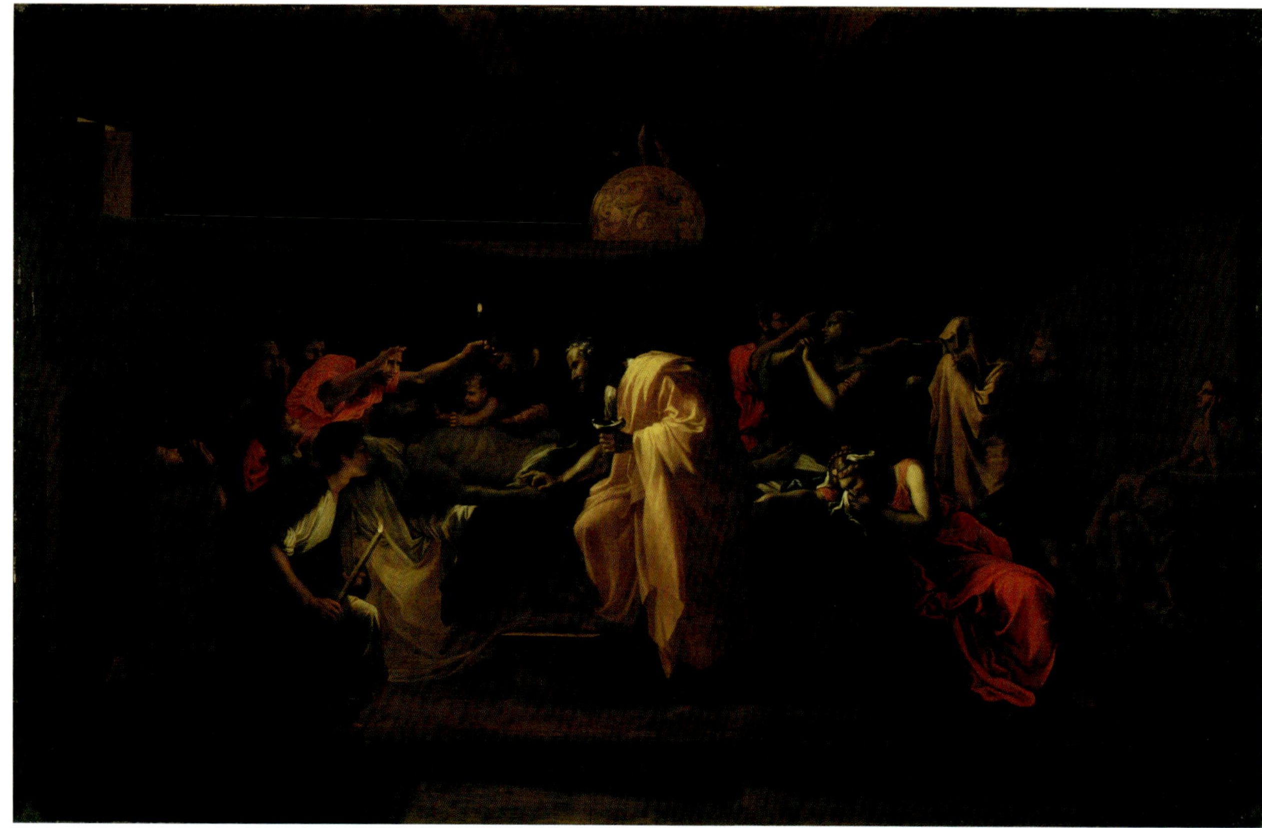

Fig. 26. Nicolas Poussin (French, 1594–1665, active in Italy), *The Sacrament of Extreme Unction*, from *The Seven Sacraments for Paul Fréart de Chantelou*, 1644. Oil on canvas, 46 x 70⅛ in. (117 x 178 cm). National Gallery of Scotland, Edinburgh. Bridgewater Loan, 1945

transformation of his prototype with a different arrangement of figures and enhanced expression render it novel. The poet Marino had previously formulated these sentiments when accused of literary theft, and even the antiquarian Lukas Holste likewise explained the difference between acknowledged translation and poetic imitation in a letter to Dal Pozzo.[76] Poussin's application of the maxim to Domenichino's altarpiece certainly reflects, above all, his own propensity for self-emulation. From the 1620s through the 1640s, the painter habitually treated the same subject twice, the second version always evincing a rigorous reformulation of the first. The second series of *Sacraments* is a sustained implementation of Poussin's unique conception of pictorial originality.[77]

The Dal Pozzo and Chantelou versions of *Extreme Unction*, like the Saint Jerome altarpieces, share a common subject matter and general composition (fig. 26). But gazing upon the later version in the artist's studio, Cassiano must have readily perceived how Poussin cultivated a greater monumentality, economy, and force of expression, not to mention a more profound sense of archaeological rigor,

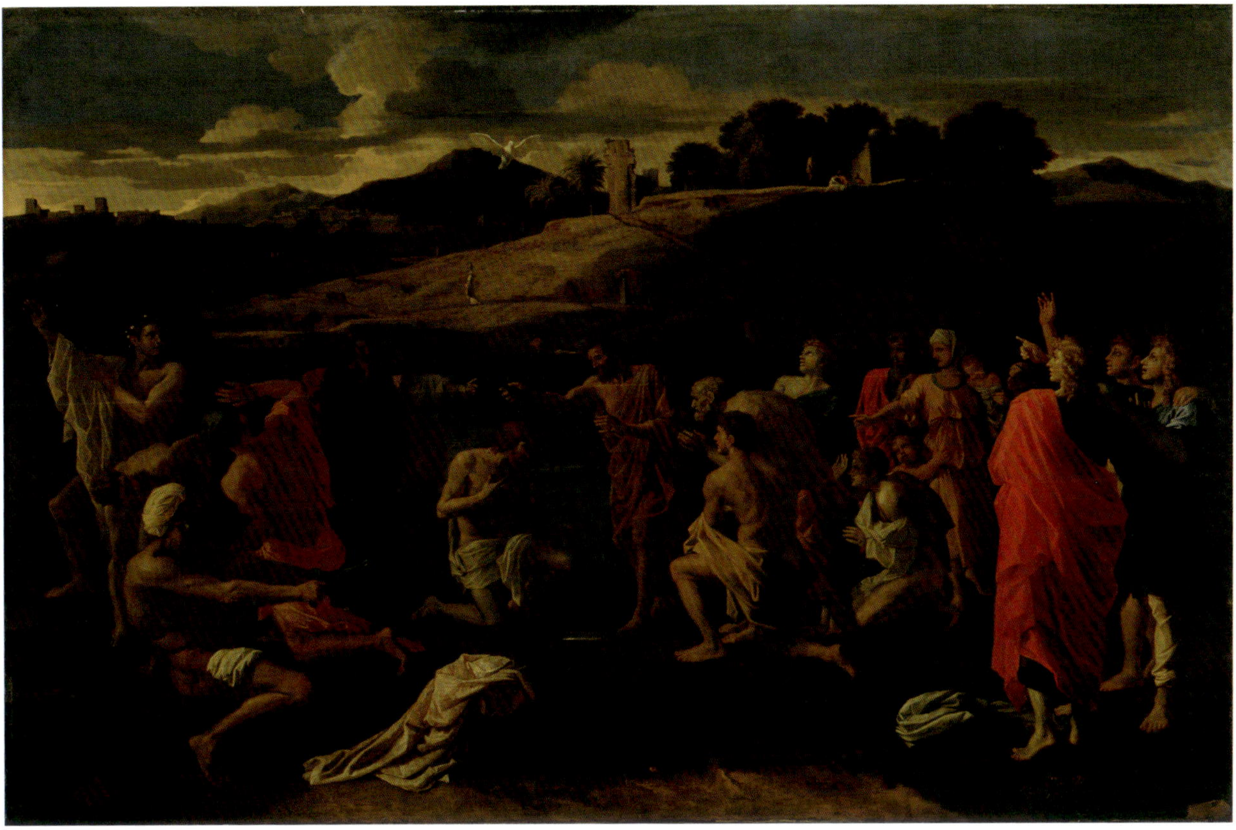

Fig. 27. Nicolas Poussin (French, 1594–1665, active in Italy), *The Sacrament of Baptism*, from *The Seven Sacraments for Paul Fréart de Chantelou*. 1646. Oil on canvas, 46 x 70⅛ in. (117 x 178 cm). National Gallery of Scotland, Edinburgh. Bridgewater Loan, 1945

than in his own painting. The daytime bustle that leavened the solemnity of the earlier scene gives way to a nocturnal vigil, where all of the figures fixate on the body of the dying man illuminated in the glow of candlelight and variously anoint and grieve. Behind the curtains, a mounted golden shield shimmers, its Chi-Rho blazon designating the deceased as a soldier in Constantine's armies.[78]

The same rigorous reinvention characterized the remaining *Sacraments*.[79] *Confirmation*, which followed *Extreme Unction* in late 1645, exhibits the most radical reworking of its subject, involving archaeological research that also characterizes the *Ordination* of 1647, both to be discussed later. The scene depicted in the Chantelou *Baptism* of 1646 is identical to the Dal Pozzo version, though Poussin now centers the ritual event and integrates the frieze of figures more harmoniously with the landscape (fig. 27).[80] Conforming to the festive subject of the Virgin's marriage, Poussin alleviates the symmetry of the Dal Pozzo *Marriage* with landscape views, nuptial festoons, and a more casually elegant grouping of figures (fig. 28).[81] This was the last canvas, delivered in March 1648.

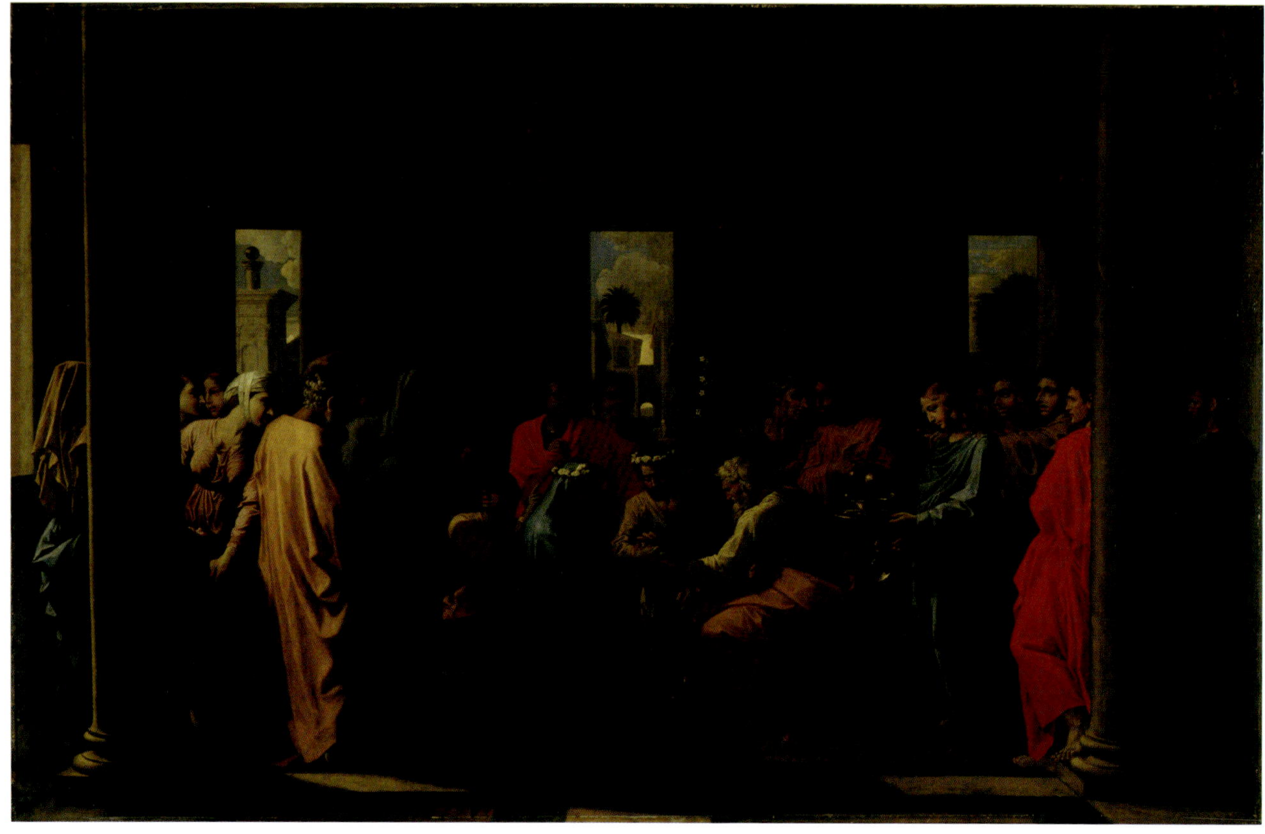

Fig. 28. Nicolas Poussin (French, 1594–1665, active in Italy), *The Sacrament of Marriage*, from *The Seven Sacraments for Paul Fréart de Chantelou*, c. 1647–48. Oil on canvas, 46 x 70⅛ in. (117 x 178 cm). National Gallery of Scotland, Edinburgh. Bridgewater Loan, 1945

As with the Dal Pozzo banquet scenes, the remade *Penance* and *Eucharist* stage the Feast in the House of Simon the Pharisee and the Last Supper around a triclinium. In *Penance*, delivered in 1647, Poussin relocates the banquet into an austere hall, a *caenaculum*, adorned with Ionic columns and niches (fig. 29). Christ and the Pharisee now physically parallel one another in the foreground, as they recline to have their feet washed and anointed. Christ's generous blessing of the lovingly contrite Magdalene contrasts with the Pharisee's haughty scorn at his acceptance of her penance. The Pharisee and his companion wear on their foreheads what Poussin understood as phylacteries—small boxes containing slips of scripture—inscribed in Hebrew with a variation of Psalm 25.15: "Mine eyes are ever toward the Lord." Poussin thereby ironically underscores the rabbi's blind incomprehension of the new age of mercy embodied in Christ.[82]

In the *Eucharist*, Poussin heightens the dramatic concentration by having eleven apostles plus

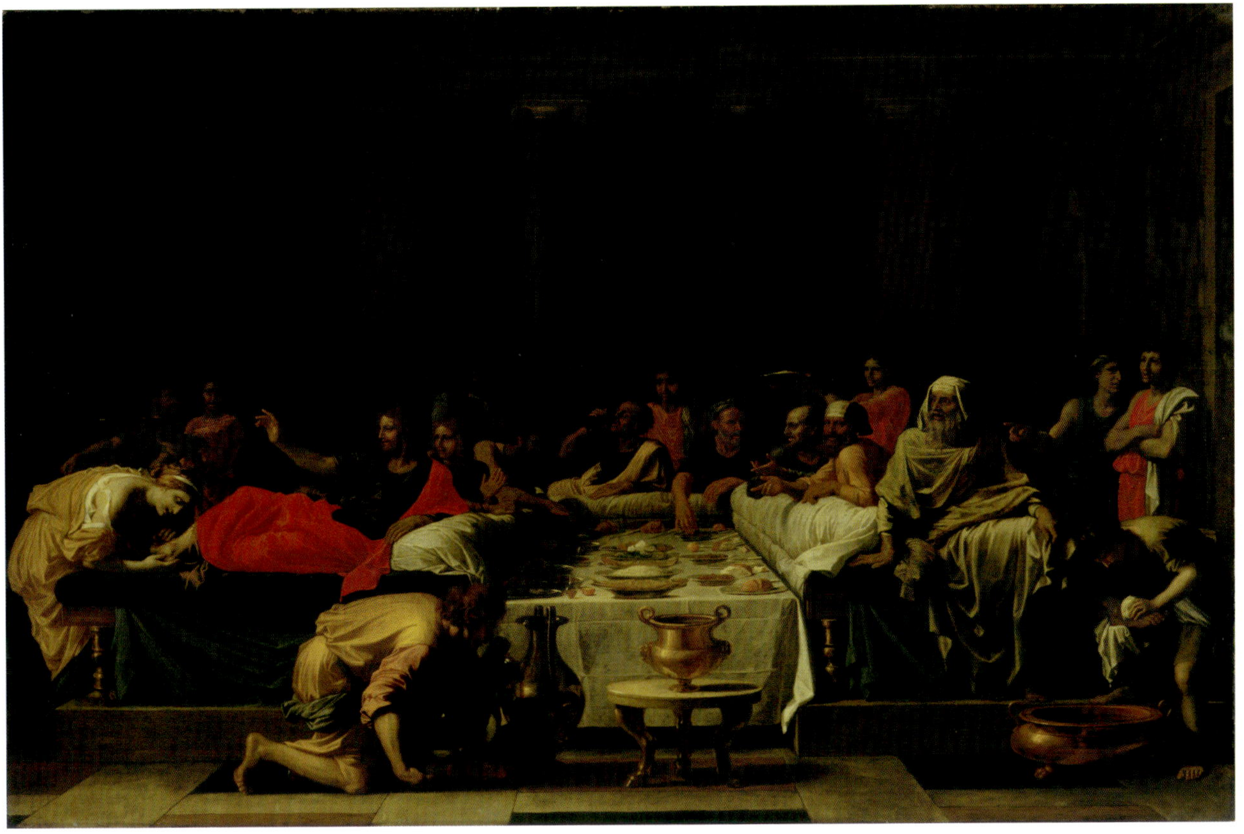

Fig. 29. Nicolas Poussin (French, 1594–1665, active in Italy), *The Sacrament of Penance*, from *The Seven Sacraments for Paul Fréart de Chantelou.* 1647. Oil on canvas, 46 x 70⅛ in. (117 x 178 cm). National Gallery of Scotland, Edinburgh. Bridgewater Loan, 1945

Christ recline on couches along all four sides of the table (fig. 30). Though this arrangement deviates from the ancient practice of having one edge of the sunken table accessible, it allows for an even distribution of figures per side, conforming to Baronio's claim that only Peter and John shared the couch with Christ. As the initial communicants raise bread to their mouths as in early Christian practice, Christ points directly to his breast—"This is my Body."[83] His scarlet pallium (cloak) indicates the significance of the cup he holds. With Judas exiting treacherously into the shadows, the apostles' agitated expressions likely respond to Christ's final utterance before the group: "I will not drink henceforth of this fruit of the vine, until that day when I drink it new with you in my Father's Kingdom" (Matthew 26:29).[84]

One of the most perceptive early viewers of the *Sacraments* was Chantelou's brother, Roland Fréart de Chambray. In his treatise *Idée de la perfection de la peinture* of 1662, Chambray hails

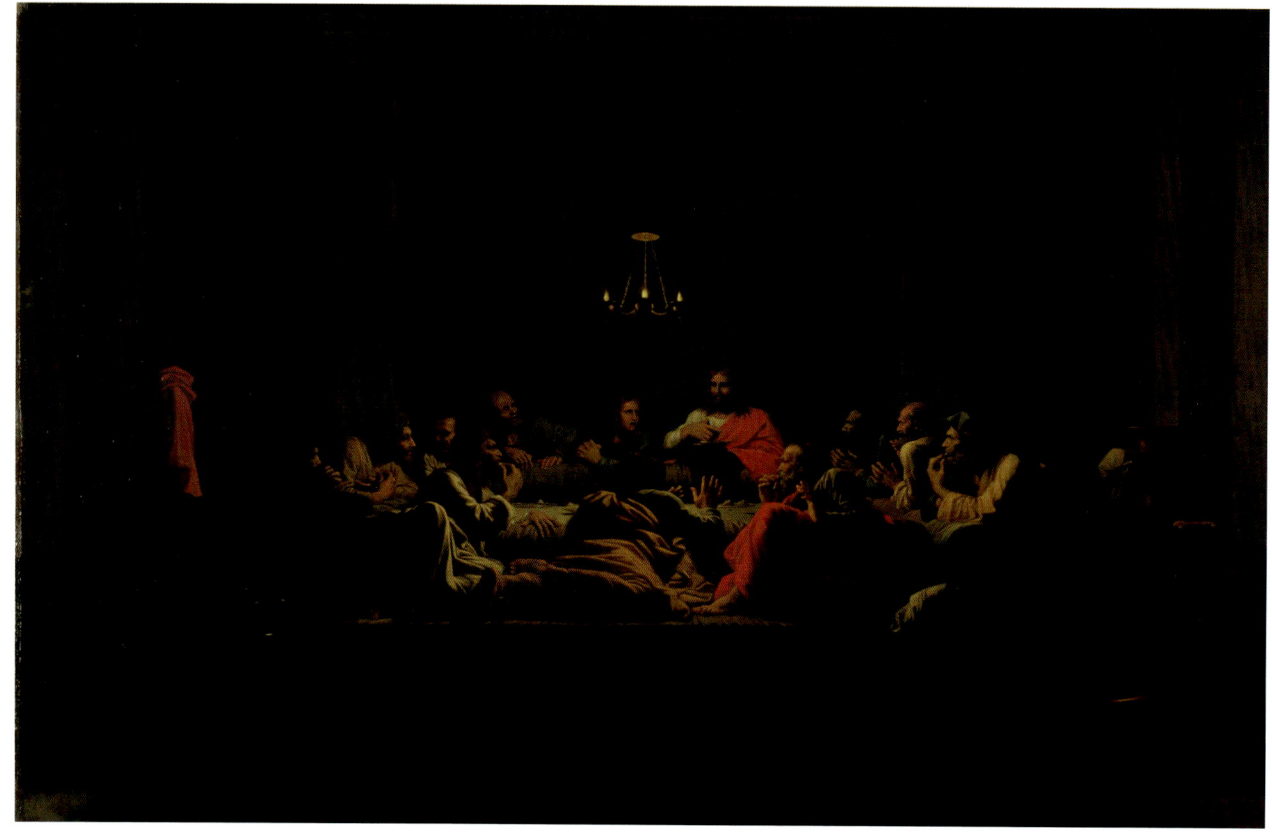

Fig. 30. Nicolas Poussin (French, 1594–1665, active in Italy), *The Sacrament of the Eucharist*, from *The Seven Sacraments for Paul Fréart de Chantelou*, c. 1647. Oil on canvas, 46 x 70⅛ in. (117 x 178 cm). National Gallery of Scotland, Edinburgh. Bridgewater Loan, 1945

Poussin's works, and the *Sacraments* in particular, as nothing less than the epitome of painting, based not only on their quality but also on their use of appropriate historical setting, behaviors, and garments, which Chambray claims is the hallmark of true pictorial knowledge.[85] For instance, Poussin's historically informed use of the triclinium exemplifies this "esprit raisonnable," since it allows Saint John to appear at Christ's breast level, awake—not inexplicably slumbering.[86] The display of Chantelou's *Sacraments* compelled a heightened concentration on the part of the beholder to detect such nuances. Unlike Cassiano's cluttered gallery, Chantelou reserved a room for the *Sacraments* alone, each shielded by a curtain that was drawn aside to contemplate a single picture at a time, following the artist's recommendation. Witnessing the cycle in the ideal environment of his brother's gallery, Chambray understood the essence of Poussin's achievement: "For although each picture can be taken on its own, and separated from the ensemble, or rather, this encyclopedia of Sacraments . . . the principal intention of our painter

[was] to form a mystical body of these seven sacred members, which is the most noble idea that can be born in the mind of a Christian painter."[87]

Perhaps the most discerning visitor ever to Chantelou's gallery was Gian Lorenzo Bernini (1598–1680), whom the collector escorted during his sojourn in Paris to oversee designs for the Louvre. Seeing the works of Poussin in Parisian private collections aesthetically reinvigorated Bernini during an otherwise politically fraught attempt to impose his artistic vision on the French court. Bernini immersed himself in each *Sacrament*, responding with both animated engagement and deep meditation. Afterwards, Bernini stated, according his host, that their "effect on him was like that of a great sermon, to which one listens with the deepest attention and goes away in silence while enjoying the inner experience." He then exclaimed, with feigned modesty but genuine admiration: "Today you have caused me great distress by showing me the talent of a man who makes me realize that I know nothing."[88]

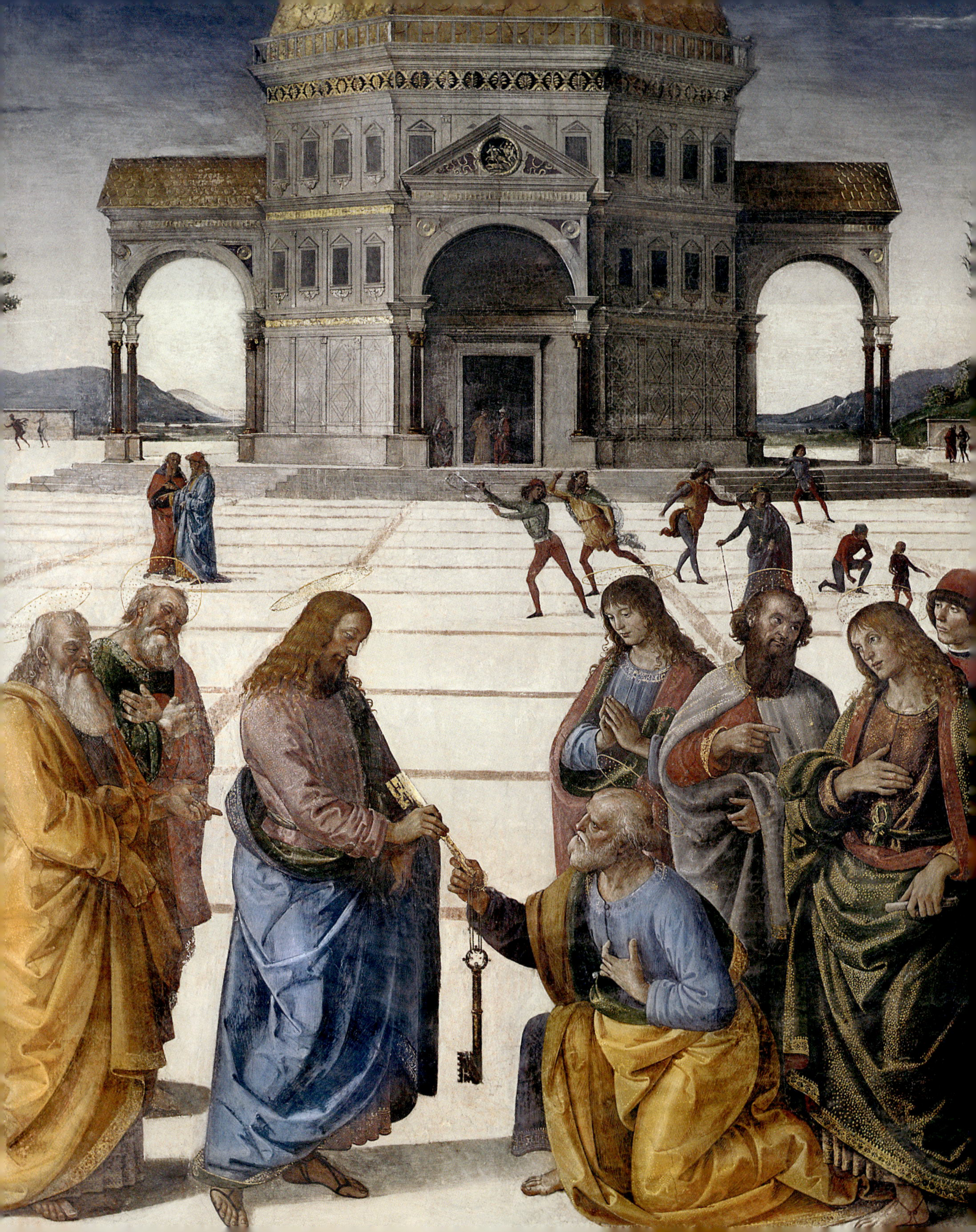

Staging the Ordination: Papal Supremacy and the Sistine Chapel

O F THE SEVEN SACRAMENTS, ORDINATION WAS BY FAR THE MOST CONTROVERSIAL FROM the standpoint of the Counter Reformation. While Protestants might criticize the administering of the Eucharist, they could hardly impugn its sacramental status, even if disputes raged over the doctrine of transubstantiation. Instead, the exclusivity of the priesthood in celebrating the ritual and consecrating the host, and thereby in dispensing the purported source of grace, were the primary Protestant targets. Martin Luther viewed ordination as licensing a corruptible priestly caste whose exclusive privilege to celebrate the re-enactment of Christ's sacrifice invested them with the power to dispense redemption over those who were already entitled to commune with the Lord directly.[89] Worse still, as John Calvin argues, the priest-based administration of the ritual denies the singular power of Christ's sacrifice to grant all of the faithful universal atonement for their sins.[90] Furthermore, ordination, in consecrating the priesthood and instituting clerical privilege and hierarchy, provided the ultimate justification for the most odious feature of the Catholic Church: the institution of the papacy and its divine charge in ruling over the faithful.[91]

The decrees of the Council of Trent, issued in 1563, rejected such reasoning and fully endorsed the sacramental status of ordaining priests to grant them the requisite sanctity to perform the mystical sacrifice of the Lord's body and blood, as they claimed Christ had instructed following the example of Jewish rites.[92] One of Philips Galle's 1576 engravings, *Orders*, describes in visual terms the Counter-Reformation Church's dictates on the subject, surveying the many scriptural justifications for the sacrament (fig. 31).[93] Beyond the central illustration of the sacrament as performed in the contemporary liturgy are various scenes of Old Testament priesthood: the institution translated into the New Covenant. A monumental figure of David stands opposite Paul, underscoring this continuity. Above the principal scene, Galle depicts the Last Supper, since the institution of the Eucharist consecrated the apostles as priests to perpetuate and officiate the ritual—"do this in remembrance of Me" (Luke 22:19).[94] To the right, the apostolic deed most clearly associated with ordination appears, the transfer

Perugino, *Christ Consigning the Keys to Peter*, detail of fig. 33

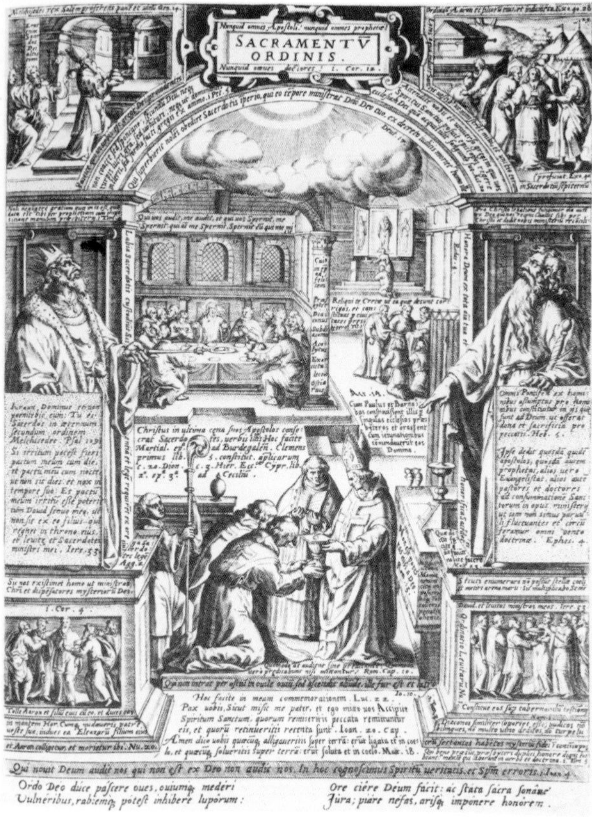

Fig. 31. Philips Galle (Flemish, 1537–1612), *Sacramentum ordinis*, from *Septem novae legis Sacramenta*, 1576. Engraving, 10 x 7 ½ in. (25.4 x 18.9 cm). Graphische Sammlung Albertina, Vienna

of evangelizing authority through the laying of hands—here illustrated by a scene of Paul and Barnabas deputizing church leaders (Acts 13:2–3). Paul himself reminds the disciple Timothy of the power of this act: "stir up the gift of God, which is in thee, by the putting on of my hands" (2 Timothy 1:6). Many Catholic apologists upheld the laying of hands as the earliest manifestation of the transfer of the Holy Spirit among proselytizers of the faith.[95] There was even archaeological evidence of this: Bosio reproduces a catacomb painting showing an enthroned Christ extending his hand upon a young acolyte assuming the gesture of prayer and flanked by elder disciples, which he views as a possible image of sacerdotal ordination (fig. 32).[96]

Yet despite the range of scriptural and iconographic prototypes, Poussin, in the Dal Pozzo *Ordination*, does not focus on ordaining the clergy in general. (Even Calvin acknowledged the necessity of pastoral leaders to evangelize and gain admission to the ministry, a "special rite for a certain function," though "Popish priests may not plume themselves upon it").[97] Instead, in an intentionally polemical decision, he depicts the scriptural passage that invests the absolute authority in the most important priest of all: the pope.

Ordination, at the various ranks, confers upon the priest three fundamental powers: the consecration of the Eucharist, pronouncing the remission of sin, and the governance of the Church. Whereas Poussin's paintings of *Penance* and *Eucharist* address the sacerdotal authority over forgiveness and Christ's body and blood, *Ordination* depicts the Lord's foundation of the Church and his establishment of its titular authority by elevating one apostle above the rest.[98] This emphasis on the ultimate doctrinal precedent for ecclesiastical hierarchy likely resonated with Dal Pozzo, who was not only trained in canon law but was, after all, a servant of Pope Urban VIII and had accompanied the official missions to France and Spain to wield the papal authority descended from Peter.[99]

The Dal Pozzo *Ordination* (fig. 1) depicts Christ addressing the apostles gathered outside the gates of the ancient Roman city Caesarea Philippi, asking, "Whom do men say that the Son of man is?" (Matthew 16:13). Baffled, some replied with various prophets—Elias, or John the Baptist, or Jeremiah. Christ then makes clear that he is speaking of himself: "But whom say ye that I am?" (16:15). Only Peter, then known as Simon, revealed his superior faith by answering: "Thou art the Christ, the Son of the living God" (16:16). At this utterance, known as the *confessio Petri*, Christ realizes that Simon could not have perceived such truth, that it must have been revealed to him by the Lord, designating him as elect among the apostles: "Blessed art thou, Simon Bar-Jonah. For flesh and blood hath not revealed it unto thee, but my Father which is in Heaven" (16:17). "Bar-Jonah" literally means son of John, but church fathers such as Jerome note its phonetic and etymological equivalence with "dove" and "grace of the Lord" in Greek and Hebrew, suggesting that Peter is specially blessed with the Holy Spirit.[100] Jesus then christens the enlightened disciple "Petrus," homonymous with "rock": "That thou art Peter, and upon this rock I will build my church; and the gates of hell shall not prevail against it. And I will give unto thee the keys of the kingdom of heaven: and whatsoever thou shalt bind on earth shall be bound in heaven: and whatsoever thou shalt loose on earth shall be loosed in heaven" (16:18–21). For the Catholic faith, this episode was tantamount to Christ anointing Peter the first pope, invested with absolute authority as the rock-solid foundation of the church on earth, much as Christ would hold dominion in Heaven. Jerome emphasizes that Christ here confers an office, adjudicating the righteous and wicked, much like the rabbinical prerogative to separate the clean and unclean.[101] In the *Annales*, Baronio emphasizes Matthew's account of Peter's *confessio* over the rituals of pastoral initiation as the foundation of Church hierarchy and judicial authority, invested in the pope through the keys. Baronio also stresses the importance of the pair of keys that ultimately appears on the papal coat of arms: a gold one signifying the power to forgive sins and a silver one to bind trespasses.[102]

In staging Christ's bestowal of the keys, Poussin naturally consulted the most authoritative, if not ancient, pictorial models—those adorning the Sistine Chapel, the site of the election of each new pope, which determines the notional transfer of the keys through the succession of Saint Peter. Given the importance of this episode in ordaining the pope's power, it appears twice in the chapel. In

Fig. 32. *Christ Enthroned with Elders and Neophyte, from the Catacombs of Saints Hermes, Basilla, Protus, and Hyacinth*, engraving in Antonio Bosio's *Roma sotterranea*, plate 565, published 1632

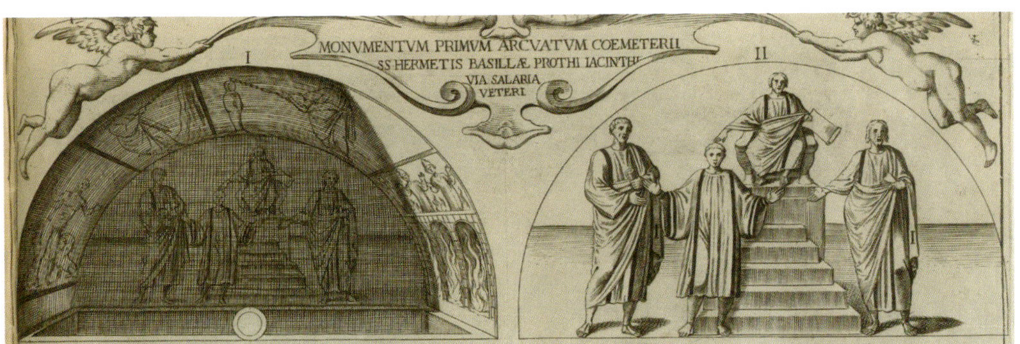

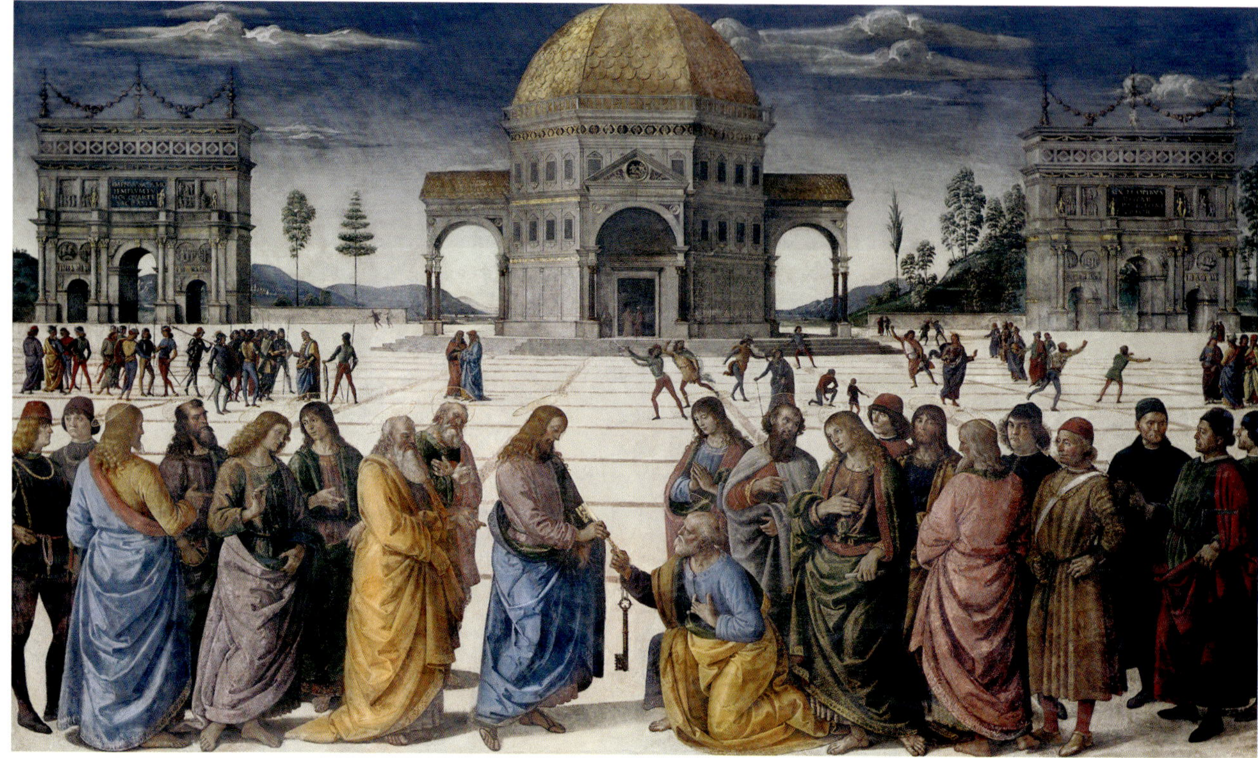

Fig. 33. Perugino (Italian, c. 1450–1523), *Christ Consigning the Keys to Saint Peter*, 1482. Fresco, 130 x 220 in. (330 x 550 cm). Sistine Chapel, Vatican Museums, Vatican City

the early 1480s, Pope Sixtus IV had the interior adorned with a cycle of murals depicting the lives of Moses and Christ, which culminated in Perugino's *Christ Consigning the Keys to Saint Peter* (fig. 33).[103] The fresco solemnly plots the apostles along the frontal plane before a grand piazza, where a church dominates pagan triumphal arches. With the isolated key placed on axis with the centralized church and the vanishing point to which all of the orthogonals recede, the perspectival construction itself proclaims that Christ's dominion, passed to Peter, extends through the church to infinity.[104]

To complement the earlier murals, not to mention Michelangelo's frescoes on the vault, Pope Leo X commissioned Raphael in 1515 to produce a series of monumental tapestries depicting the acts of Saints Peter and Paul to adorn the Sistine Chapel's lower walls.[105] Reaffirming the message of Perugino's painting, Raphael's "Feed my Sheep" tapestry and its preparatory cartoon stage a related post–Resurrection event, when Christ appears on the coast of the Sea of Tiberias before a group of apostles out fishing (figs. 34, 35). Initially, they do not recognize him, but he soon reveals himself through their massive haul of fish. Upon their reunion on the shore, Christ queries Peter: "'Simon, son of Jonas, lovest thou me more than these [others]?" Peter replies: "Yea Lord, thou knowest that I love thee," to which Christ says, "Feed my Lambs" (John 21:15). After repeating this query twice more, and receiving Peter's insistent pledge of love, Christ charges him to "Feed my Sheep" (21:16–17). The post-Resurrection apparition reaffirms the earlier consignment of the keys and further invests Peter, and his papal progeny, with ultimate authority over the Christian flock. Raphael conflates this text with the canonical verses from the gospel of Matthew to underscore the primacy of Peter. The shoreline landscape and fishing boat certainly reprise the setting of John's final chapter, as does Christ's clearly resurrected appearance. Nonetheless, Peter genuflects and grasps the keys in verification of the earlier donation. Furthermore, Raphael sets Christ's designation of Peter before ten witnessing apostles, with only the absence of

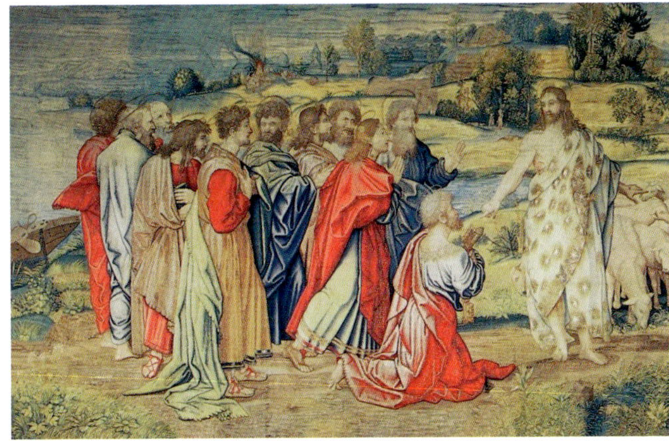

Fig. 34. After Raphael (Italian, 1483–1520), *Christ's Charge to Peter (Feed My Sheep)*, c. 1518–19. Tapestry made for the Sistine Chapel, 135 x 209⅜ in. (343 x 532 cm). Vatican Museums, Vatican City

Fig. 35. Raphael (Italian, 1483–1520), *Christ's Charge to Peter (Feed My Sheep)*, cartoon for the Sistine Chapel tapestry, c. 1515–16. Bodycolor over charcoal underdrawing on paper, mounted on canvas, 135 x 209⅜ in. (343 x 532 cm). Victoria and Albert Museum, London. On loan from Her Majesty Queen Elizabeth II

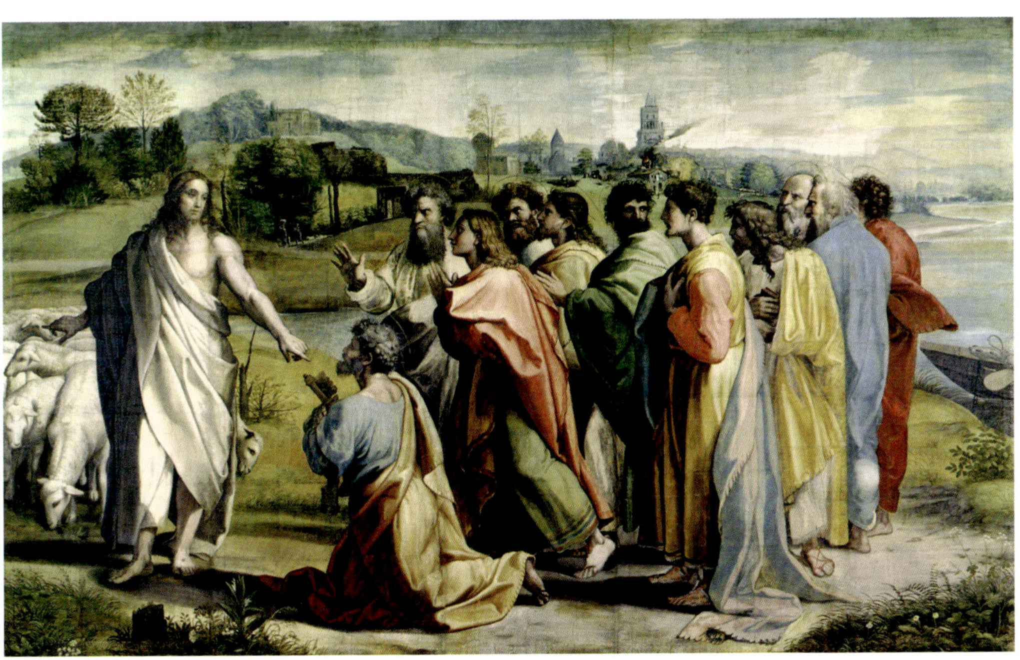

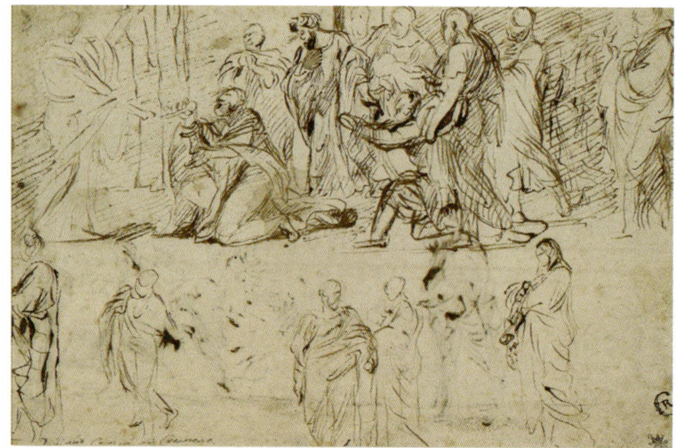

Fig. 36. Attributed to Poussin, *Compositional Studies for the Ordination*, c. 1636 (or later). Pen and ink, 5⅞ x 8¹³⁄₁₆ in. (15 x 22.4 cm). The Pierpont Morgan Library, New York. Gift of a Trustee in honor of Miss Felice Stampfle

Fig. 37. Raphael (Italian, 1483–1520), initial design for *Christ's Charge to Peter (Feed My Sheep)*, c. 1514. Red chalk (offset), 10⅛ x 14¾ in. (25.7 x 37.5 cm). The Royal Collection, Windsor Castle

Judas signaling the post–Resurrection time frame, rather than the seven that John's Gospel situates at the miracle.[106]

In composing the Dal Pozzo *Ordination*, Poussin drew from both Perugino's and Raphael's Sistine works to invest his scene with an artistic pedigree that reinforces the message of papal authority. Raphael's cartoons for the tapestries left for England the year before Poussin arrived in Italy, but the painter certainly knew the tapestry itself, as well as various engravings after it.[107] Among the most obvious debts the Dal Pozzo *Ordination* pays to the tapestry is its elegant grouping of figures in dignified ancient dress before a verdant landscape.[108] Yet Poussin's apostles, strung out along the breadth of the pictorial field so that all but one is largely visible,

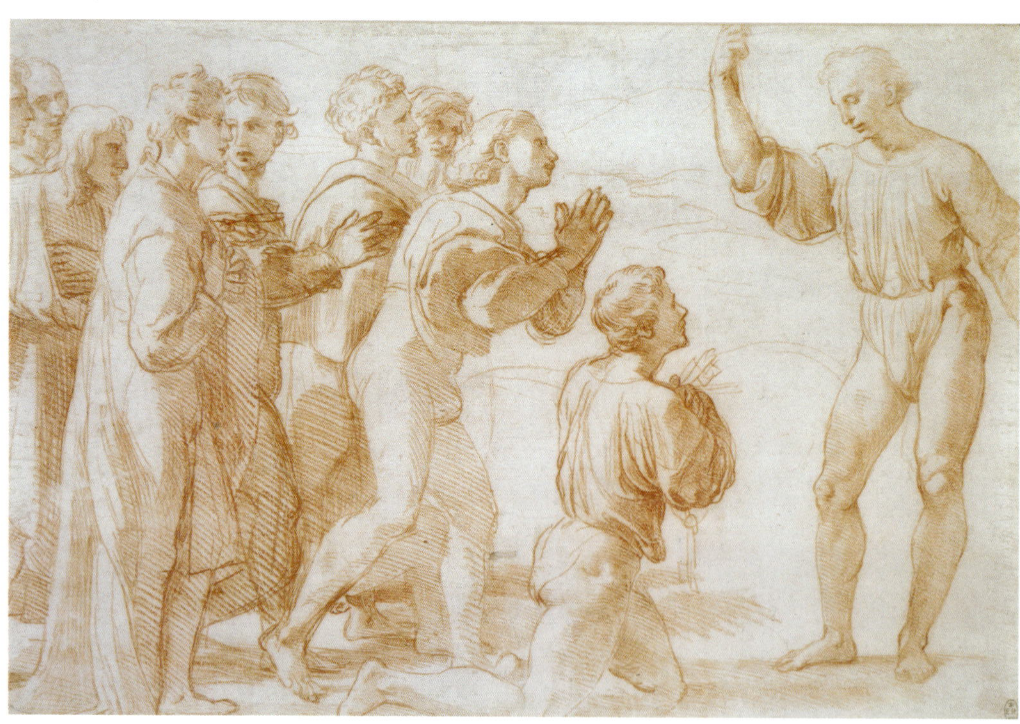

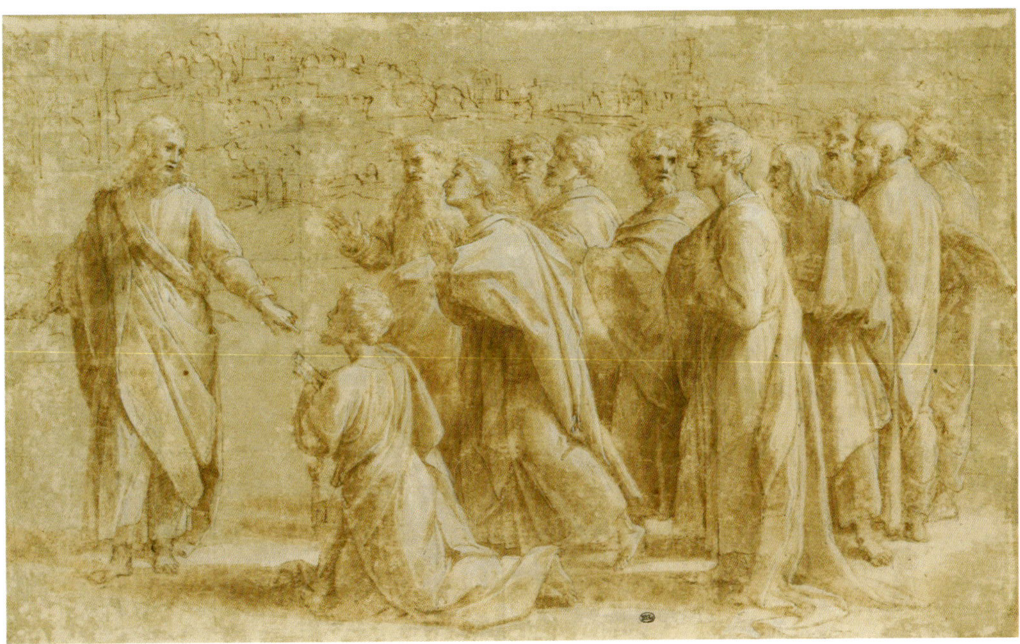

Fig. 38. Raphael (Italian, 1483–1520), compositional design for *Christ's Charge to Peter (Feed My Sheep)*, 1516. Pen and ink, 8¾ x 14 in. (22.2 x 35.4 cm). Musée du Louvre, Paris

owe more to Perugino's calibrated plotting than to Raphael's densely overlapping bodies and aligned faces. Indeed, Poussin's figures echo those of Perugino in their proportion relative to the field, their arrangement along roughly parallel rows, and their delicate gestures of reverence and reflection. Certainly the pose and orientation of Jesus, the consigning action, and even the relative position of gold and silver keys approximate Perugino's Christ. A doubled-sided drawing attributed to Poussin contains several sketches of the figure groupings and the pose of Christ (fig. 36). One can chart a gradual departure from Raphael's block of apostles, although Poussin determined the profile view of the Lord's commanding gesture and bold stride early on.[109] This profile stance and Christ's raised left arm pointing to the heavenly source of his paternity approximate Raphael's own early solution for the tapestry's design, as seen in a chalk drawing (fig. 37). While it is uncertain whether Poussin knew this drawing, he was certainly familiar with Raphael's study for the final composition, owned by his friend, the painter Jacques Stella (fig. 38).[110] The most obviously Raphaelesque aspect of the Dal Pozzo *Ordination*, the exquisite color harmonies of pastel vermillion, cerulean blue, mauve, peach, and various hues of green, yellow, and ocher among the draperies must be fortuitous. The cartoon was already in England—with the tapestry adopting a denser and richer color scheme.

Poussin's choice of a pure landscape setting for the consignment of the keys is highly motivated, as it deviates significantly from the scripture's specification that the event took place outside the city of

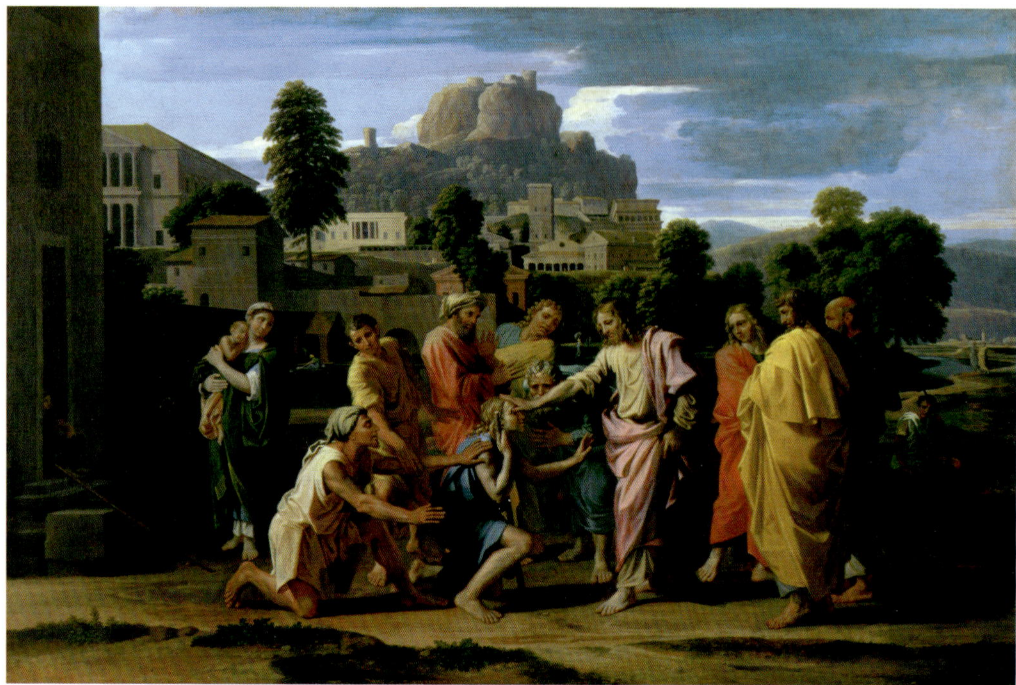

Fig. 39. Nicolas Poussin (French, 1594–1665, active in Italy), *Christ Healing the Blind at Jericho (Capernaum?)*, 1650. Oil on canvas, 46⅞ x 69¼ in. (119 x 176 cm). Musée du Louvre, Paris

Caesarea Philippi. Though he usually included classically inspired structures to indicate the appropriate urban locale, as in *Christ Healing the Blind at Jericho* (fig. 39),[111] in *Ordination*, he uses only trees and hills to set off the figures, in a manner similar to some of his earlier pagan-themed works, like *The Triumph of Pan*. This reference is likely purposeful; the sylvan environment and its lounging occupants may harbor pagan associations and provide a temporal and conceptual contrast to the foreground biblical event. For Anthony Blunt, the landscape represented a philosophers' grove, as it does in later paintings of that theme by Salvator Rosa (fig. 40).[112] The philosophers symbolize the pagan order that will be supplanted in the age of grace initiated by Christ's advent and the permanent institution of his church through the papacy. This may be one way in which Poussin subtly acknowledges the biblical setting, since the charge to Peter transpired on the borders of Jewish Palestine, in a largely pagan territory with a shrine to Pan. Thus even the locale of Peter's elevation signals the future enfranchisement of the Gentiles into the church.[113] The way one of the philosophers points forward toward the apostolic assembly anticipates this. A bearded figure who strides past Christ at the left edge of the composition, his bowed head absorbed in his book, might suggest continuities between the epochs: pagan mysteries yield to the sacraments as the instruments of divine communion with humanity. Some scholars have suggested that the figure is an embodiment of the Old Testament, perhaps one of the Pharisees that Christ had recently censured for blindly seeking portents (Matthew 16.1–12), though an alternate theory will be examined in a following chapter.[114]

The screen of trees, apart from any pagan associations, reiterates in arboreal terms the theme of deputizing to spread the message of divine truth through Christ's ministry. The loftiest trunk aligns with Christ's striding form, as a smaller, leafy tree extends his gesture up toward the heavenly gate that the keys unlock. The paired major and minor tree shafts articulate the transfer of ministerial authority. Another tree to the right echoes the largest tree, reiterating the dual-figure exchange, and punctuates the group of five apostles whose physical expressions of veneration mimic Peter's genuflection and register the gradual comprehension of their evangelical roles. To the right of the apostle who kneels even more deeply than Peter, another group of six articulate more varied reactions through their gesticulations—perhaps reflecting their earlier confusion when questioned about Jesus's identity. Behind them, the allée of diagonally receding trees both helps alleviate the composition's insistent lateral organization and aligns these apostles with the inquisitive pagans. Incorporating the same colors as Christ and Peter, but in a slightly different key, a youthful disciple reorients Christ's right hand gesture toward his neighbor, whose vigorous contrapposto and sharp profile balance those of Jesus, bracketing the elegantly varied apostle group between them. Isolated from this enclosed ensemble, another figure lingers in the shadows, significantly realigning Christ's pointing gesture from heaven to his own neck, his green garments reflecting his invidious complexion. He can only be Judas, whose ultimate suicidal fate is foreshadowed in the rocky ledge and gallows–shaped stump

Fig. 40. Salvator Rosa (Italian, 1615–1673), *The Grove of Philosophers*, c. 1642–45. Oil on canvas, 57⅞ x 87 in. (147 x 221 cm). Galleria Palatina, Palazzo Pitti, Florence

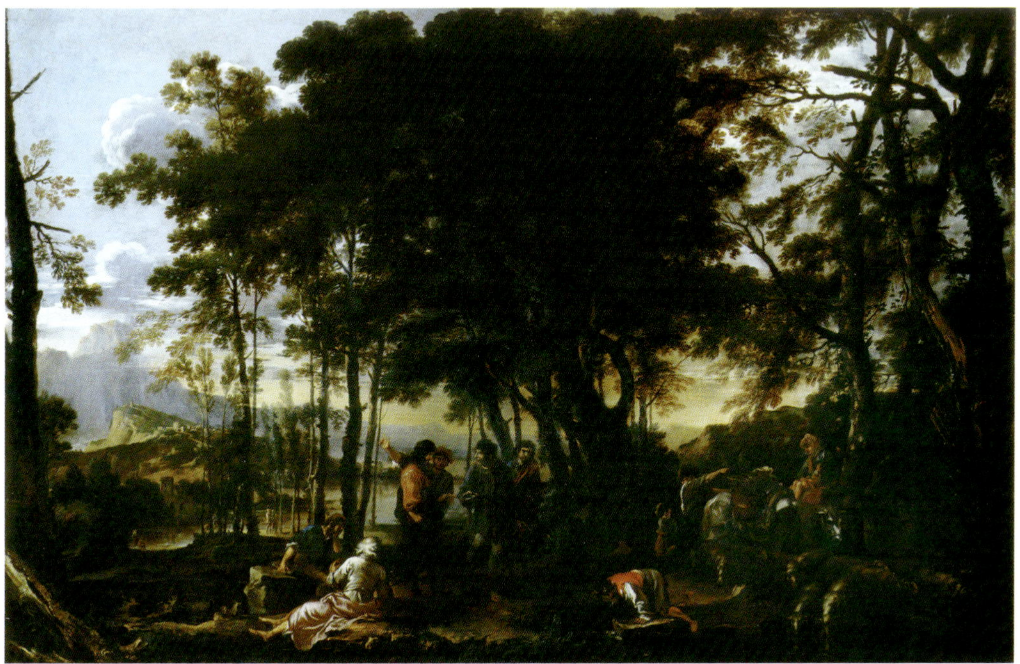

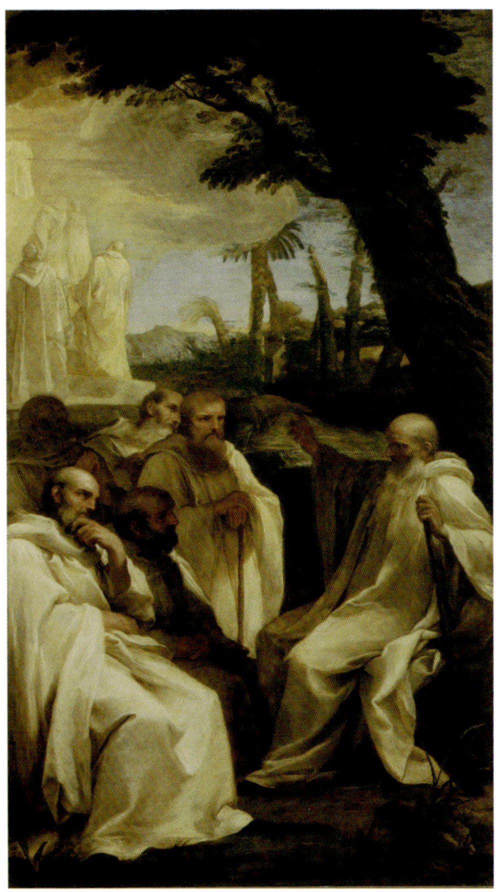

Fig. 41. Andrea Sacchi (Italian, 1599–1661), *The Vision of Saint Romuald*, 1631. Oil on canvas, 122 x 68.9 in. (310 x 175 cm). Vatican Museums, Vatican City

rising above him.[115] The stone cliff and barren limb of self-annihilation contrast with the verdant boughs above Christ and the conspicuous rock below him—the foundation of the Church as the conduit to the eternal life of heaven.

Poussin lavished exceptional care on the characterizations of the apostles. Their noble physiognomy and placid reverence recalls contemporary paintings by Andrea Sacchi, in whose drawing studio Poussin studied earlier in the decade (fig. 41). Not coincidentally, Cassiano owned a reduction of an altarpiece by Sacchi in which the protagonist, Saint Romuald, resembles the penultimate apostle to the right.[116] Apart from the contested sheet of compositional studies, only one drawing, comprised of three head studies, relates directly to the Dal Pozzo *Ordination* (fig. 42).[117] With light pen contours, minimal hatching, and feathery strokes for hair, Poussin fashions the noble profile of Christ, the cocked, inquisitive

Fig. 42. Nicolas Poussin (French, 1594–1665, active in Italy), *Head Studies of Christ and the Apostles* (verso), c. 1636–40. Pen, ink, and wash, 5 x 8⅝ in. (12.6 x 22 cm). The Cleveland Museum of Art, Leonard C. Hanna, Jr. Fund

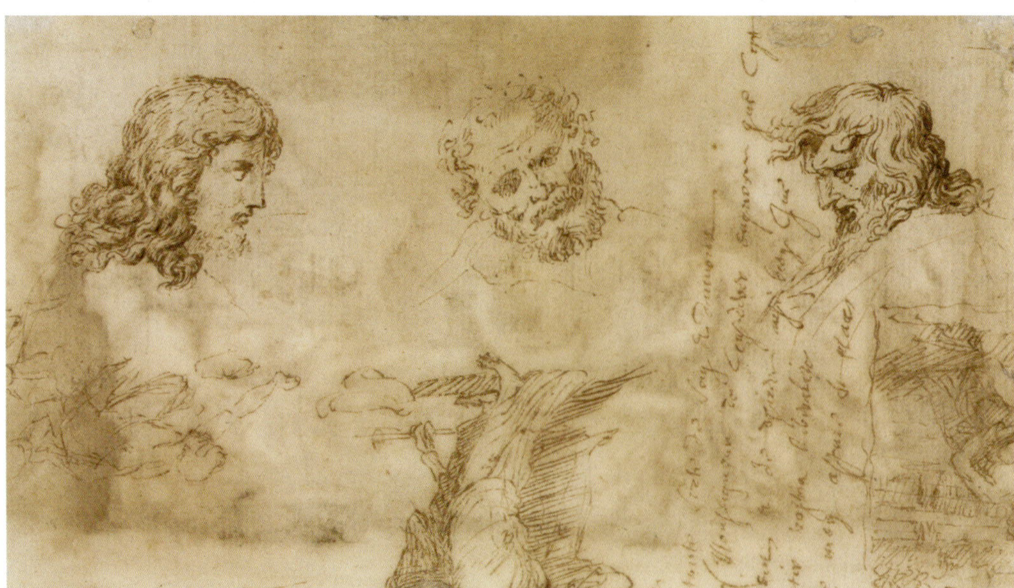

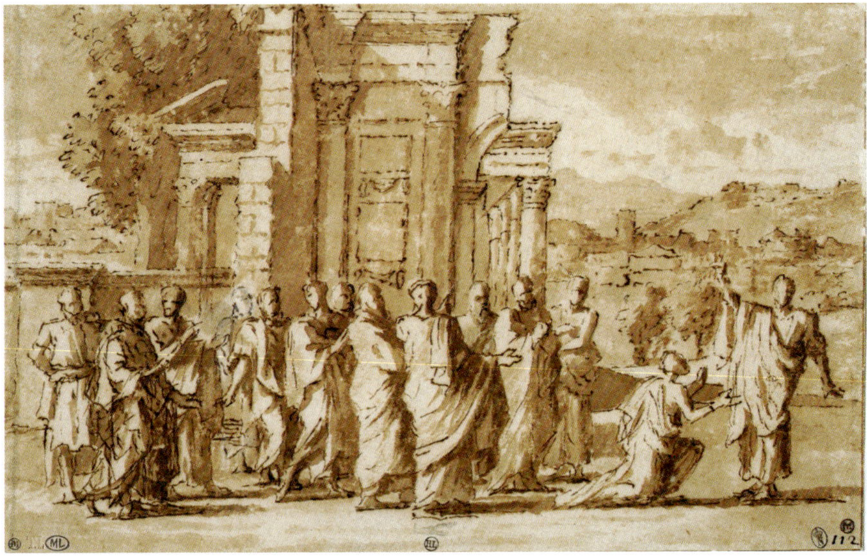

Fig. 43. Nicolas Poussin (French, 1594–1665, active in Italy), *Study for the Sacrament of Ordination*, c. 1646–7. Pen, ink, and wash study, 5⅜ x 8⅜ in. (13.7 x 21.2 cm). Musée du Louvre, Paris

head of the bearded apostle directly behind Peter, and the bowed, angular visage of Judas. These sketches constitute the unique example of detailed facial studies among Poussin's surviving graphic oeuvre and reveal his determination to convey the solemnity of Christ's charge, the curiosity yielding to reverence among the apostles, and the shameful depravity of Judas.[118] The head study of Christ may also indicate a desire to capture an authentic likeness of his true portrait, based on purported eyewitness descriptions included in Counter-Reformation treatises like Borromeo's *De Pictura Sacra* and featured on countless medals.[119]

Unlike the Dal Pozzo *Ordination*, there are extensive preparatory drawings that chart the evolution of the design for the Chantelou version. These typify Poussin's compositional method and demonstrate his characteristic cultivation of a novel solution to a repeated subject. In the earliest study, Poussin begins with the raw material of the Dal Pozzo composition, retaining the lateral frieze of apostles but reversing their orientation and slightly varying their placement (fig. 43).[120] Characteristic of his pen, ink, and wash studies, the artist uses drawing almost exclusively to fix possible figural dispositions before the architectural backdrop or landscape rather than to work out details of facial expression or clothing. Indeed, he may have drawn the mannequin-like figures after modeled wax figurines placed on an enclosed miniature stage box, as was his habit, according to early commentators.[121] The swaths of chiaroscuro made with wash may record the lighting experiments that Poussin is reported to have controlled through apertures in the side of the box. The extra thirteenth apostle that appears in the drawing indicates its experimental quality. In this first study, Poussin bases Christ's dramatic three-quarters stance more closely on Raphael's Christ; he gestures in dual directions, though one arm is still upraised, as in the Dal Pozzo painting. Poussin now represents the prior pagan age through

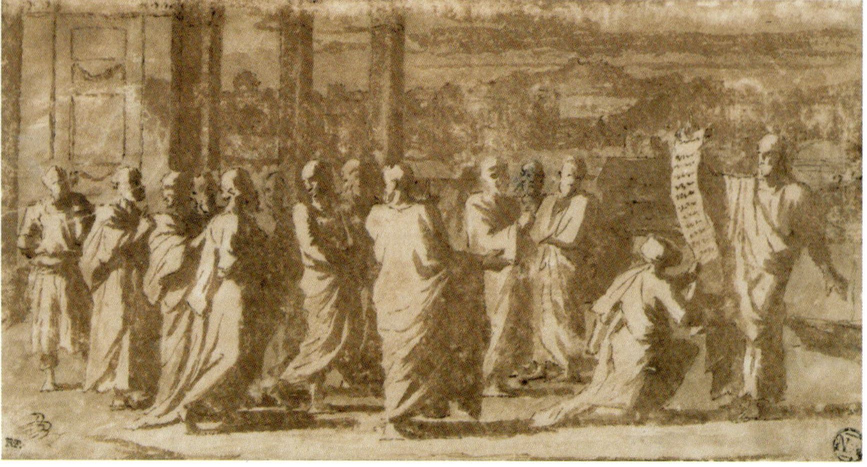

Fig. 44. Nicolas Poussin (French, 1594–1665, active in Italy), *Study for the Sacrament of Ordination*, c. 1646–7. Pen, ink, and wash study, 5¼ x 9⅝ in. (13.3 x 24.5 cm). Musée du Louvre, Paris

an exquisitely rendered ruined temple with receding Corinthian columns. The geometric forms of the structure create an almost cubist still life, animated by a subtle play of light through the expert manipulation of wash and exposed paper.

Poussin's second study focuses on the figural groups, with the temple colonnade now extended horizontally (fig. 44). There are still thirteen posed figures besides Jesus. The major shift here is that Christ now holds an unrolled scroll in his upraised right hand, which he bestows upon Peter, a reference to the laws of the Church.[122] The final pair of compositional studies approximates the final design of Chantelou's picture (figs. 45, 46). These indicate a fundamental shift in conception, as Poussin distributes the now twelve apostles into roughly equal groups on either side of Christ, who dominates the center of the composition before a hilly landscape of tombs, monuments, and a distant city gate.[123] Poussin must have realized that Christ's expansive gesture, borrowed from Raphael, made more sense placed centrally, engaging both groups of apostles; his left arm now points heavenward as in the Dal Pozzo picture.

Fig. 45. Nicolas Poussin (French, 1594–1665, active in Italy), *Study for the Sacrament of Ordination*, c. 1647. Pen, brown ink, and brown wash on paper, 7 5/16 x 10 in. (18.7 x 25.5 cm). The Pierpont Morgan Library, New York

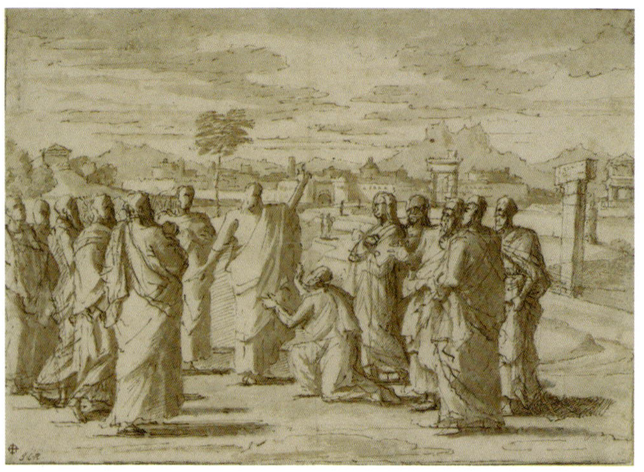

In the finished painting, Poussin places the keys prominently in each of Christ's hands and adjusts some of the poses, especially those of the elegant figures in the right group (fig. 47).[124] Saint John now spreads his arms and gazes heavenward in awe, and his companion echoes Christ's left arm gesture while pointing outward to the beholder. Though somewhat severe, the composition is a masterpiece of color distribution. Poussin repeats the primary triad of red, blue, and yellow three times in the figures at far left and right, as well as in the central group of Christ and Peter. Flanking them, three apostles wear the secondary colors

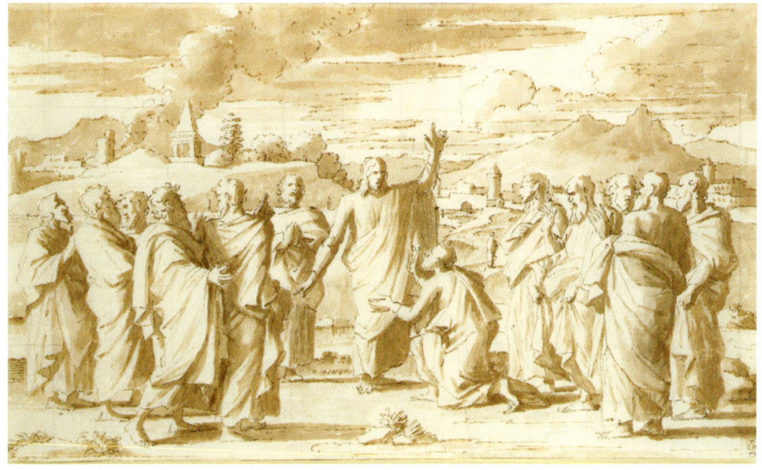

Fig. 46. Nicolas Poussin (French, 1594–1665, active in Italy), *Study for the Sacrament of Ordination*, c. 1647. Pen, ink, and wash studies, 7¾ x 12⅞ in. (19.8 x 32.7 cm). The Royal Collection, Windsor Castle

of green and orange. Compared to the drawings, the architectural elements—a pyramidal tomb, a bridge, a turret, and a pier curiously inscribed with an "E"—are far more dominant and designate the sanctity of the space.

Fig. 47. Nicolas Poussin (French, 1594–1665, active in Italy), *The Sacrament of Ordination*, from *The Seven Sacraments for Paul Fréart de Chantelou*, 1647. Oil on canvas, 46 x 70⅛ in. (117 x 178 cm). National Gallery of Scotland, Edinburgh. Bridgewater Loan, 1945

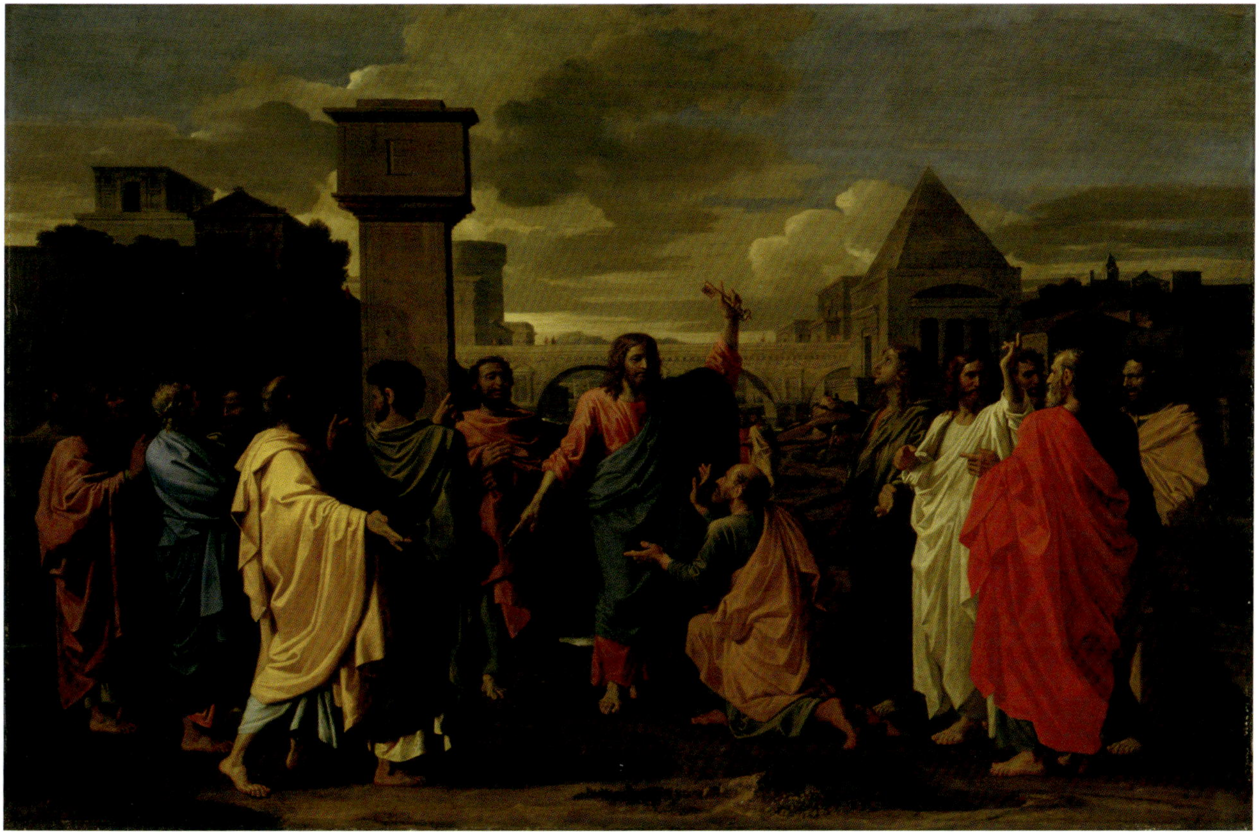

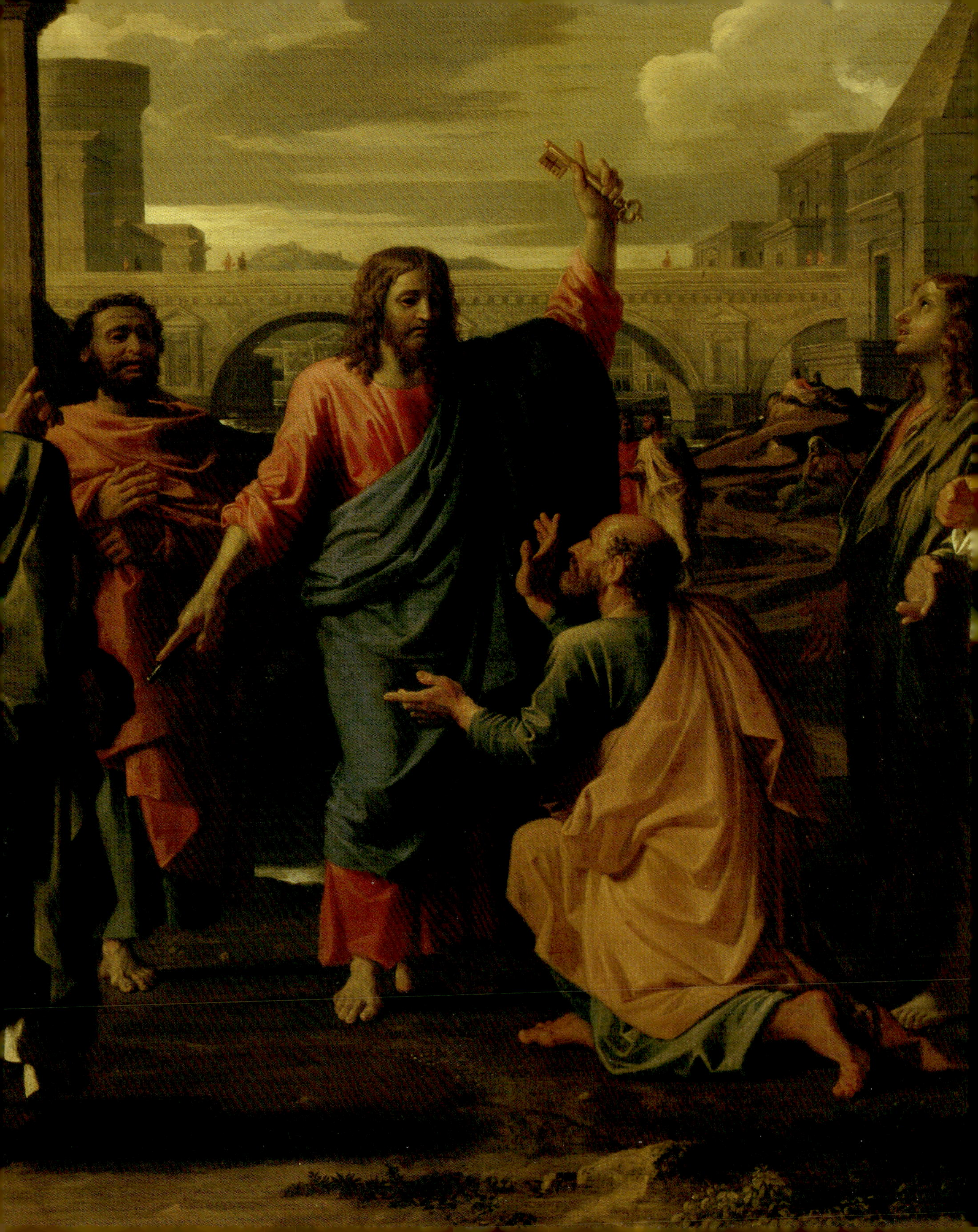

Peter, Paul, and the Early Church

I N THE TRANSITION BETWEEN THE FIRST AND SECOND SERIES OF *SACRAMENTS*, POUSSIN INTENSIFIES his quest for historical and archaeological accuracy. In particular, the transformation between the two versions of *Confirmation* introduces a degree of historical specificity that further illuminates the scope of each *Ordination* painting. Unlike most of the other sacraments, confirmation lacks an exemplary biblical narrative. Instead, Poussin depicts the administering of the sacrament according to the rite of the primitive church. In the version painted for Dal Pozzo, a white-robed bishop anoints a young communicant with consecrated oil, while another priest binds a youth with a fillet, or headband, before a paschal candle indicating Easter (fig. 48). On the left, mothers encourage their children to watch, and two older witnesses seem to debate what is unfolding; the turban that one wears might designate them as suspicious Pharisees. The costumes and setting read as generically antique, though Poussin bases the architecture on the sixteenth-century church of Sant'Anatasio dei Grechi in Rome.[125]

By contrast, the Chantelou version could hardly be more rigorous in its reconstruction of a paleo-Christian environment, as Charles Dempsey has shown (fig. 49). The scene now transpires in an ancient Roman catacomb. In the distant shadows, a body is laid out between a pair of sarcophagi barely illuminated by oil lamps. Between them is a baptismal font, since confirmation followed immediately upon baptism in early Christian ritual.[126] It is not a typical catacomb, carved from raw subterranean tufa stone and lined with mortuary niches (*cubicula*). Rather the grand columns and marble pavement identify the space as the catacombs under the Baths of Novatus. The baths were part of the opulent palace of the Roman Senator Pudens, who hosted the apostles Peter and Paul during their Roman ministry before their martyrdom under Nero.[127] The kneeling confirmant wears a toga, dyed red to designate high status, over which extends a horizontal band, a reference to the *latus clavus*—a sign of senatorial rank. This detail was based on scholarly opinion, which Cassiano dal Pozzo

Nicolas Poussin, *The Sacrament of Ordination*, from *The Seven Sacraments for Cassiano dal Pozzo*, detail of fig. 47

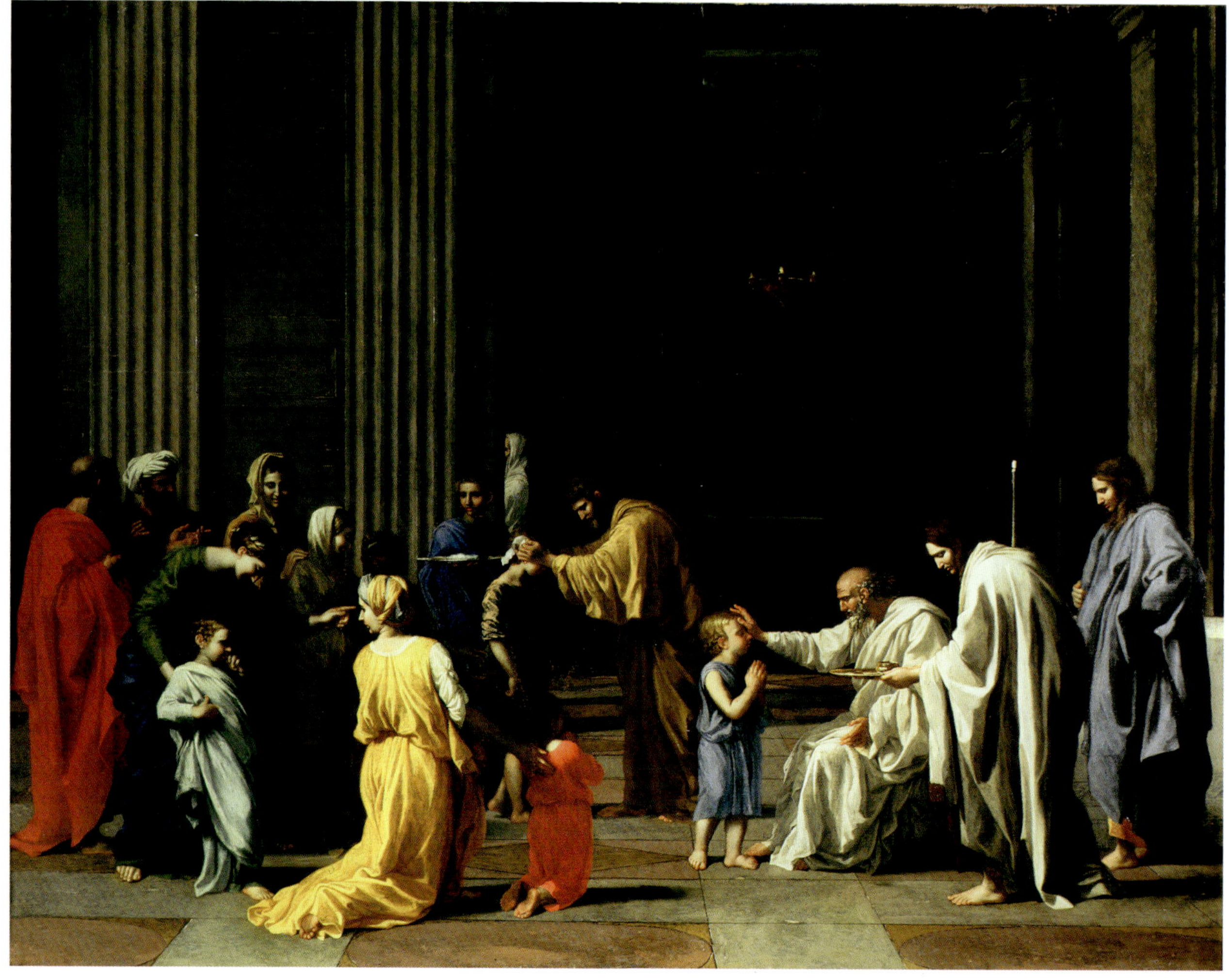

Fig. 48. Nicolas Poussin (French, 1594–1665, active in Italy), *The Sacrament of Confirmation*, from *The Seven Sacraments for Cassiano dal Pozzo*, c. 1636–1640. Oil on canvas, 37⅝ x 47⅝ in. (95.5 x 121 cm). The Duke of Rutland's Poussin Settlement, Belvoir Castle, Leicestershire, England

endorsed, that the *latus* was a separate band worn across the chest, as illustrated in drawings from the Paper Museum. The fact that the *latus* was actually a vertical fold with a distinctly colored hem hardly detracts from Poussin's objective to cast the confirmant as a senator, namely Pudens. The officiating priest, wearing an embroidered bishop's *latus clavus*, can only be Saint Paul, who resided and preached in the house above. As Paul anoints the senator, his sainted daughters Praxedes and Pudentiana await their turn. Timothy, to whom Paul addressed two epistles, has already been anointed and receives the fillet. At the right, the Roman newcomer Peter, with his typical grey beard and bald head, enters the scene, being blessed with holy water.[128] In the church that still exists on the site of Pudens's palace, Santa Pudenziana, the fifth-century apse mosaic depicts Paul, Peter, and Christ all wearing, ironically enough, a correctly rendered *latus clavus* fold with hem (fig. 50).[129] Poussin thus referenced the most advanced archaeological researches into the ancient church to invest the post-evangelical sacrament of confirmation with the venerable patina of the apostolic age and place its celebration under the auspices of Peter and Paul.

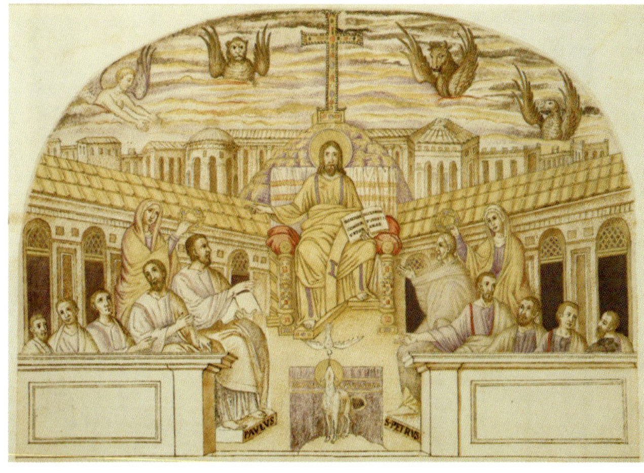

Fig. 50. Antonio Eclissi (Italian, active 1627–1644), *Fifth-Century Apse Mosaic of Santa Pudenziana, Rome*, from the Museo Cartaceo of Cassiano dal Pozzo, 17th century, watercolor. The Royal Collection, Windsor Castle

Fig. 49. Nicolas Poussin (French, 1594–1665, active in Italy), *The Sacrament of Confirmation*, from *The Seven Sacraments for Paul Fréart de Chantelou*, 1645. Oil on canvas, 46 x 70⅛ in. (117 x 178 cm). National Gallery of Scotland, Edinburgh. Bridgewater Loan, 1945

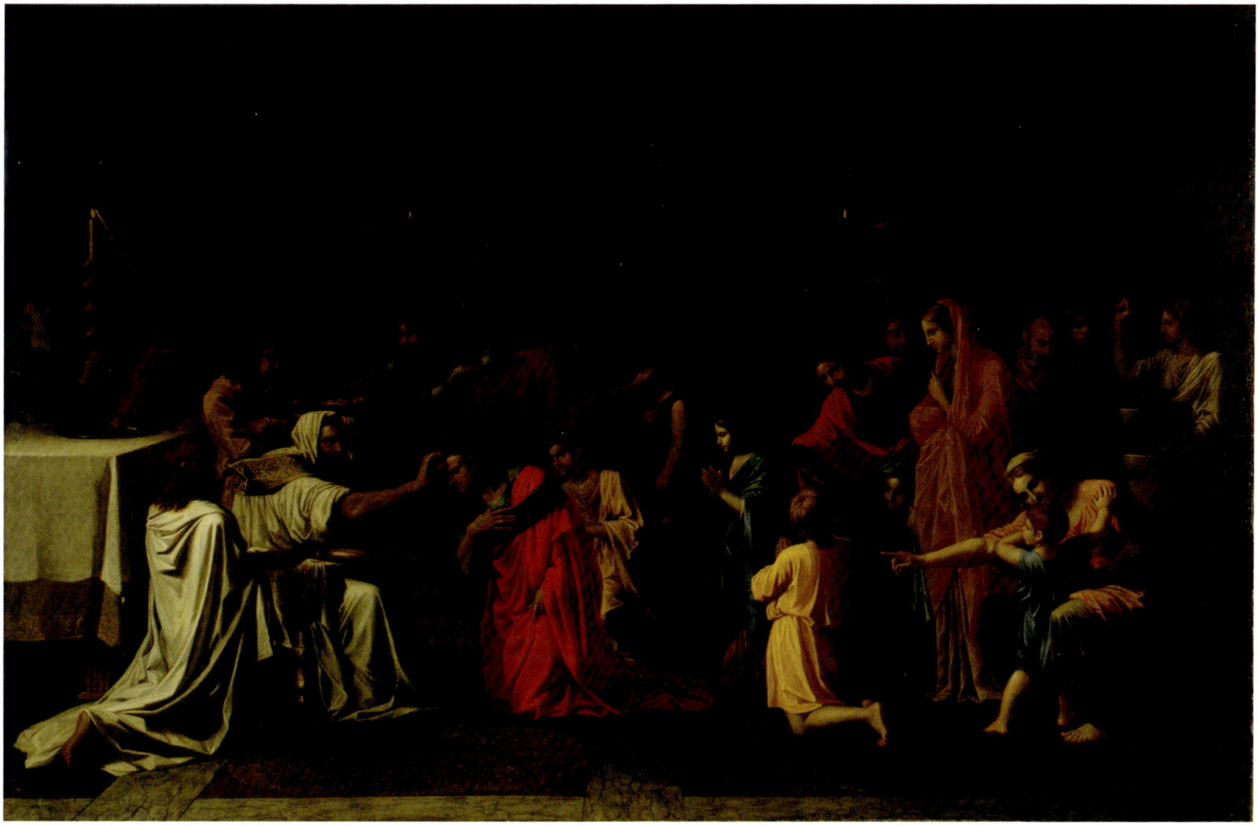

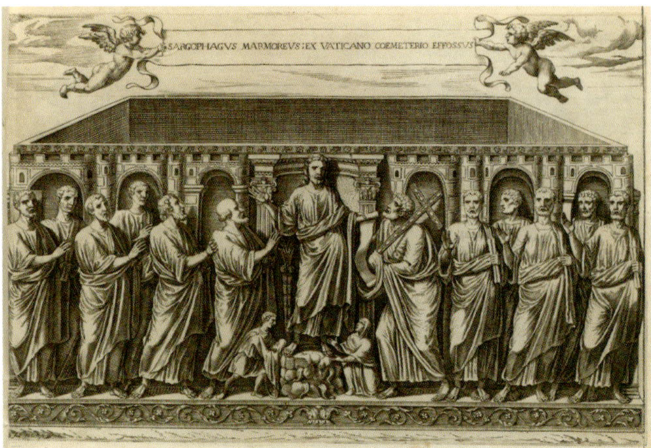

Fig. 51. *Fourth-Century "Traditio Legis" Sarcophagus*, now in the Musée du Louvre, engraving in Antonio Bosio's *Roma sotterranea*, plate 69, published 1632

Fig. 52. *Fourth-Century "City Gate" Sarcophagus from the Catacombs*, from the Museo Cartaceo of Cassiano dal Pozzo, 17th century, pen-and-ink drawing. The Royal Collection, Windsor Castle

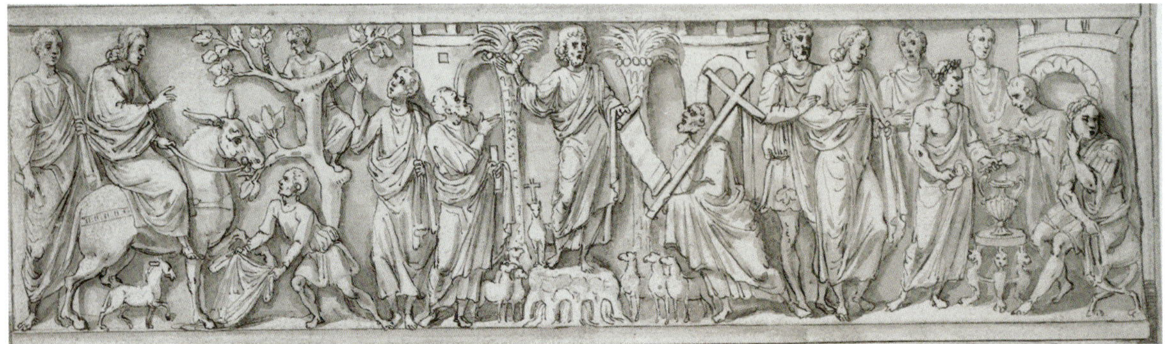

In the *Ordination* for Chantelou, Poussin also enriched the scene in ways conversant with recent paleo-Christian researches. As previously mentioned, at one stage in the evolution of the design Poussin had Christ hold up a scroll instead of a key. This motif references the *traditio legis*, or transfer of the law, which was prevalent in the earliest official Christian imagery. As commonly seen in sarcophagus reliefs, Christ stands frontally on the mount of Paradise, extending the scroll of the law to Peter and flanked by Paul on the right (fig. 51). The composition extends laterally to include either the other apostles before Jerusalem (known as the "City Gate" type) or additional Gospel episodes.[130] A drawing of the Gospel-episode type, after a sarcophagus discovered in the excavations for the new Saint Peter's Basilica, appears in the Museo Cartaceo and perhaps formed the basis for the corresponding engraving in Bosio's *Roma sotterranea* (fig. 52).[131] A drawing by Poussin copies the central motif of a seated Christ extending the law to a bowing Saint Peter from another Bosio plate, though he likely studied the original sarcophagus as well.[132] The scroll contains the Christian teachings that now supplant the

Law of Moses, to be promulgated in the new church headed by Peter and expanded through Paul. That the type draws on Roman imperial iconography of lawgiving emphasizes the newly official recognition of the church after Constantine.[133] Although Poussin abandons the scroll in the final design of the *Ordination*, Anthony Blunt maintains that Poussin adhered to the formal symmetrical grouping of the sarcophagus type to lend the overall composition paleo-Christian authority.[134] Charles Dempsey further argues that Poussin retains the basic concept of the *traditio legis*—both through the figures' symmetrical arrangement and the inclusion of Paul, whom Dempsey identifies as the figure behind Christ's arm on his right side. Shown with Paul's characteristic dark, short hair and beard, his stepping into the scene might be an elegant way of suggesting Paul's belatedness as an apostle, called and converted after Christ's death and resurrection.[135]

Furthermore, Dempsey argues that the setting is not just generically antique but shows Rome as it appeared in the apostolic age from the Vatican, the enduring seat of Christ's church and the popes that succeed Peter. The arches of the Pons Triumphalis, now the Ponte Sant'Angelo, extend behind Christ, connecting the pyramidal tomb of Scipio Africanus with a rounded turret of the Mausoleum of Hadrian, later transformed into the Castel Sant'Angelo.[136] Isolating Christ's dramatic pose before the arched bridge and open sky, Poussin emphasizes the keys as eternal symbols of papal authority.[137] Christ's lower hand extends not directly to Peter, but to the base of a pier supporting a block inscribed with a capital E. The inscription is variously thought to refer to the Greek "Ei" ("thou art"), as inscribed at the Sanctuary of Apollo at Delphi—which could refer to either Christ's pronouncement, "thou art Peter" or Peter's *confessio*, "thou art the son of the Living God"—or, in Dempsey's view, to "Ecclesia," the church built upon the rock of Peter. According to this interpretation, Christ indicates the Roman locale of Peter's church, the great basilica that Constantine will erect above the apostle's grave. Indeed, the inscribed pier reads as a tomb marker, the Christian counterpart to the mausoleum of the pagan general on the opposite bank.[138]

Dempsey's analysis of the composition as conforming to the abstract *traditio legis* of the Church and set in its Roman dominion raises some questions. Can the gathering be totally extracted from the historical moment when Christ consigned the keys to Peter—the foundational event of the sacrament? Also, why do the apostles number twelve, unlike in the earlier preparatory drawings, where the thirteen figures might indicate the addition of Paul?[139] According to Dempsey, Paul's presence as the counterpart to Peter in the ahistorical scene would preclude Judas's presence, even though the swarthy apostle at far right somewhat resembles the fated betrayer. Arguably, Poussin's conflation of Raphael's "Feed my Sheep" tapestry design—which omits Judas due to its post-Resurrection setting—and the abstract *traditio legis* pairing Peter and Paul could credibly account for the substitution. Perhaps the most compelling argument for the identification of Paul in the Chantelou *Ordination*, however, is that Poussin similarly included Paul in his earlier *Ordination* for Dal Pozzo, in a clever foreshadowing of the twin apostolic authority of Peter and Paul over the eternal church.

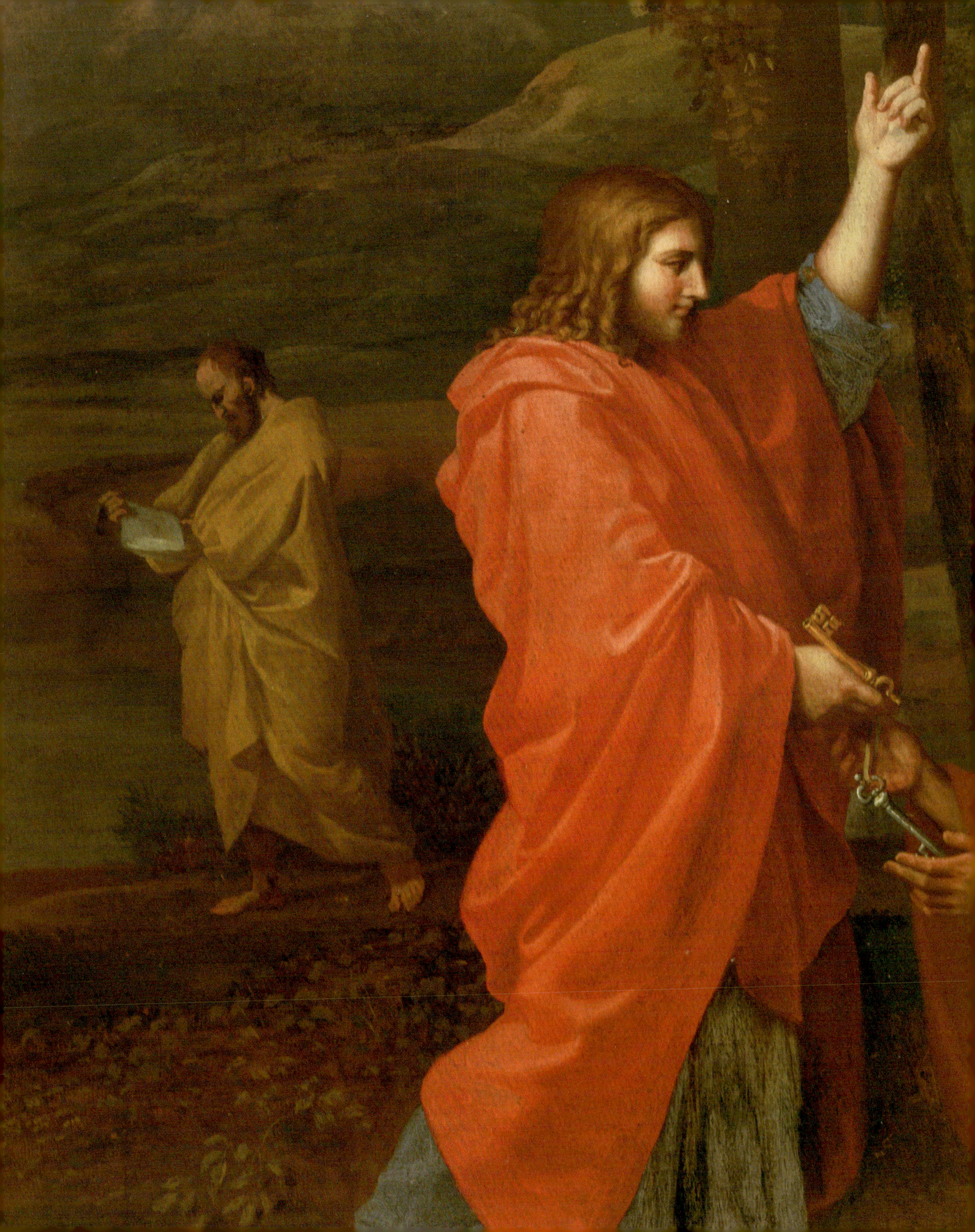

Paul and the Dal Pozzo *Ordination*

Whereas the figures in the philosophers' grove in the background of the Dal Pozzo *Ordination* suggest an earlier pagan age, the lone figure at the far left, paralleling Christ's form even as he walks in the opposite direction, is too conspicuous to be simply another of the philosophers' company. Rather, he must be Paul. Poussin uses compositional clues to express the historical position of Paul at this moment with amazing precision. He shows Paul—or Saul of Tarsus, as he was known before his conversion—an educated Jew and Roman citizen, turning away from Christ. This is appropriate, as Paul played no part in the earthly ministry of Jesus. Indeed, the figure is the embodiment of the Old Law. After Christ's Passion, Saul would conspire with the Pharisees and become the foremost persecutor of the very apostles shown here. It is therefore fitting that he forms the counterpart to Judas the betrayer, on the opposite side of the composition. Poussin also compositionally signals Saul's future state as Paul. Saul was converted when the Lord blinded and then healed him on the Road to Damascus, after which he became the most fervent of apostles and evangelizers.[140] Accordingly, Poussin has Paul's pose and orientation echo that of the apostles.[141] As Paul later reminisces in his epistle to the Galatians (1:13–16): "beyond measure I persecuted the church of God . . . being more exceedingly jealous of the traditions of my Fathers. But when it pleased God . . . to reveal his Son in me, that I might preach him among the heathen; immediately I conferred not with flesh and blood."

As indicated in the passage, the Lord summoned Paul to serve as the apostle to the Gentiles, paving the way for a marginal Jewish sect to become, over time, the official faith of Rome. To foreshadow this in the Dal Pozzo *Ordination*, Poussin ingeniously places Paul at the background point to which the hill of the pagan philosophers descends, but with his figure horizontally aligned with the still-Jewish apostles. As the Jewish zealot Saul, he was more theologically proximate to Christ's messianic fulfillment of the Old Testament prophets than to the pagans, even if he initially turned away from the message. As the proselytizer to the pagan world, Paul famously debated Stoic and Epicurean

Nicolas Poussin, *The Sacrament of Ordination (Christ Presenting the Keys to Saint Peter)*, detail of fig. 1

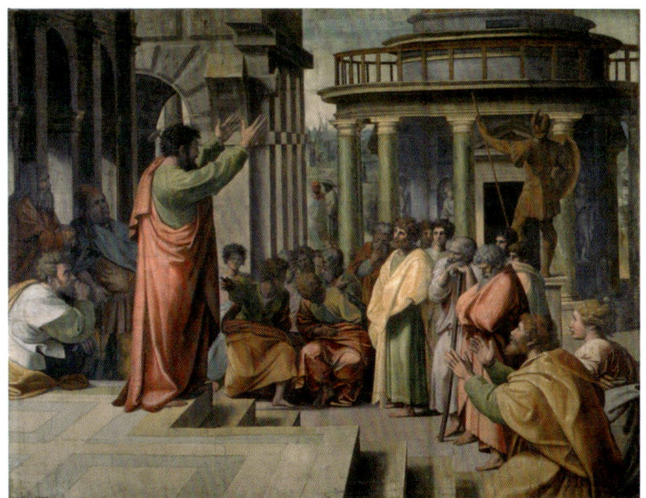

Fig. 53. Raphael (Italian, 1483–1520), *Paul Preaching to the Philosophers in Athens*, cartoon for a Sistine tapestry, 1516–18. Bodycolor over charcoal underdrawing on paper, mounted on canvas, 135 x 174 in. (343 x 442 cm). Victoria and Albert Museum, London. On loan from Her Majesty Queen Elizabeth II

philosophers in Athens, where he mocked their shrine to "an unknown God," exhorted them to abandon their idols, and revealed the path through Christ to a mystical God (Acts 17: 28–30). Raphael's cartoon of Paul preaching in the Athenian agora stages this ideological confrontation, juxtaposing the exhortative apostle with a circular temple adorned with graven idols (fig. 53). Recognizing the fundamental compatibility with Platonic idealism, Dionysius the Areopagite undergoes his conversion in the foreground. [142]

In portraying Paul, who serves as the mediator between the apostles of Christ and the heathen scholars in the grove, Poussin references definitive prototypes for the saint's features: the earliest known representations of the apostle in Roman catacomb paintings discovered in the late-sixteenth century. Drawings of motifs from frescoes in various catacombs indicate Poussin's familiarity with these sites (see fig. 22). [143] In fact, Poussin's Paul shares identical features with a representation of the saint on a mid-fourth-century fresco from the catacomb of Domitilla: a short pointed beard, a prominent forehead, closely cropped hair, and a somewhat receding hairline (fig. 54). In the fresco, Paul holds a scroll, drawn from an adjacent capsa, or basket. [144] Poussin's drawing even reproduces the motif of the capsa, inscribed "volumni," from the apsidal niche fresco of the cubiculum (burial chamber) dei Pistores in this

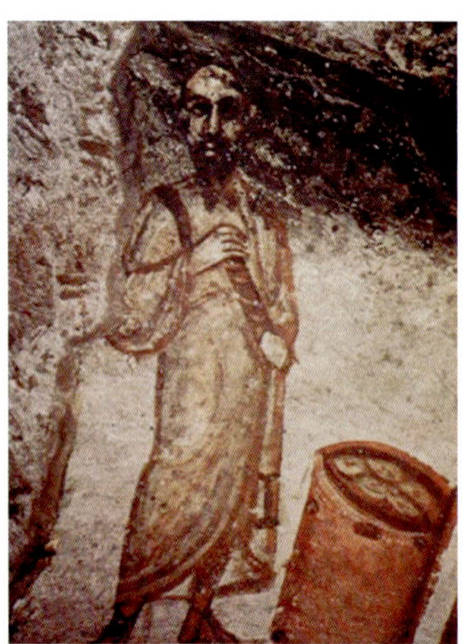

same catacomb. This fresco depicts Christ enthroned among the apostles; a seated Paul in profile likewise conforms to the figure in the Dal Pozzo *Ordination* (fig. 55). [145] A similar scene, with Christ seated above the sainted occupants of the tomb, flanked by Saints Peter and Paul—the latter bearing the same physiognomic features as Poussin's apostle—adorns the cubiculum vault of the Saints Marcellinus and Peter catacomb (fig. 56). [146] A fragment of the head of Paul from a thirteenth-century fresco depicting the Dream of Constantine on the portico of the Old Saint Peter's Basilica testifies to the endurance of this physiognomic type well

Fig. 54. *Saint Paul*, 4th century AD, fresco. Catacomb of Saint Domitilla, Rome

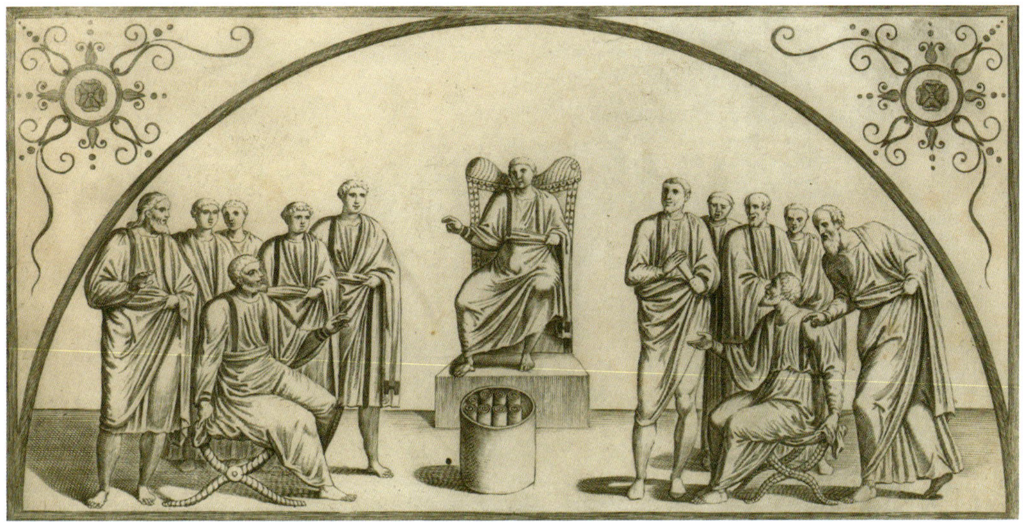

Fig. 55. *Christ with the Apostles, Peter, and Paul, from the Cubiculum dei Pistores, Catacomb of Saint Domitilla, Rome*, engraving in Antonio Bosio's *Roma sotterranea*, plate 221, published 1632

into the later medieval period. Again, the background figure in the *Ordination* conforms completely to the portrayal of Paul on the fragment, then owned by Poussin's patron Vincenzo Giustiniani.[147]

Poussin's Paul substitutes a book for the scroll, which is also common in early Pauline imagery, such as on the summit of the fifth-century triumphal arch mosaic at Santa Maria Maggiore (fig. 57).[148] Both scroll and book signify Paul's status as a scholar. His features also attest to his learned status; the

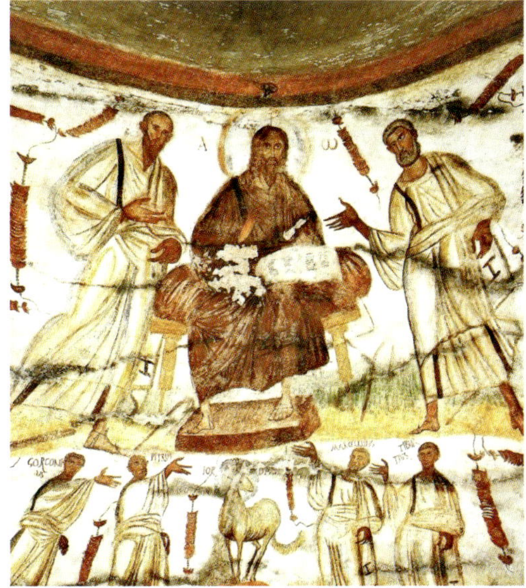

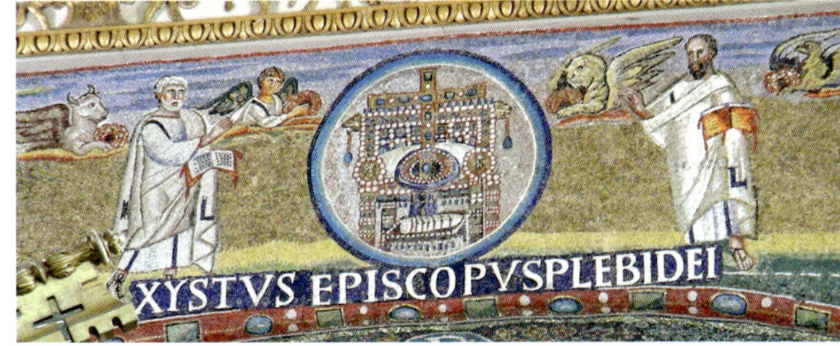

Fig. 56. *Christ with Peter, Paul, and Saints*, 4th century AD, fresco. Catacombs of Saints Peter and Marcellinus, Rome

Fig. 57. *Peter and Paul*, 5th century AD, mosaic. Detail of the triumphal arch in Santa Maria Maggiore, Rome

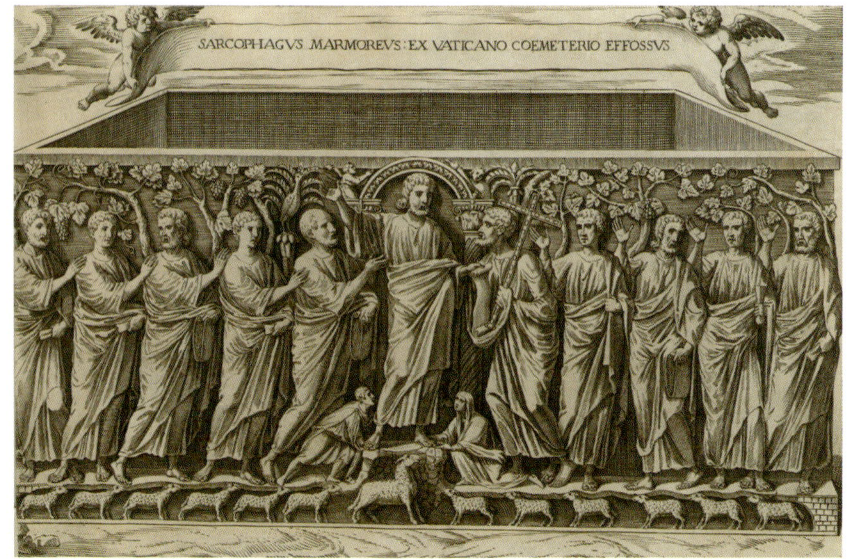

58 **Fig. 58.** *"Traditio legis" Sarcophagus,* now in the Vatican Museums, engraving in Antonio Bosio's *Roma sotterranea*, plate 75, published 1632

iconography of Paul evolved from ancient portraits of philosophers, including Socrates and especially the Neoplatonist Plotinus.[149] The resemblance of Poussin's Paul to Raphael's Socrates in the *School of Athens* reaffirms the kindred origin of the portrait type. This association further justifies Paul's placement between the pagan philosophers and Christ's apostles in the Kimbell painting.

Paul's proximity to Christ allows Poussin to re-create the triad of Christ, Peter, and Paul that pervaded early Christian imagery, while Paul's smaller scale and reverse orientation reinforce that, at the time of the consigning of the keys, the triad is merely virtual and does not replicate the law-giving scenario. Nonetheless, the features of Poussin's Paul accord with venerable examples of the *traditio legis* image type, including a sarcophagus relief with a striding, toga-clad, and balding Paul. Here the apostles are gathered before grapevines that evoke the screen of trees in the Dal Pozzo *Ordination*—and Christ assumes a similarly dynamic pose with upraised arm (fig. 58). Since this sarcophagus marked the grave of the four Pope Leos in the Vatican, all vehement defenders of the temporal powers of the church, it furnished a particularly potent image of papal authority and primacy.[150]

Poussin's Paul also conforms to the facial features and profile orientation of the saint in the most ancient monumental example of the *traditio legis*: a mid-fourth century apse mosaic in the mausoleum of Constantina, today Santa

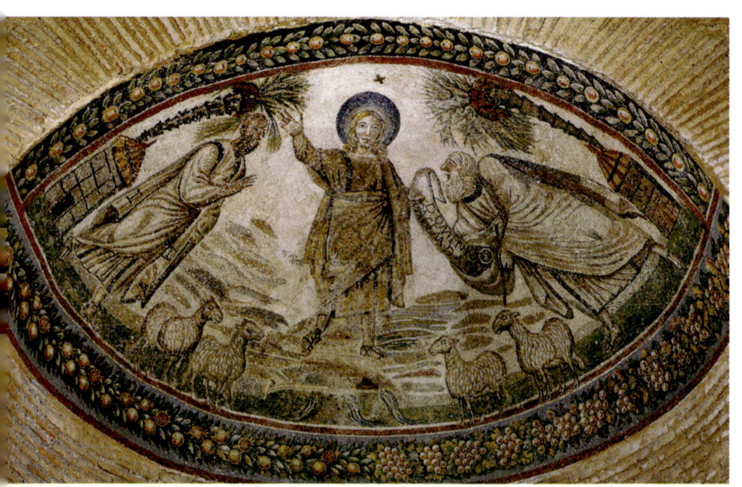

Fig. 59. *Peter Receiving the Law from Christ in the Company of Paul*, 4th century AD, mosaic. Eastern niche of Santa Costanza, Rome

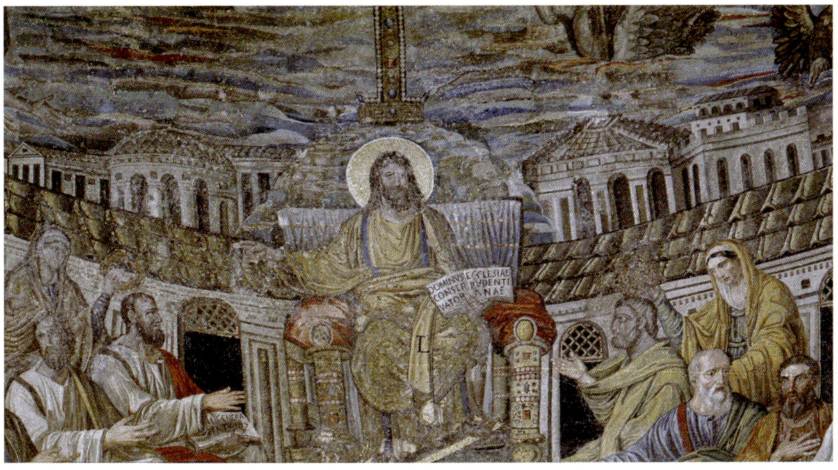

Fig. 60. *Christ Enthroned Instructing the Apostles* (detail), c. 400 AD, mosaic. Apse of Santa Pudenziana, Rome

Costanza (fig. 59). This image of Christ on the Mount of Paradise unfurling the scroll of the law toward a bent, humbled Peter to his left while raising his right arm in benediction over Paul formed a prototype for the central group of numerous apse decorations.[151] In the earliest monumental Church apse mosaic still intact, at Santa Pudenziana, Christ occupies a regal throne, flanked by profile views of Peter, on the left, and Paul, on the right, before assembled apostles (fig. 60). Personifications of the churches of the Gentiles and the Jews crown each apostle, designating the compass of their evangelizing mission—an idea Poussin emphasizes through situating Paul in the pagan grove, while aligning his pose with his future apostolic brethren.[152] In the adjacent oratory adorned with medieval frescoes depicting the conversion of the Pudens family, Paul similarly conforms to this type.[153] The Santa Pudenziana Paul was the most artistically accomplished early Christian prototype, with the possible exception of the spectacularly imposing apse mosaic from the basilica of Saints Cosmas and Damian (fig. 61).[154]

In addition to the actual monuments, Poussin was also able to study at close hand the many drawings of them in Cassiano's Paper Museum, largely by Antonio Eclissi. These drawings were often byproducts of restoration projects; others recorded deteriorating frescoes such as those in

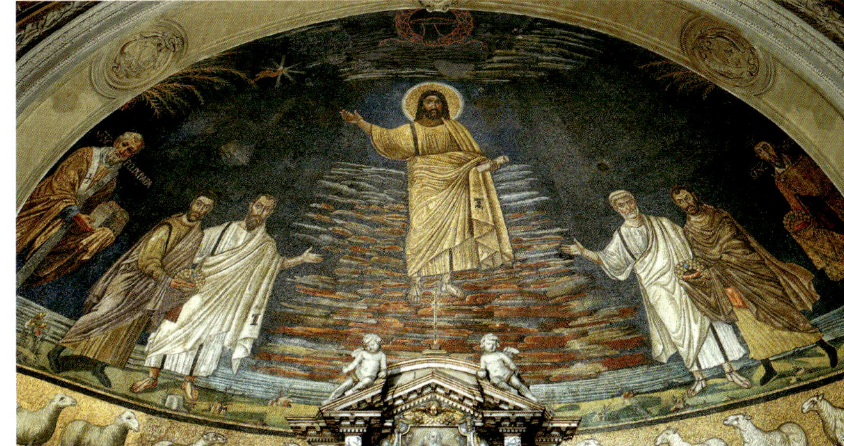

Fig. 61. *Christ Flanked by Saint Peter, Saint Paul, and Titular Saints*, c. 530 AD, mosaic. Apse of Santi Cosma e Damiano, Rome

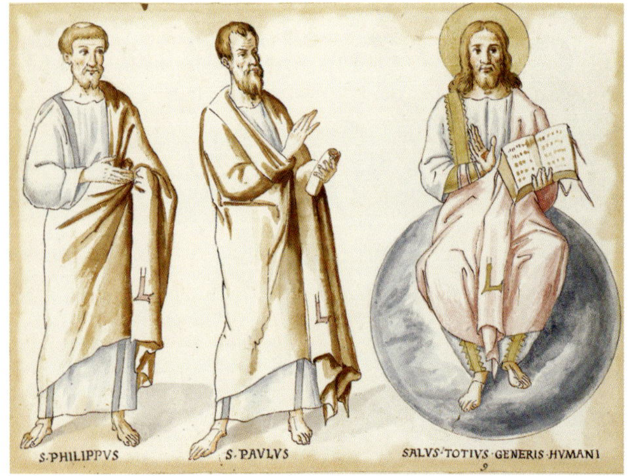

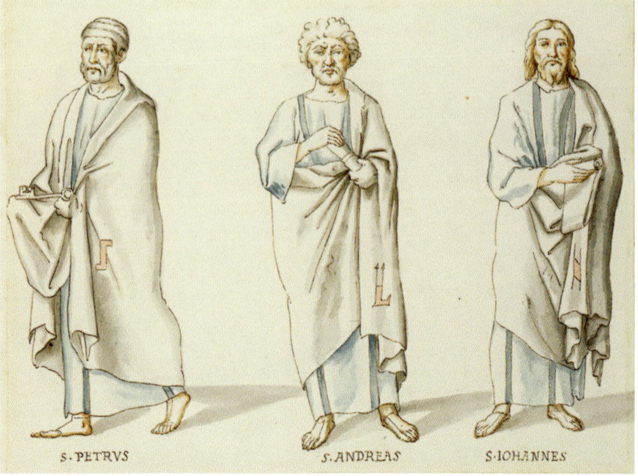

Fig. 62. Antonio Eclissi (Italian, active 1627–1644), *Lost Apse Mosaic of Sant'Agata, Rome,* from the Museo Cartaceo of Cassiano dal Pozzo, 17th century, watercolor. The Royal Collection, Windsor Castle

the oratory of Santa Pudenziana and depicted lost cycles known through earlier engravings.[155] For instance, in one watercolor, Eclissi reconstructs a previously documented and lost apse mosaic of Christ and the apostles from Sant' Agata, where Paul again recalls Poussin's figure quite closely (fig. 62).[156] The triumphal arch mosaics at San Lorenzo fuori le Mura offer another example: Paul, with receding hairline and pointed beard, grasps a book with toga-covered arms and steps forward, as in the Dal Pozzo *Ordination* (fig. 63).[157] A triumphant Christ flanked by Peter and Paul, accompanied by titular saints, adorned many venerable early Christian apses in Rome, including the Old Saint Peter's Basilica and Santa Cecilia in Trastevere, both duly recorded in the Museo Cartaceo (fig. 64).[158] Even Poussin's own parish church of San Lorenzo in Lucina contained an apsidal fresco of Christ flanked by Paul and Peter, paired with the later patron saints of the church (fig. 65).[159]

In nearly all these apse decorations, Paul is placed on the privileged right side of Christ, since he was the designated apostle to the Gentiles who evangelized throughout the

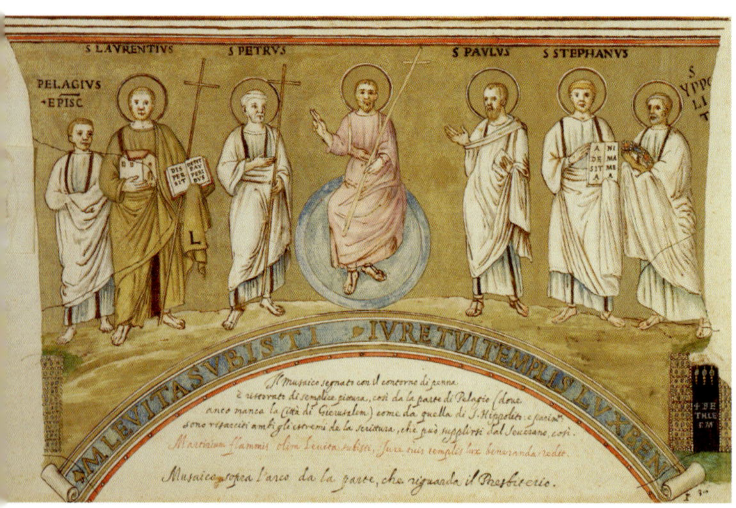

Fig. 63. Antonio Eclissi (Italian, active 1627–1644), *Apse Mosaic of San Lorenzo fuori le Mure, Rome,* from the Museo Cartaceo of Cassiano dal Pozzo, 17th century, watercolor. The Royal Collection, Windsor Castle

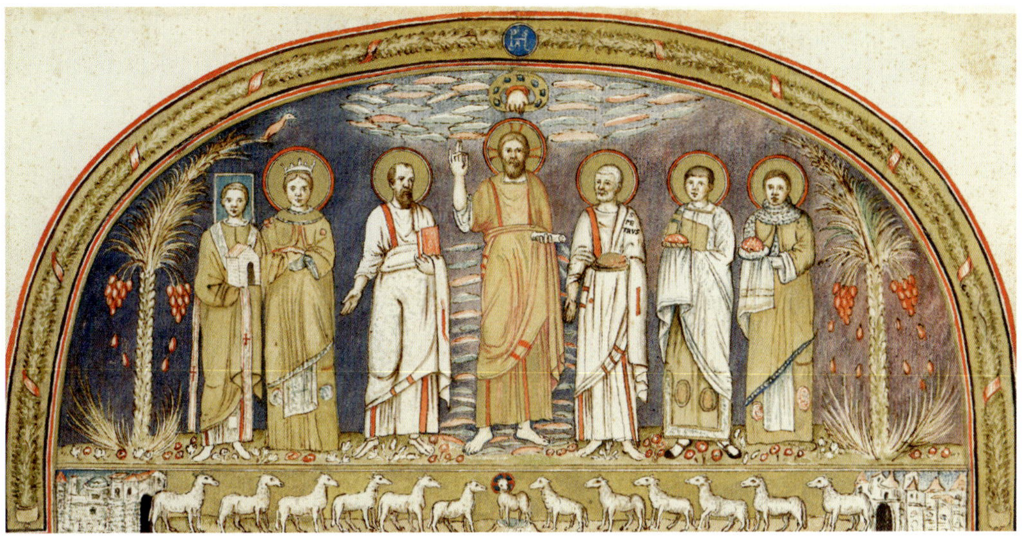

Fig. 64. Antonio Eclissi (Italian, active 1627–1644), *Apse Mosaic of Santa Cecilia, Rome,* from the Museo Cartaceo of Cassiano dal Pozzo, 17th century, watercolor. The Royal Collection, Windsor Castle

Fig. 65. Antonio Eclissi (Italian, active 1627–1644), *Lost Apse Fresco of San Lorenzo in Lucina, Rome,* from the Museo Cartaceo of Cassiano dal Pozzo, 17th century, watercolor. The Royal Collection, Windsor Castle

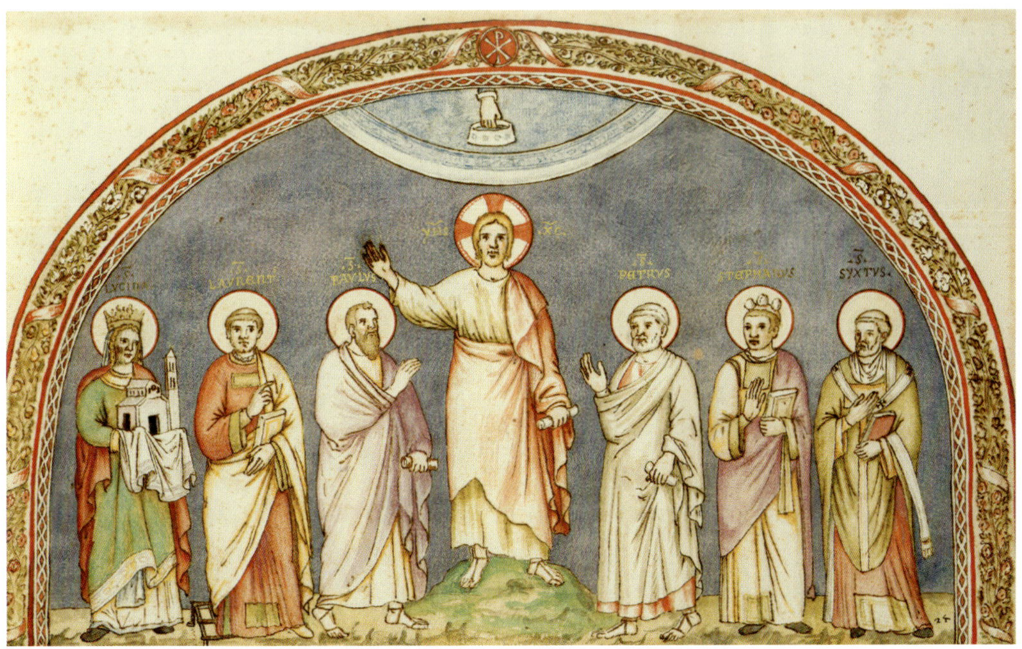

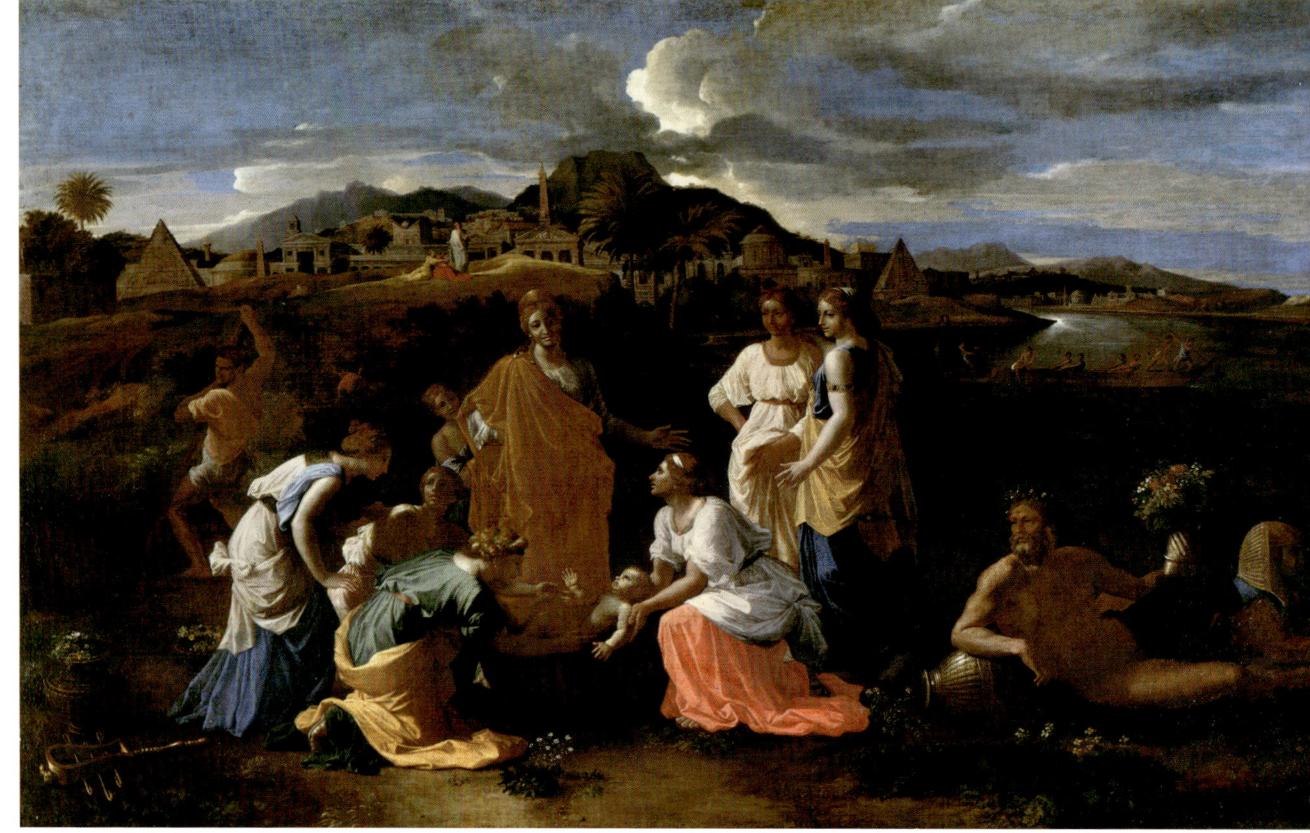

Fig. 66. Nicolas Poussin (French, 1594–1665, active in Italy), *The Finding of Moses*, 1647. Oil on canvas, 47¼ x 76¾ in. (120 x 195 cm). Musée du Louvre, Paris

Roman world. The implicit primacy, or at least parity, of Paul in these decorations was troublesome for Counter-Reformation historians, especially given the influence of Paul's emphasis on divine grace and justification by faith on reformers like Luther. Calvin even cites Paul's statements that none other than Christ founded the church and served as its cornerstone (1 Corinthians 3:11; Ephesians 2:20) to denounce the foundation of the church in Christ's donation to Peter as a blasphemous contrivance of papal tyranny.[160] But the Dal Pozzo *Ordination*, of course, accords due prominence to Peter, the first pope, with Paul's role discretely implicit.

Compared to the Dal Pozzo *Ordination*, the second version for Chantelou further emphasizes Paul's presence by aligning his proportions with those of Christ and Peter and adopting the more frontal position of the great early Christian mosaic apses and the *traditio legis* formula. Paul is still at Christ's right side, and occupying a seemingly coextensive space at a congruent scale, but his "just-arriving" stride yields primacy to the kneeling Peter.[161] The panorama of Rome, as it appeared in the apostolic age, displays the forum of Paul's mission to the Gentiles, much as Paul ambles within the pagan landscape in the Dal Pozzo version. Yet something of the elegance of the first *Ordination* is lost in the Chantelou version: the combination of the Gospel narrative of the consigning of the keys at Caesarea, a setting that recreates Rome in the apostolic age and alludes to the Vatican, and Paul's anachronistic presence in the central grouping seems overly didactic and almost jarringly disjunctive.

Chantelou himself was somewhat disappointed with his *Ordination* despite the prominence accorded his namesake Paul, perhaps due in part to his familiarity with the enchanting landscape in the earlier version for Dal Pozzo. A letter from Poussin records Chantelou's jealousy of a rival patron, Jean Pointel, who had just received Poussin's exquisitely lyrical *Finding of Moses* (fig. 66). The elegant ensemble of beautiful maidens attending the graceful Egyptian princess Bithiah as she is presented with the heaven-sent infant before a delightful Nile landscape must have made the solemn groups of apostles and edifying backdrop seem rather austere indeed. Exasperated, Poussin explains that the paintings' different subjects mandate distinct manners of representation: "Can you not see that it is the nature of the subject that has caused this effect, and disposition, and that the subjects represented in your pictures require a different manner altogether? The whole artifice of painting lies in this."[162] Poussin then explains that the subject matter, pictorial style, and calculated emotional effect together conform to a particular mode, as in ancient Greek music.[163] He then defines the characteristics of the mode that pertains to the *Ordination*: "The ancients would call Dorian that mode which was firm, grave, and severe, and they applied it to subjects that were grave, severe, and full of wisdom." *The Finding of Moses*, on the other hand exemplifies the Hypolidian mode, which is defined by a "suavity and sweetness that fills the soul of the spectator with joy."[164] Contrary to this absolute modal distinction, Poussin, in the Dal Pozzo *Ordination*, balances the solemnity of the ritual with the sheer visual enchantment of the composition and its natural setting.

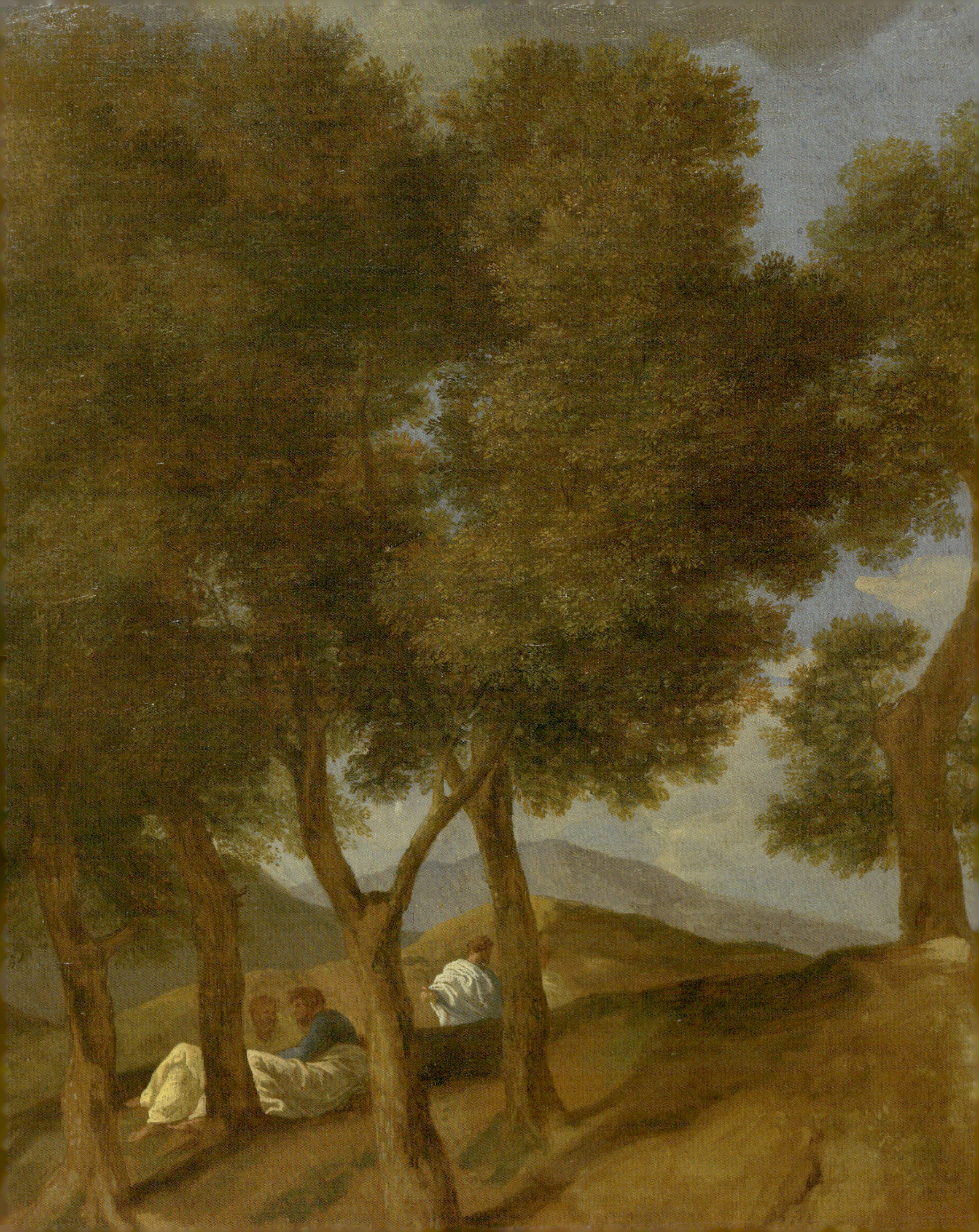

The Sacred Landscape
and the Apostolic Mission

IT IS PRECISELY POUSSIN'S USE OF LANDSCAPE THAT INVESTS THE DAL POZZO *ORDINATION* WITH AN inherent aesthetic unity. A similar integration of figural drama and landscape characterizes other compositions painted during the same years Poussin was at work on the Dal Pozzo *Sacraments*, including *The Israelites Gathering Manna*, his earliest picture for Chantelou (fig. 67). In the painting, Poussin stages the complete story of the famine afflicting the Israelites, the miracle of the falling manna, whose heavenly origin Moses invokes with his outstretched arm, and the resulting salvation within the unified space of the pictorial field. In a letter that accompanied the painting, the artist advised Chantelou: "If you would examine the picture as a whole, I believe that you will easily recognize those who languish, who admire, those who take pity, who offer charity . . . since the first seven figures on the left side will tell you all that is written here and all the rest is more of the same: Read the story and the picture, in order to know if everything is appropriate to the subject."[165] Scanning the picture from left to right, like a text, one registers the significance of each group, which, taken together, reconfigures the temporal sweep of the narrative from deprivation to deliverance, like a complete plot.[166] The pictorial foundation for narrative unity was the visual continuity of the barren Sinai landscape, obliquely centered on a natural arch. Poussin based its design on an ancient fresco of a grotto, discovered during excavations for the Palazzo Barberini and recorded in the Museo Cartaceo (fig. 68). Lukas Holste, a renowned classical scholar in Dal Pozzo's circle, identified the landscape with the cave of the nymphs from the *Odyssey*, which the ancient Neoplatonist Porphyry interpreted as an allegory of the site where souls generate their earthly veils.[167] As Poussin plots the full dramatic unfolding of the Exodus miracle of heavenly nourishment—the prototype for the salvational function of the Eucharist as the "Bread of Life"—the pagan spiritual associations of the landscape underscore the magnitude of grace that revives the Christian soul.[168]

Likewise, the landscape of the Dal Pozzo *Ordination*, with the trees and sloping hills structurally

Nicolas Poussin, *The Sacrament of Ordination (Christ Presenting the Keys to Saint Peter)*, detail of fig. 1

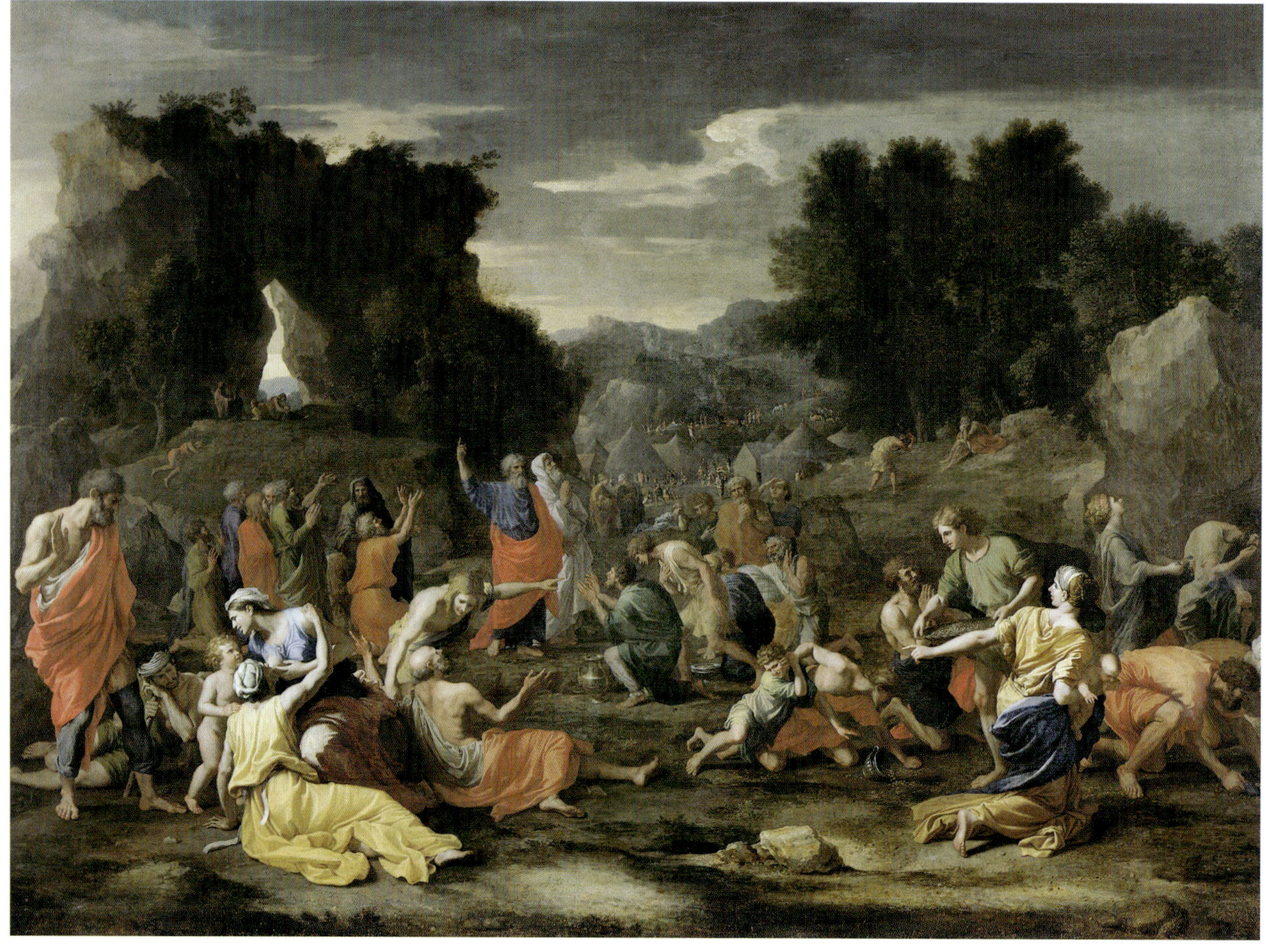

Fig. 67. Nicolas Poussin (French, 1594–1665, active in Italy), *The Israelites Gathering Manna*, 1638. Oil on canvas, 58⅝ x 78¾ in. (149 x 200 cm). Musée du Louvre, Paris

anchored to the row of foreground apostles, creates a spatial synchronicity, despite the anachronism introduced by Paul's presence. Nature provides a harmonious stage for the biblical narrative's distinct temporal implications, similar to that of *The Israelites Gathering Manna*: a landscape associated with pagan philosophy provides the backdrop to an event that links the Jewish foundations of the church with the sacramental manifestation of divine grace. While Paul is unaware of Christ's charge in the historical moment depicted in the *Ordination*, his orientation foreshadows his later elevation to apostolic rank. Furthermore, the landscape itself symbolizes the ecumenical purpose and scope of Paul's mission, as stated in his own words.

In the Letter to the Romans, Paul meditates on the various constituencies of the apostolic ministry, reinforcing his commitment to the Gentiles, while expressing his wish to also convert

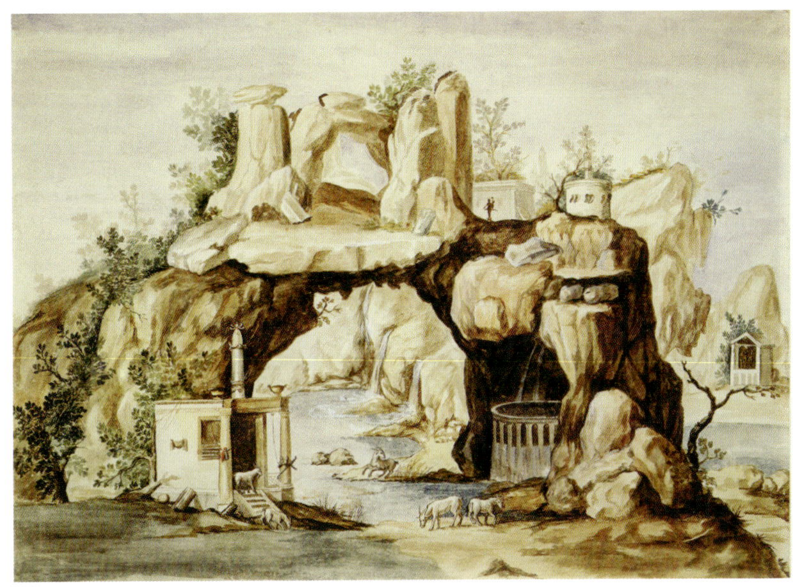

Fig. 68. *The Barberini Landscape*, after an ancient fresco, from the Museo Cartaceo of Cassiano dal Pozzo, c. 1630, watercolor. The Royal Collection, Windsor Castle

the brethren of his ancestry. He likens the sacred Jewish tradition to the root of a tree, which has a few branches that are likewise holy, but many others that have withered and broken, in refusing to accept the nourishment of the messianic revelation of Christ. In their place, the new communities of Christ are boughs of wild olive, signifying pagan origin, grafted onto the fecund trunk: "if the root be holy, so are the branches. And if some of the branches be broken off, and thou, being a wild olive tree, wert graffed in among them, and with them partakest of the root and fatness of the olive tree" (Romans 11:16–17). But Paul warns the Gentiles to guard against arrogance for receiving the gift of salvation in Christ and tells them that the once-rooted Jews who were cut off may yet, through God's grace, be grafted back upon the tree, like the spliced Gentile branches: "For if thou wert cut out of the olive tree which is wild by nature, and wert graffed contrary to nature into a good olive tree: how much more shall these, which be the natural branches, be graffed into their own olive tree?" (Romans 11:24).

It can hardly be a coincidence that Poussin extends the line of Christ's arm and heavenward-pointing finger with a slender tree, whose distinct pointy foliage resembles that of an olive tree. The gesture of Christ and the kneeling figure of Peter both overlap the tree, their bodies anchoring it to the ground, forming the holy root of Jewish tradition. In addition, the two larger trees on either side display both a severed branch and minute sprigs that appear almost grafted onto the more imposing trunk. In contrast to the dense copse of trees shading the philosophers, the specimens rising directly behind Christ and the apostles to the left exhibit an insistent rhythm of hoary and slender trunks, broken boughs and vibrant sprigs that evoke the venerably rooted and wildly grafted spiritual epochs of Paul's letter. Indeed, particularly leafy boughs extend beyond the tree behind Christ leftward toward Paul—the Jew who, after persecution and spiritual conversion, will join Jewish "root" to Gentile "branch," establishing the broadly ecumenical—indeed Catholic—church that Peter's pontifical heirs will inherit.

Poussin's inflection of the exquisitely rendered, naturalistic landscape with Paul's arboreal imagery may actually result from his research into an authentic paleo-Christian likeness of the apostle. In the final book of the *Roma sotterranea*, Bosio catalogues decorative motifs encountered in the frescoes and artifacts unearthed in the catacombs, including tree branches. Thinking of works such as the *traditio legis* sarcophagus showing the apostles aligned with a grape arbor (fig. 58) and a frescoed funerary niche from the catacomb of Sant'Agnese depicting the triad of Christ, Peter, and Paul before a row of trees (fig. 69), Bosio observes:

> Several images of Apostles next to Our Lord provide us with material for discussion, in which one sees behind these heads, and almost extending from them, branches of trees. And although this might be the caprice of the sculptor or painter, nonetheless these could have symbolic significance; perhaps alluding to the branches grafted in Christ, of which Paul speaks (Rom. 11), saying: "thou, being a wild olive tree, wert graffed in among them, and with them partakest of the root and fatness of the olive tree."[169]

Bosio acknowledges that Paul's metaphor contradicts reality: in horticultural practice, a cultivated fruit-producing bud or shoot is grafted upon a wild plant to jump-start generation, not vice versa. But the unproductive wild olive signifies innate human impoverishment, especially of the pagan Gentiles,

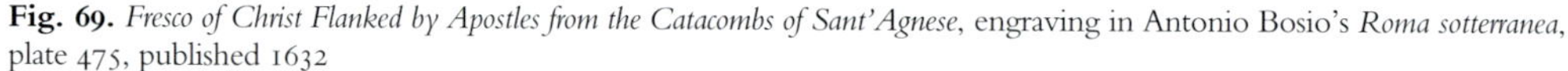

Fig. 69. *Fresco of Christ Flanked by Apostles from the Catacombs of Sant'Agnese*, engraving in Antonio Bosio's *Roma sotterranea*, plate 475, published 1632

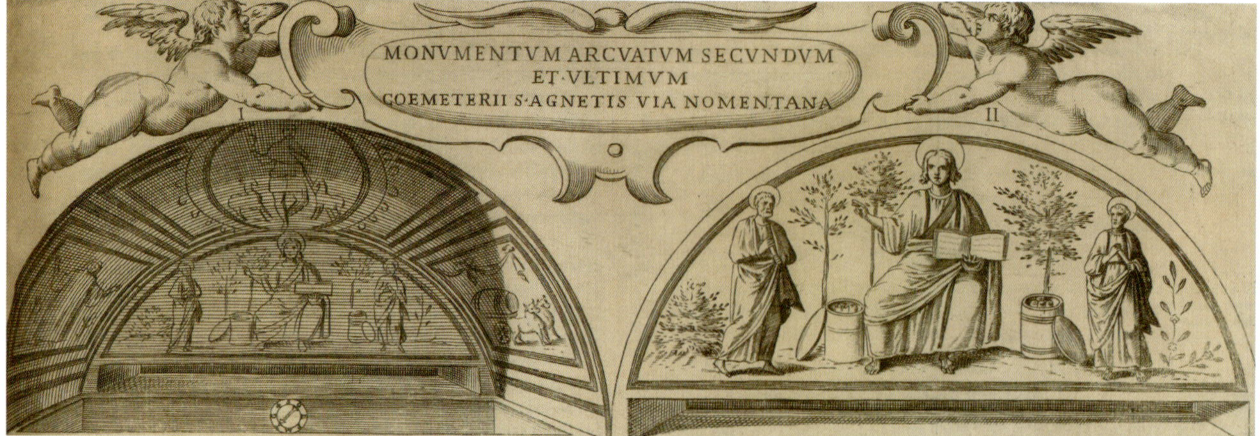

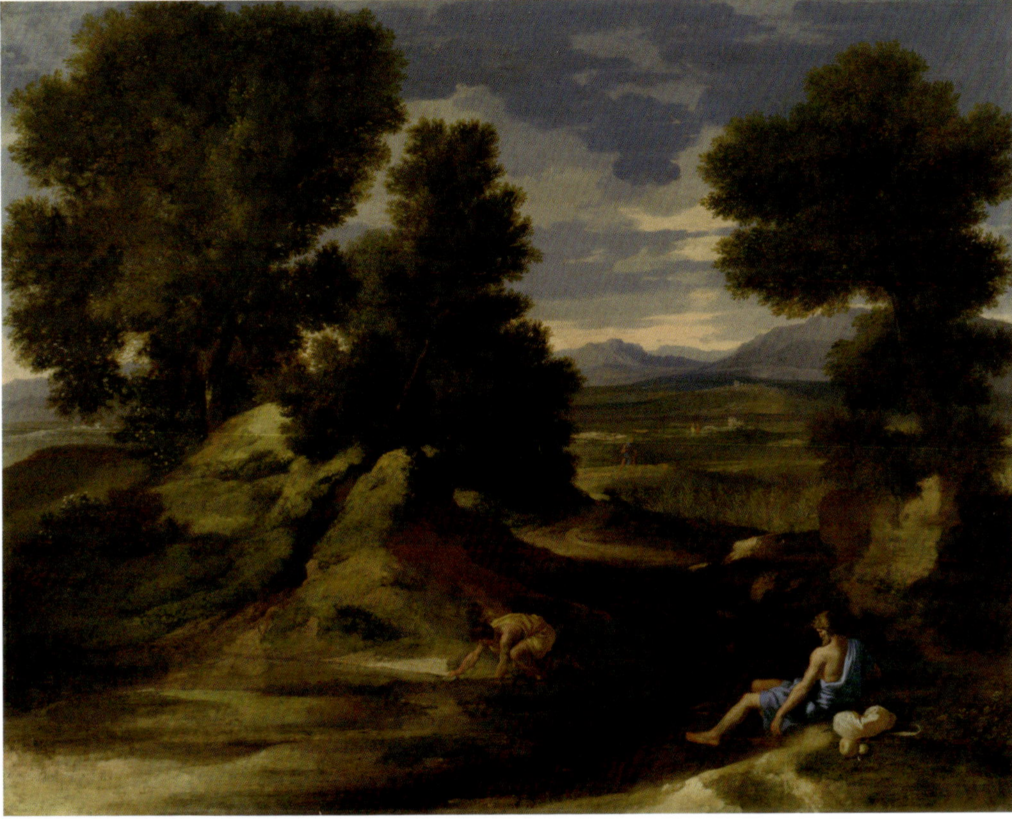

Fig. 70. Nicolas Poussin (French, 1594–1665, active in Italy), *Landscape with a Man Scooping Water from a Stream*, c. 1637. Oil on canvas, 24¾ x 30⅝ in. (63 x 77.7 cm). The National Gallery, London

which only the grace of the Lord, who consolidates the root and the tree, can render miraculously fruitful. Thus Bosio concludes that the branches seen with the apostles "signify that they, being grafted in Christ, produce the fruits of the conversion of the world, for which Christ had come."[170] Poussin's beautifully transcribed forms of nature become a sacred landscape symbolizing the promise of redemption through the Church, much like Paul's wild olive miraculously yields the spiritual fruit of the traditions embodied in Christ.

The Dal Pozzo *Sacraments* coincide with Poussin's development as a landscape painter. While working on them, he also painted several landscapes for Dal Pozzo that correspond in spirit to the pagan philosophers' grove in the background of the *Ordination*.[171] The *Landscape with a Man Scooping Water from a Stream*, for example, probably depicts the cynic philosopher Diogenes, who denounced all worldly comforts, realizing the superfluity of his drinking bowl when seeing a youth manually scooping water (fig. 70). In this and two companion landscapes, Poussin emphasizes the noble, densely foliate trees that punctuate the panoramic view to the horizon. The landscapes complemented the *Sacraments*, with which they were displayed in Dal Pozzo's palace, epitomizing his complementary interests in antiquity and nature.[172]

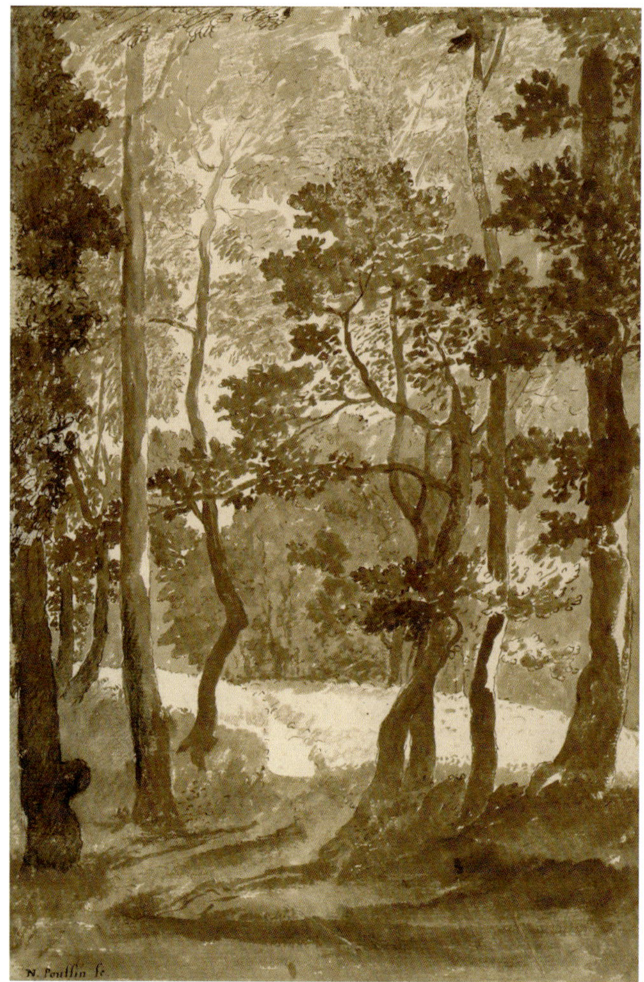

Fig. 71. Nicolas Poussin (French, 1594–1665, active in Italy), *A Path Leading into a Forest Clearing*, c. 1635–40. Pen and brown ink and brown wash, 15³⁄₁₆ x 9¹¹⁄₁₆ in. (38.5 x 24.6 cm). The J. Paul Getty Museum, Los Angeles

Fig. 72. Claude Lorrain (French, 1604–1682, active in Italy), *View in the Park of the Villa Madama; Landscape with Trees, Hills in the Distance to the Left* (recto), c. 1638. Brush drawing over brown wash, over graphite, 12½ x 8¾ in. (31.6 x 22.1 cm). British Museum, London

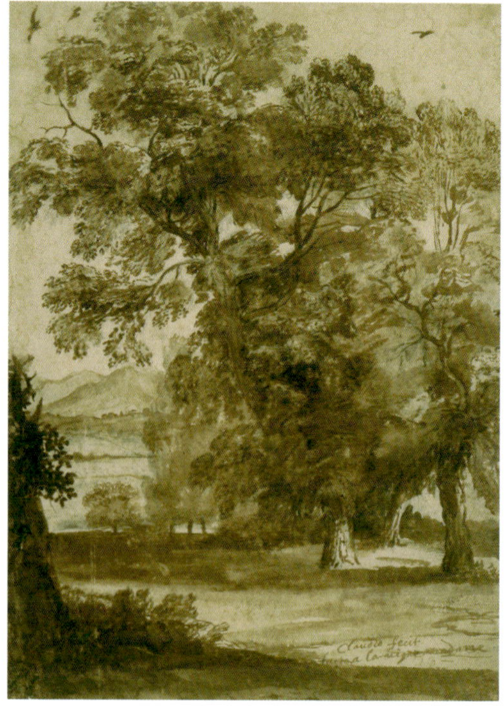

These landscapes testify to Poussin's close artistic relations with Claude Lorrain, the foremost French master of landscape painting, who, after settling permanently in Rome in 1626, became a lifelong friend of Poussin. The two ventured frequently into the Roman countryside to sketch the landscape.[173] The pen-and-ink studies of trees Poussin made on these trips show a marked affinity with Claude's, especially in their abbreviated foliage patterns (figs. 71, 72). Both artists manipulate bold gradations in wash to create a silhouetting effect in the trees that screen an otherwise luminous view into a wood or onto distant hills.[174] Claude's finished landscapes from this period encompass topographical views of Rome, rustic landscapes, harbor scenes, and pastoral idylls. Occasionally, he includes a sylvan mythological theme, such as Europa mounting the bull (fig. 73), but such vignettes are incidental to Claude's true subject matter: how sunlight and atmosphere transform the landscape at dawn or dusk; how a silhouetted grove of trees and distant horizon trace an immeasurable panorama and virtual pilgrimage. By contrast, Poussin's subject matter invariably determined the character of the landscape, rather than vice versa, as evident in both versions of the *Ordination*.

In 1634–35, King Philip IV of Spain ordered a series of landscapes with hermits for the royal villa of the Buen Retiro in Madrid from various artists active in Rome, including both Poussin and Claude. This commission provided the impetus for Poussin to consider landscape in terms of sacred retreat and spiritual meditation, at just the time he was conceiving the Dal Pozzo *Ordination*. Whereas Claude's quartet of paintings for the series characteristically apportion the sacred themes to the times

Fig. 73. Claude Lorrain (French, 1604–1682, active in Italy), *Coast Scene with Europa and the Bull*, 1634. Oil on canvas, 67¼ x 78⅜ in. (170.8 x 199.7 cm). Kimbell Art Museum, Fort Worth

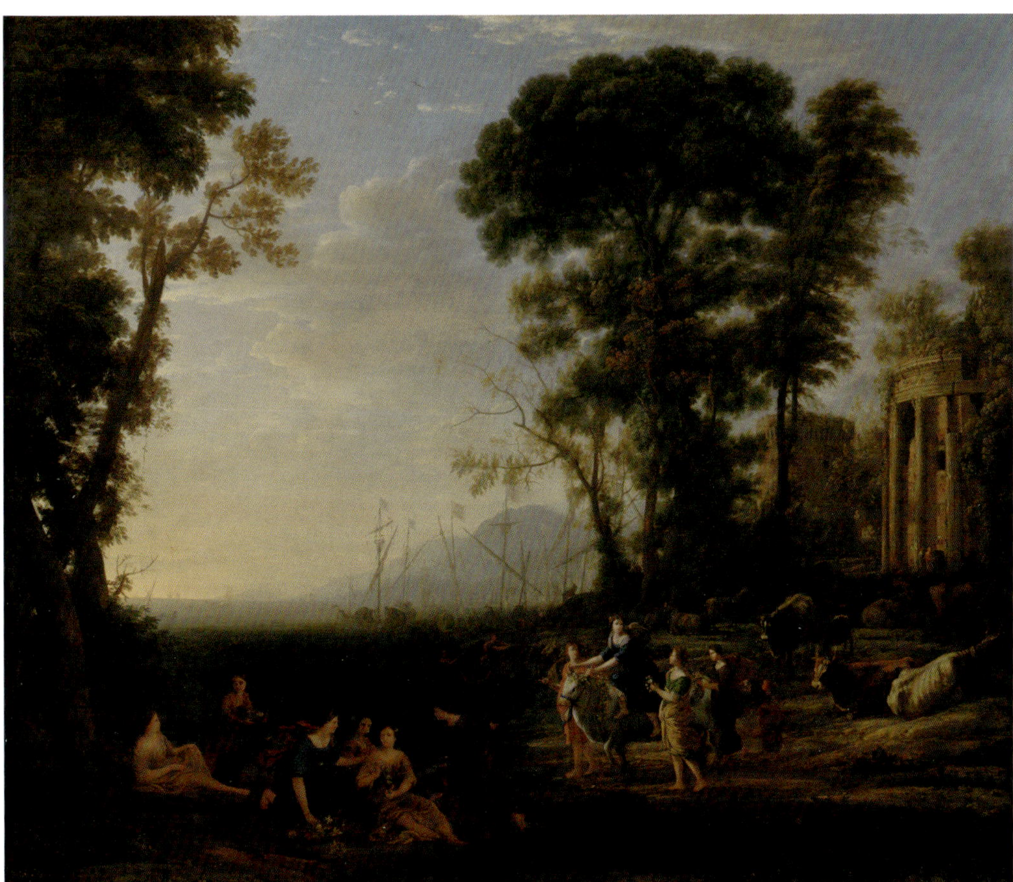

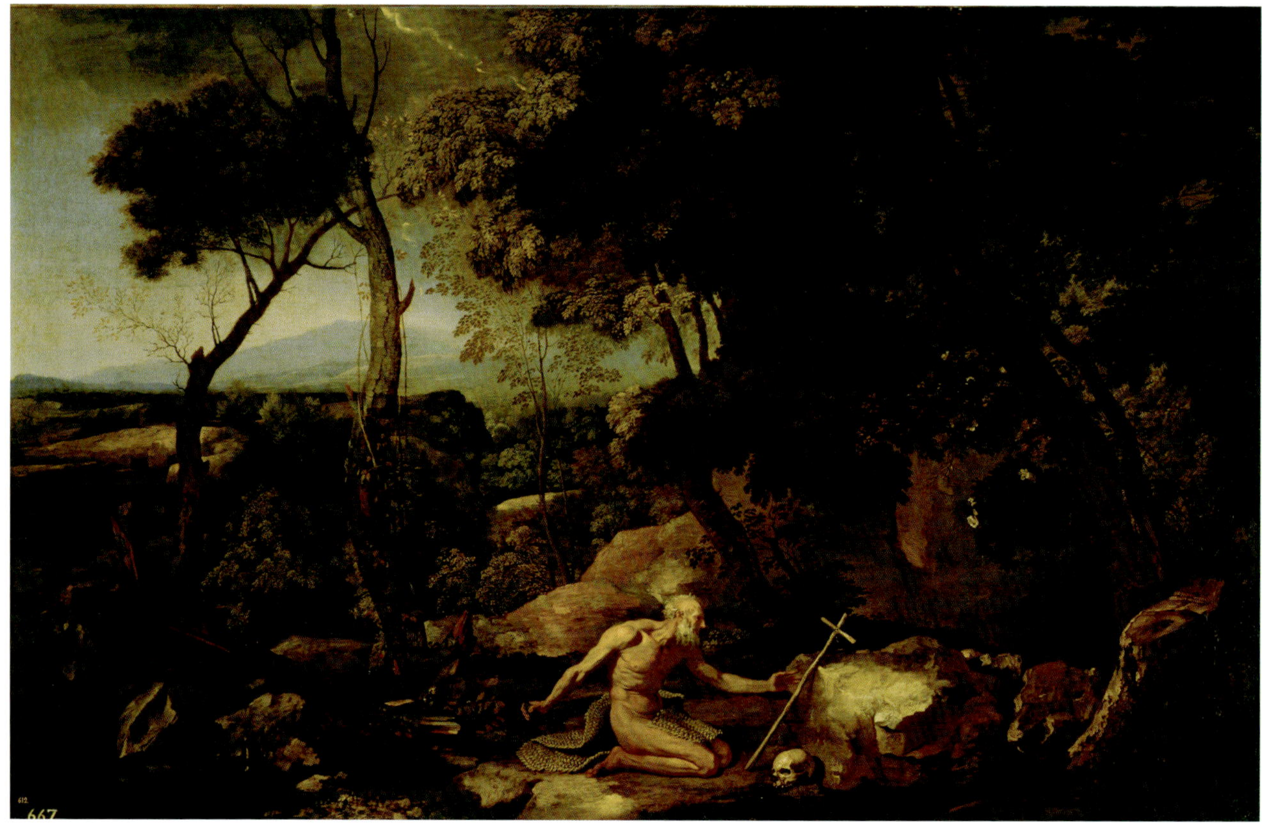

Fig. 74. Nicolas Poussin (French, 1594–1665, active in Italy), *Landscape with Saint Jerome*, c. 1635–7. Oil on canvas, 61 x 92⅛ in. (155 x 234 cm). Museo del Prado, Madrid

of the day, Poussin's one contribution presents a wild and tenebrous landscape of rugged trees and jagged stones that expresses the profound solitariness of Saint Jerome (fig. 74).[175]

In Renaissance art theory, landscape was viewed as an accessory to the loftier didactic purpose of narrative painting and was often dismissed as the particular province of the highly naturalistic painters of Northern Europe.[176] Early in the century, Annibale Carracci and Domenichino transformed landscape into a structured stage for lofty biblical and classical themes, as evident in their complementary treatments of *The Flight to Egypt* (fig. 75).[177] The theoretical advocate of both Carracci and Domenichino, Giovanni Battista Agucchi, believed that artists must elevate nature to an ideal of harmony and balance. By the late 1620s, another theorist, Giulio Mancini, recognized that the landscapes of the Bolognese masters exemplified a distinct genre: "paesi perfetti," or "perfect(ed) landscapes."[178] Soon after completing the *Ordination*, Poussin cultivated his own variation of this approach to landscape in two paired landscapes with Evangelists showcasing an elevated viewpoint, a series of diagonal planes to give the scene depth, arboreal signposts marking each division, and reflective aquatic features (figs. 76, 77).[179] Poussin situates Matthew and John, and their respective symbolic companions of the angel and eagle, among ruins and intact ancient cityscapes, suggesting the eternal dimension of the divine revelations each Evangelist records.

The artist's Parisian interlude in the early 1640s and the second series of *Sacraments* caused a hiatus in Poussin's development as a landscape painter until 1648, when he fully committed to the genre. Soon after the completion of the second *Sacraments*, Poussin dispatched a letter to Chantelou in which he suggests an ambitious new series, whose themes, at least in part, would take shape through landscape:

> I would wish, if it were possible, that these seven sacraments were converted into seven other stories, which would represent most vividly the strangest turns that Fortune has ever played on men . . . their sight would remind men of the consideration of the virtue and wisdom that one must acquire to remain firm and immobile against the efforts of the blind madwoman. But only extreme wisdom and extreme stupidity can be exempt from her tempests, the one being above, the other below, and those in the middle rank are liable to feel her rigors.[180]

Fig. 75. Annibale Carracci (Italian, 1560–1609), *The Flight to Egypt*, 1605. Oil on canvas, 48 x 91 in. (122 x 230 cm). Galleria Doria Pamphilj, Rome

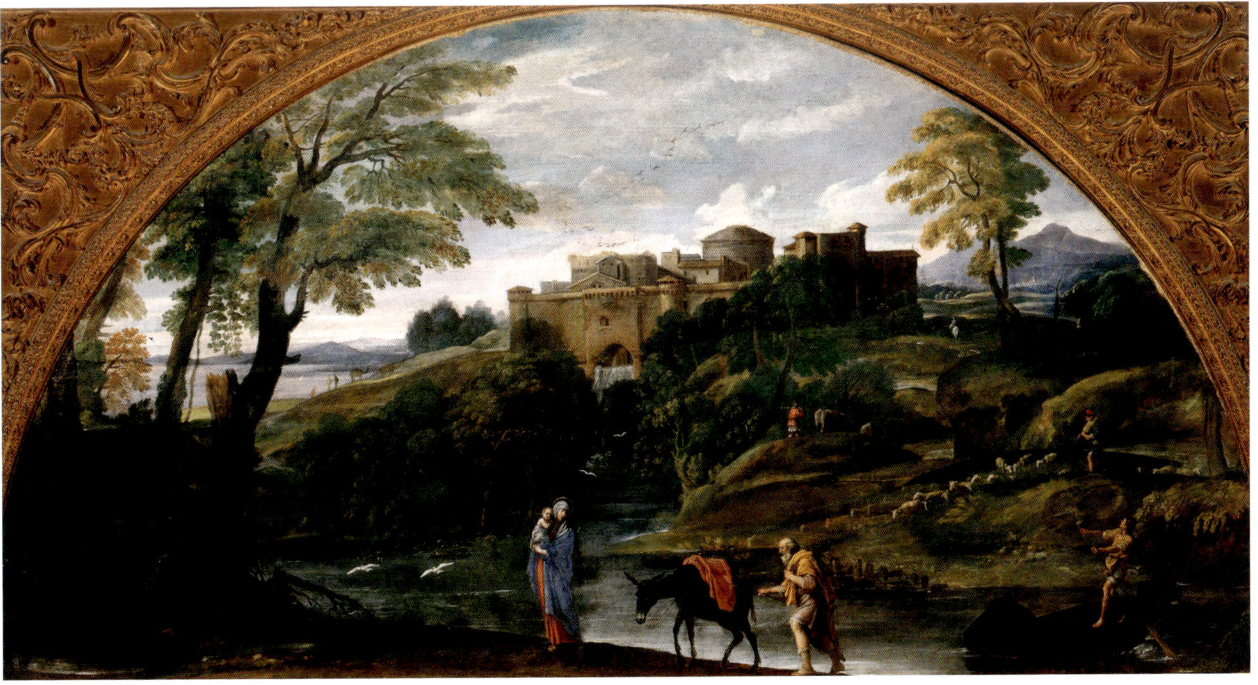

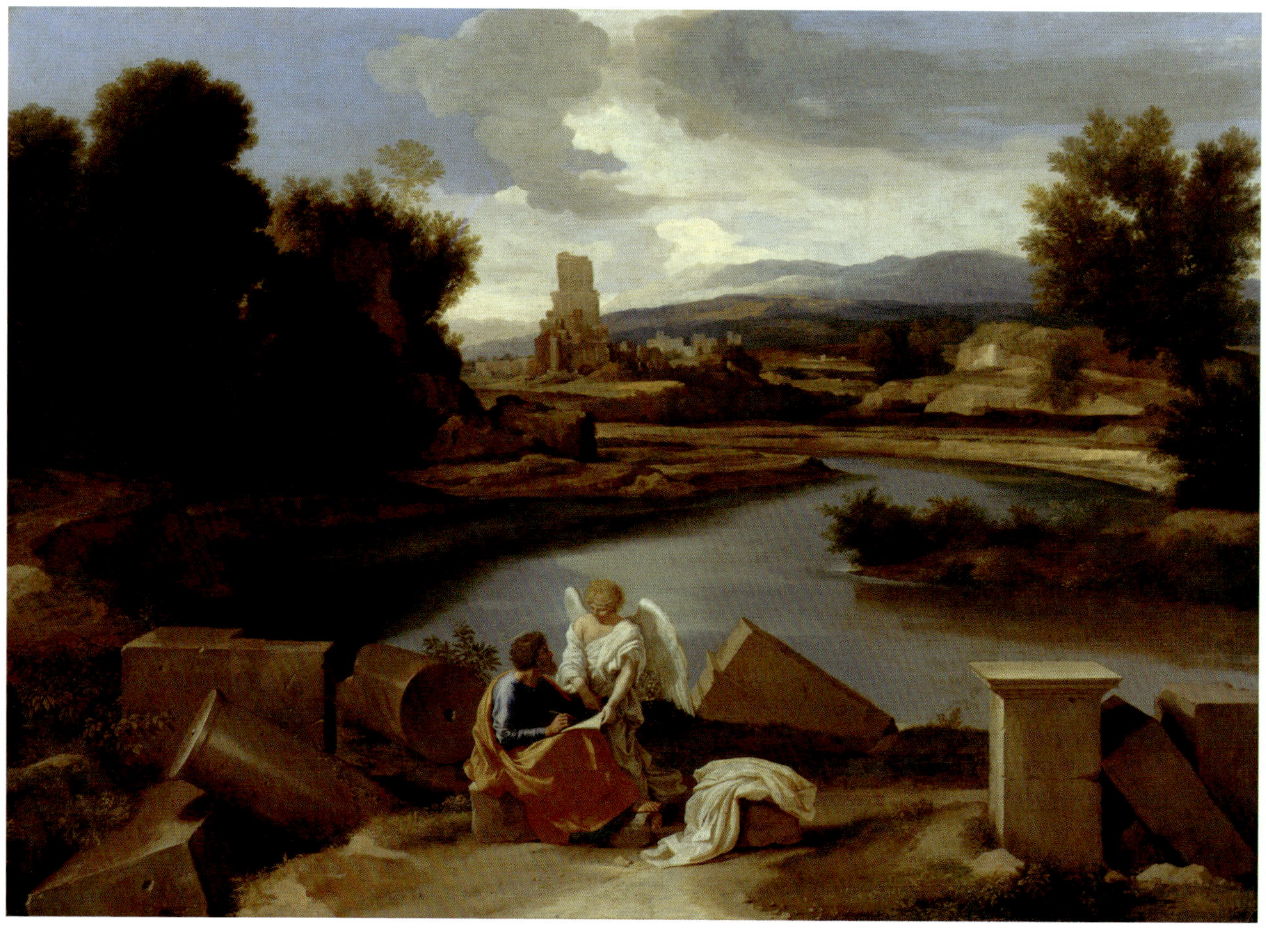

Fig. 76. Nicolas Poussin (French, 1594–1665, active in Italy), *Landscape with Saint Matthew*, c. 1639–40. Oil on canvas, 39 x 53⅛ in. (99 x 135 cm). Gemäldegalerie, Staatliche Museen, Berlin

This need to stand firm against the blows of fortune and accept with detached equanimity the injustice of worldly affairs was the mantra of neo-Stoicism, a philosophical system whose outlook on life is echoed in Poussin's letters.[181] The cryptic last line on the varying susceptibility to Fortune derives from the neo-Stoic treatise *De la Sagesse* (On Wisdom) of 1604 by Pierre Charron, which separates humanity into three social orders. The lowest is the vulgar majority, capable only of being ruled. The smaller middle rank possesses reason and can govern but often succumbs to passion and circumstance. A select few are supremely wise and transcend earthly concerns. Charron finds the ultimate confirmation of his schema in the order of nature. The lowest level corresponds to the earth, receptive to environmental conditions. The highest resembles the clarity and tranquility of the heavens. Yet the middle rank of humanity, which succumbs to Fortune's blows, is like the air, which generates meteorological disturbances and unleashes tempests.[182] Several scholars have argued that the proposed "Fortune" cycle materialized to some degree in an extraordinary group of landscapes painted from 1648 through the 1650s, several of which depict storms ("fortuna" can be a synonym of "tempesta" in Italian) or contrastingly placid vistas. While these do not constitute a literal series, painted as they were at different times, in different formats, for different patrons, several have Stoic themes, while others treat the indiscriminate wrath of fate.[183]

Poussin's initial aim that a "Fortune" series would "convert" the *Sacraments* has garnered less speculation, since thematic correspondences are inconsistent. Either of two landscapes depicting doomed lovers could be an inversion of the sacrament of marriage. In *Orpheus and Eurydice*, a snake kills the bride, and in *Stormy Landscape with Pyramus and Thisbe*, a betrothal ends in mutual suicide.

Fig. 77. Nicolas Poussin (French, 1594–1665, active in Italy), *Landscape with Saint John on Patmos*, 1640. Oil on canvas, 39½ x 53⅝ in. (100.3 x 136.4 cm). The Art Institute of Chicago. A. A. Munger Collection

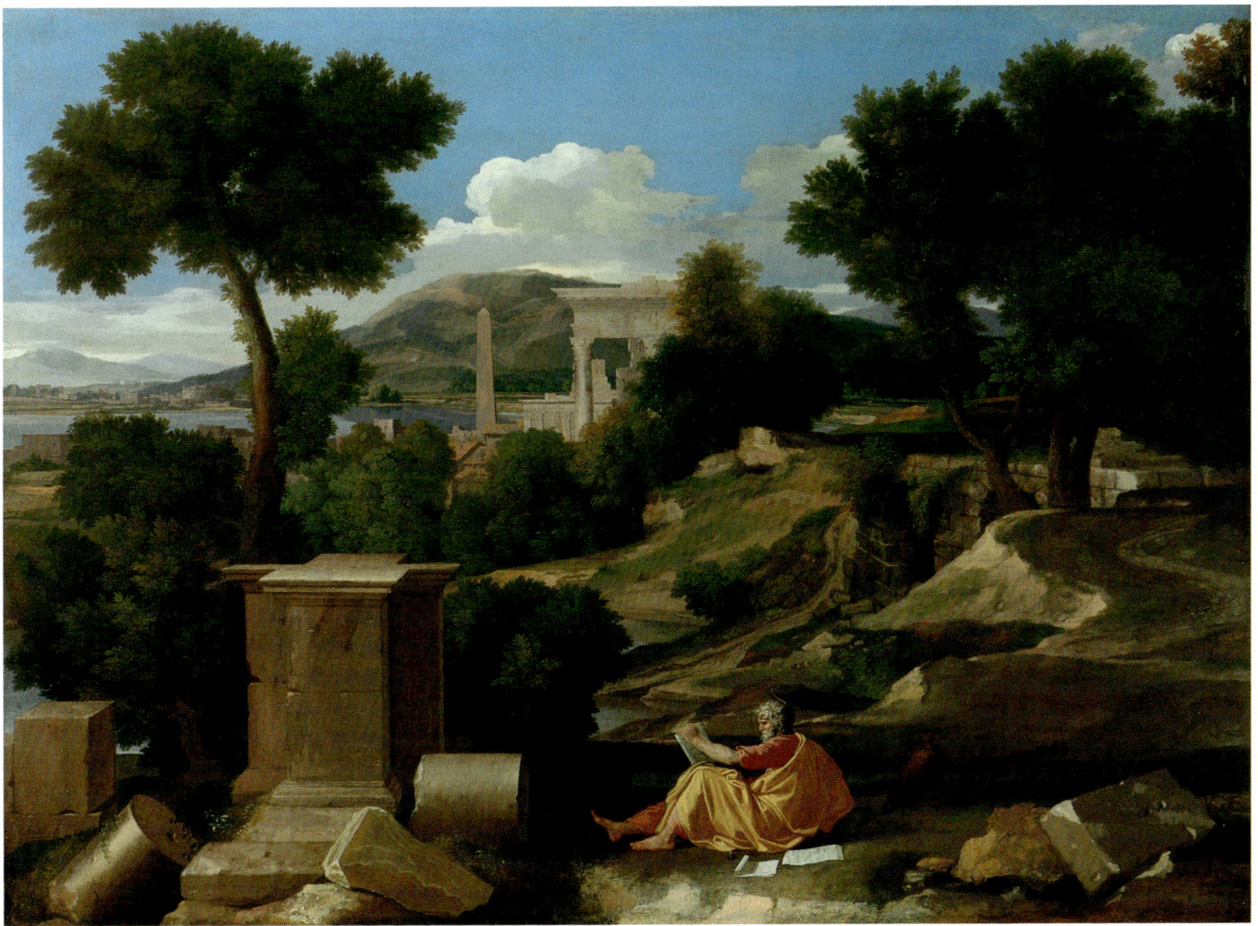

Both clearly show Fortune undermining matrimony.[184] Might it be possible, then, that the glorious *Landscape with Diogenes* (fig. 78), with its serene clarity transcending Fortune's agitations, represents the thematic converse of either *Ordination* painting?[185] By the Jubilee year of 1650, Poussin had developed a rather more skeptical attitude toward the ecclesiastical hierarchy. The papacy of Urban VIII ended ignominiously with a gratuitous, costly, and futile war to secure a Barberini fiefdom at Castro, Italy. On the eve of the pope's death in 1644, Poussin confided to Chantelou: "They say here that His Holiness is not doing well, if we lose Him, may God grant us a better one."[186] This wish went unfulfilled in the election of Innocent X Pamphilj, who drove Dal Pozzo's Barberini protectors into exile. Worse still was the ascension of the Barberini creature Cardinal Jules Mazarin, who succeeded

Fig. 78. Nicolas Poussin (French, 1594–1665, active in Italy), *Landscape with Diogenes*, c. 1648–57. Oil on canvas, 63 x 87 in. (160 x 221 cm). Musée du Louvre, Paris

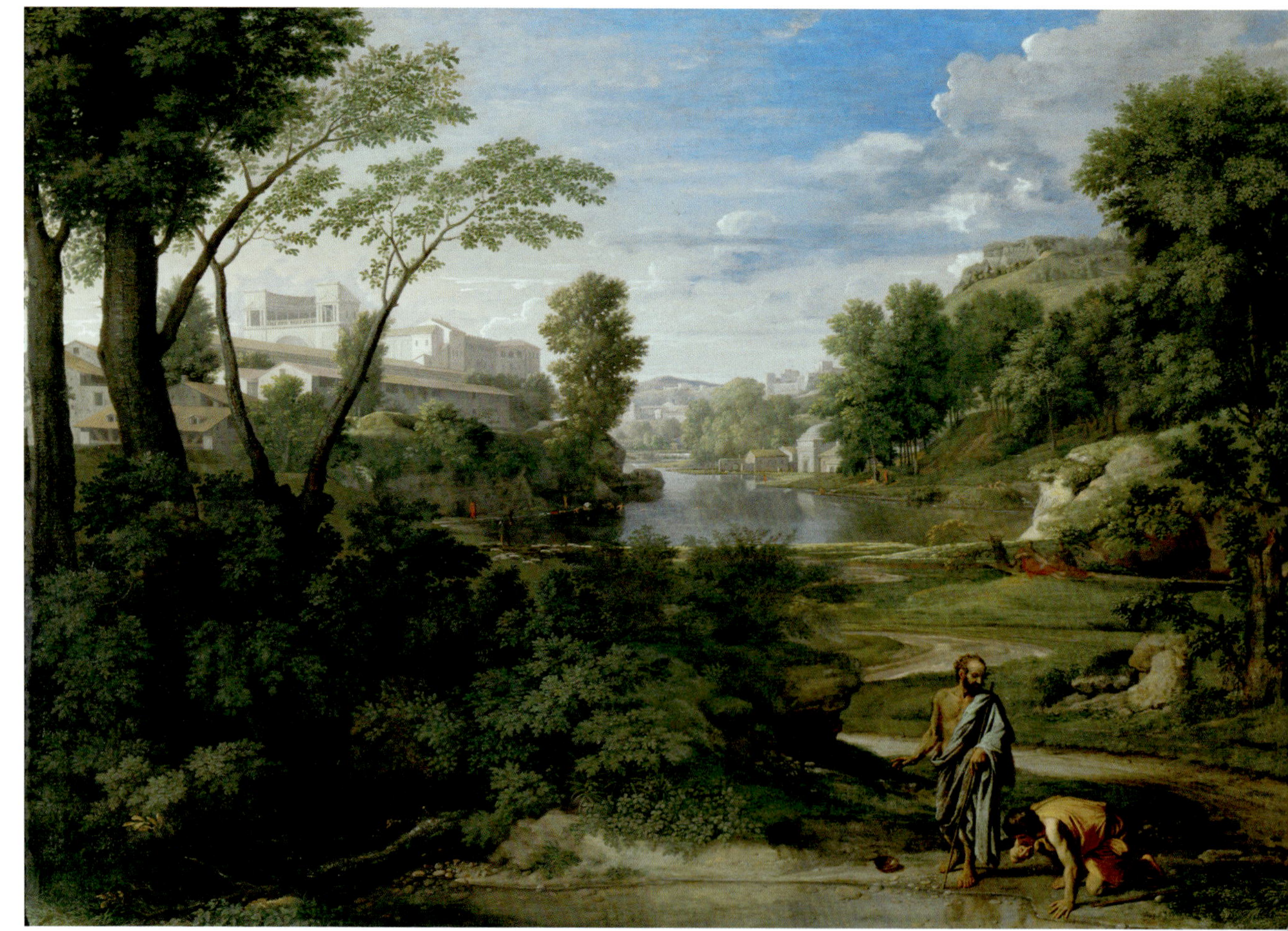

Richelieu as minister and came to dominate France while the next king, Louis XIV, was still a minor. Mazarin's engineering of the disgrace of Sublet de Noyers outraged Poussin, who ultimately blamed the cardinal's corrupt administration for the bloody civil war known as the Fronde (1648–53).[187] In the Dal Pozzo *Ordination*, the communion of ordered, reverent apostles gather before the Lord who, as shepherd, embodies spiritual rebirth transferred through the keys to the apostolic mission. In the *Diogenes*, this communion gives way to a solitary philosopher in the wilderness, where a random shepherd boy lapping at a stream offers a fortuitous lesson of further self-denial. By contrast, the unintended consequence of the power invested in the keys is exemplified through Poussin's inclusion of the Belvedere courtyard of the Vatican Palace, rising unmistakably on the promontory above the mid-ground lake. The Belvedere, a symbol of the imperial opulence of the papal court, provides an ironic foil to Diogenes's disavowal of all comforts, even a mere bowl. Perhaps the humble action of a pagan philosopher, purged of all worldly ambitions, whose rarified spirit is immune to earthly concerns and thus exempt from Fortune's wiles, offers a lesson to the very institution charged with shepherding the spiritual flock of humanity. Such would also be the message of Paul, whom Poussin in the Dal Pozzo *Ordination* portrays as a still-solitary sage immersed in nature.

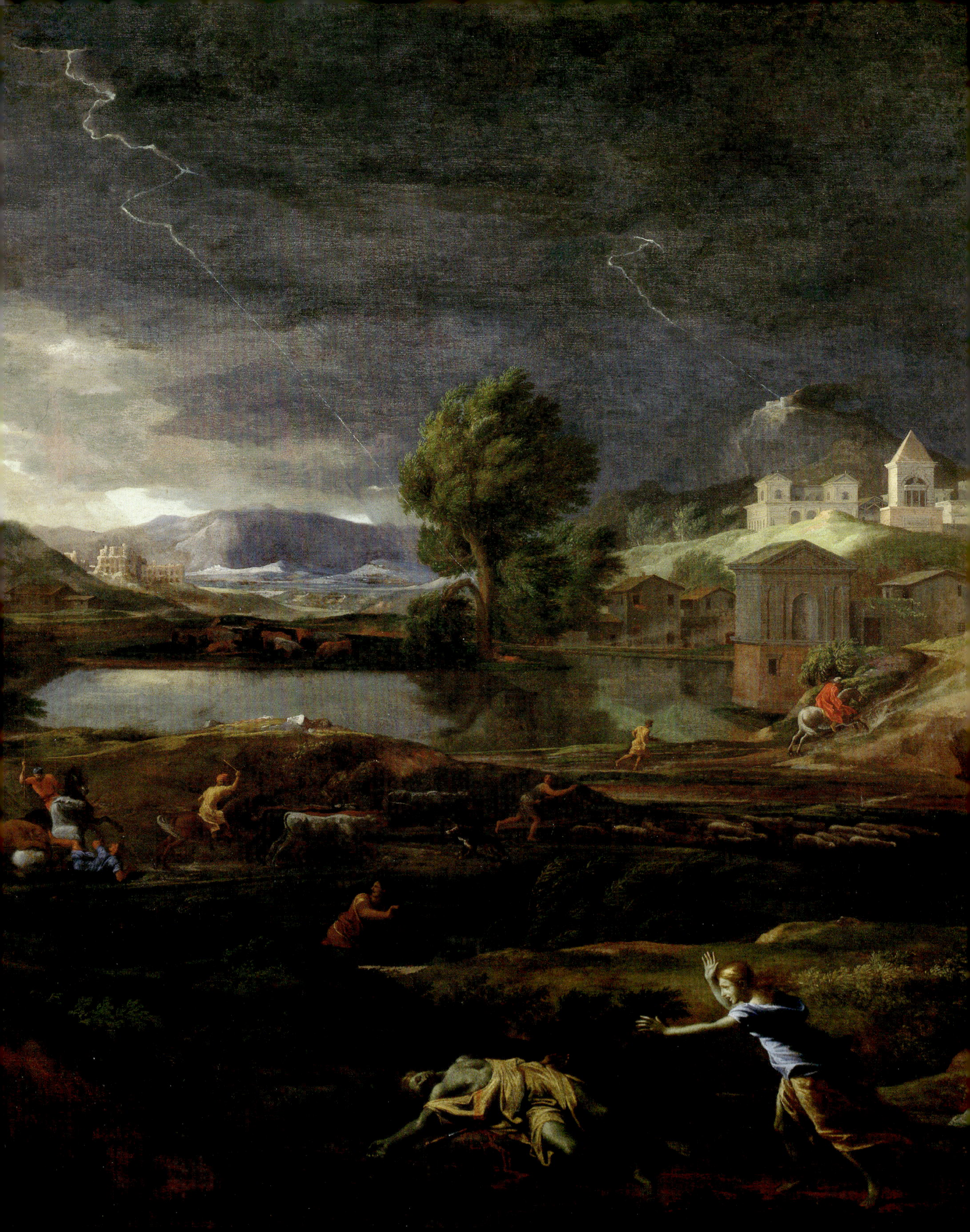

Epilogue

Poussin's final two decades of activity in Rome were monopolized by commissions from Chantelou, Pointel, and other French patrons. His life settled into an ordered routine of stoic detachment from everything but his art.[188] Despite the decidedly French orientation of his later career, Poussin managed to paint a final work for Cassiano dal Pozzo, the *Pyramus and Thisbe* of 1651 (fig. 79), by far his largest and grandest landscape. Here, the relation between figural drama, natural setting, and symbolic resonance, already evident in the Dal Pozzo *Ordination*, coalesces, as the storm-ravaged landscape amplifies the tragedy of the doomed lovers and universalizes the indiscriminate rule of fortune over human desire.[189] The sublime landscapes from the last decade of Poussin's life further distill mythological subjects into allegories of natural forces.[190] With paintings such as these, Roman colleagues acknowledged Poussin's status as an elder sage; the new generation of French artists and theorists, such as Charles Le Brun and André Félibien, revered him as an oracle of painting. The founding of the Académie royale de peinture et de sculpture under Louis XIV cemented Poussin's canonization; a frequent topic of the academy's *conférences* was deducing universal artistic precepts from the analysis of his paintings.[191]

After Cassiano's death in 1657, Poussin remained friends with his distinguished brother Carlo Antonio, who maintained and expanded his brother's collections, including the Museo Cartaceo, until his own death in 1689. The art passed to his short-lived heir, Gabriele, and then, in 1695, to his grandson Cosimo Antonio, who sold the contents of the library, including the Museo Cartaceo, to Pope Clement XI Albani in 1703.[192] Upon Cosimo Antonio's death in 1739, the *Sacraments* passed to the Boccapaduli family, into which Cosimo Antonio's daughter Maria Luisa had married. The Boccapaduli palace quickly became an obligatory stop on artistic pilgrimages to Rome, especially those increasingly undertaken by wealthy Britons on the Grand Tour.[193] By the mid-eighteenth

Nicolas Poussin, *Pyramus and Thisbe*, detail of fig. 79

century, the *Sacraments* had gained such fame that they were irresistible prospects for English collectors, who were able to take advantage of the willingness of increasingly impoverished Italian nobles and institutions to sell their substantial holdings of art and antiquities. Only the direct intervention of Pope Benedict XIV, who prohibited export licenses for the *Sacraments* as irreplaceable cultural assets, thwarted their sale to the former British prime minister and avid collector Sir Robert Walpole in the early 1740s. Benedict understood completely the incomparable artistic significance of the *Sacraments*, especially with Pompeo Batoni concurrently decorating a ceiling in the Papal palace of the Quirinale with a scene of *Christ Delivering the Keys* that takes its inspiration from both *Ordination* paintings (fig. 80). Whereas Batoni's centralized composition and the figures of Christ and Peter derive from the Chantelou *Ordination*, the varied frieze of apostles and tree alignments at the edge pay homage to the Dal Pozzo version, and the locale at the gate of Caesarea Philippi is made prosaically explicit.[194]

Fig. 79. Nicolas Poussin (French, 1594–1665, active in Italy), *Pyramus and Thisbe*, 1651. Oil on canvas, 76 x 107⅞ in. (193 x 274 cm). Städel Museum, Frankfurt

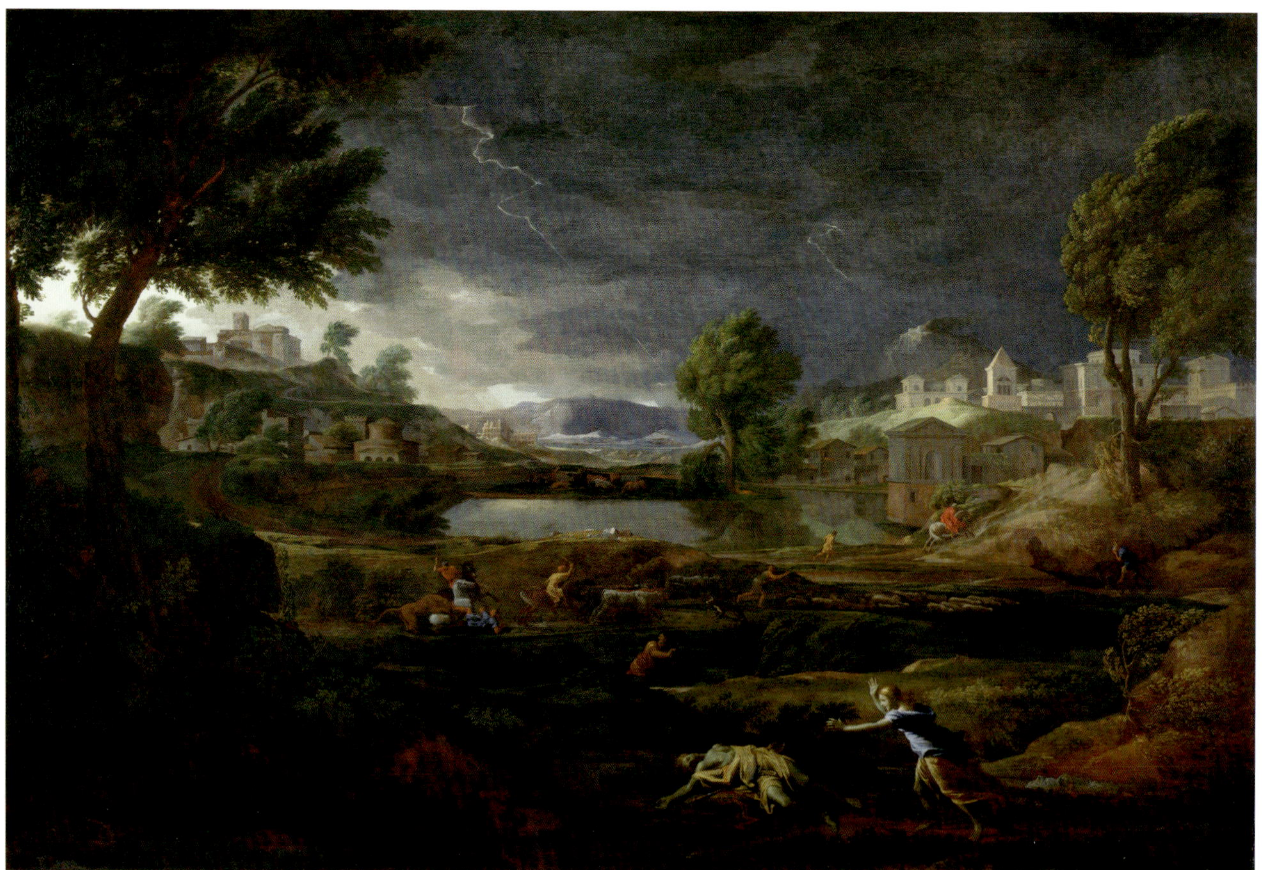

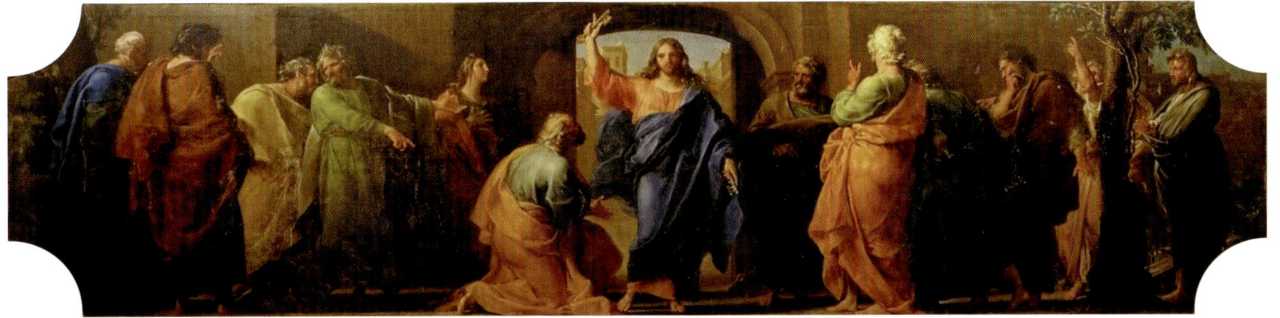

Fig. 80. Pompeo Batoni (Italian, 1708–1787), *Christ Delivering the Keys to Saint Peter*, 1742. Oil on canvas, 60 x 75 in. (152 x 144 cm). Palazzo del Quirinale, Casino del Giardino (Caffeaus), Rome

Nearly two generations would pass before a shrewd operator, the Scottish antiquarian James Byres (1734–1817), who resided in Rome and served as a guide and art dealer to elite Grand Tourists, managed to circumvent the *de facto* moratorium. In 1785, Byres, in a breathless letter to Sir Charles Manners, 4th Duke of Rutland, divulged a scheme to extricate the *Sacraments* from Rome. In an ironic twist on Poussin's and Cassiano's mutual hesitation on having the series copied for Chantelou, it was precisely well-made replicas that one by one replaced the originals in the Boccapaduli palace and enabled the paintings to come surreptitiously into Byres's possession. In the letter, Byres apprised Manners that the subterfuge was well underway, with half the decoys in place, and begged the duke's discretion, since, "were it known that they were going out of Rome, they would certainly be stopped . . . and [I] should wish that it were never known that they came through my hands, as it might bring me some trouble here."[195]

Before consenting to Byres's price of two thousand pounds for the set, the duke consulted the foremost art authority in Britain, the renowned painter, theorist, and president of the Royal Academy, Sir Joshua Reynolds (1723–1792) (fig. 81). His correspondence with the duke traces the saga of the purchase, arrival, and initial reception of the paintings in England. Less than a month after Byres's proposal, Reynolds implores the duke to go forward with the purchase, even at a "great sum, [since] a great object of art is procured by it, perhaps a greater than any we have at present in this nation. Poussin certainly ranks amongst the first of the first rank of Painters, and to have such a set of Pictures of such an artist will really and truly enrich the nation." Reynolds goes on to allay the duke's fear of being swindled by vouching for Byres's character, though Reynolds ironically had no scruples whatsoever when it came to defrauding Rome of its patrimony.[196] Indeed, in the next letter, from September 1785, Reynolds rejoices "to hear that scheme of their coming to England is in such forwardness," and reassures the duke that "the Poussins are a real national object," and "very cheap," all things considered.[197]

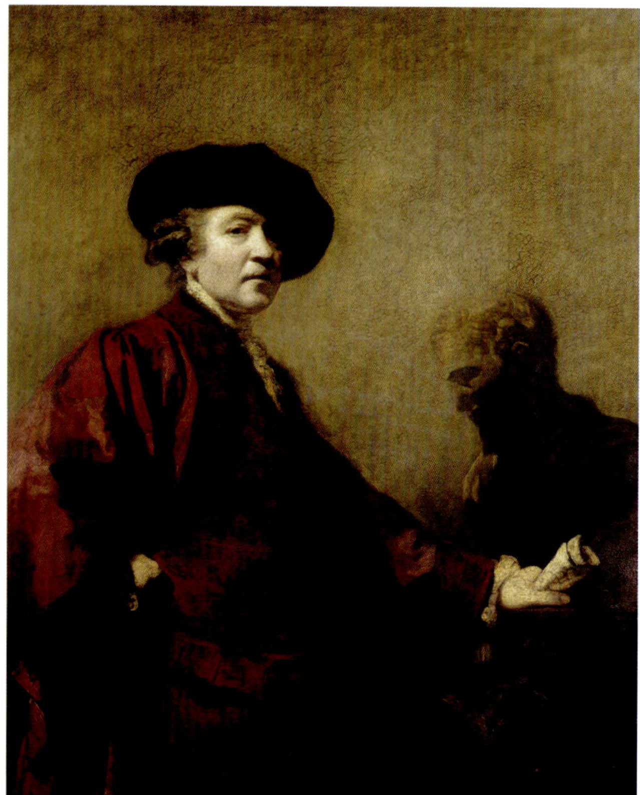

Fig. 81. Joshua Reynolds (English, 1723–1792), *Self-Portrait*, c. 1779–80. Oil on panel, 50 x 40 in. (127 x 101.6 cm). Royal Academy of Arts, London. Given by Sir Joshua Reynolds, P.R.A.

After some delays in shipping the clandestine pictures, Reynolds informed the duke of their safe arrival and fully recounted his impressions on finally seeing them in a letter of September 7, 1786: "I hang over them all day . . . this must be considered as the greatest work of Poussin, who was certainly one of the greatest painters that ever lived." He adds that "Rome . . . is now much poorer, as England is richer than it was by this acquisition."[198] This may sound like hyperbole to flatter an aristocratic patron on his sensational purchase, but Reynolds's extensive comments in this and later missives reveal his genuine admiration for the paintings. He marvels at their exceptional state of preservation, later reporting that a cleaning, which he superintended, restored them to a pristine state, as if they were still on Poussin's easel.[199] Most significantly, he extols the superior painterly quality of the Dal Pozzo *Sacraments* over those in the Chantelou series, then in the collection of the Duc d'Orleans,

which he describes as "feebly painted, though equally excellent [for] invention."[200] Reynolds later reiterates that the Dal Pozzo *Sacraments* are "not only original, but in his very best manner," while further belittling the weakness of the Chantelou set, which, though "undoubtedly original, have somewhat the appearance of copies"—a rather ironic aside under the circumstances.[201] Indeed, the visiting Italian nobleman Prince Abbondio Rezzonico, a nephew of Pope Clement XIII, was aghast at beholding the original *Sacraments* in England. He immediately notified his brother, the cardinal secretary of state in Rome, who instituted harsh punishments for picture smuggling.[202]

Having overseen the arrival and cleaning of the *Sacraments*, Reynolds petitioned the duke to allow the public exhibition of the new national treasures at the Royal Academy before their transfer to Rutland's ancestral seat of Belvoir Castle, in Leicestershire. While the duke graciously consented, Reynolds's fellow academicians protested that the spectacular "French" acquisitions would eclipse the annual salon of contemporary British art and insisted on their installation in a less august ground-floor gallery. Sequestration hardly diminished the public enthusiasm for the Poussins, which were displayed like the spoils of conquest. Reynolds personally escorted King George III through the gallery and sated his curiosity on the pictures' origins and arrival.[203] Indeed, this exhibition of the *Sacraments* corresponded with the apogee of Poussin's aesthetic influence and stature, especially outside of Italy, in the more public artistic arenas of London and Paris. Benjamin West's grand narrative pictures and Reynolds's academic discourses had primed the English audience to Poussin's idiom. At just this moment, across the channel, neoclassicism reached its zenith in the great Salon paintings of Jacques-Louis David and his peers. Poussin's legacy of antique inspiration, rigorous design, and vivid rhetorical expression begat a crystalline narrative style, as yet unburdened by its imminent appropriation for revolutionary and Napoleonic agendas.

After the exhibition, the *Seven Sacraments* left for Belvoir Castle (fig. 82), though they did not remain together for long. A fire struck part of the castle in 1816 and mercilessly claimed *Penance*, and later, in 1939, *Baptism* was sold to raise funds to maintain the estate. Similar exigencies to endow the castle's preservation fund compelled the recent sale of both *Ordination* and *Extreme Unction*, the latter to the Fitzwilliam Museum in Cambridge. With the sale of *Ordination* to the Kimbell, the tension between aristocratic impoverishment and prospective loss of national patrimony briefly played out again, minus the subterfuge. Now, *Ordination* shares an ideal museum environment with the works of Poussin's contemporaries, such as Claude, and modern acolytes, like Paul Cézanne, whose stated objective was to "redo Poussin over again according to nature."[204] But looking at *The Sacrament of Ordination*'s phalanx of cylindrical trees and sloping triangular hills as they echo the apostolic charge, join the roots and branches of faith, and overlap epochs of time, one might ask if an ideal integration of nature into painting had already been achieved.

Fig. 82. Belvoir Castle, Leicestershire, England

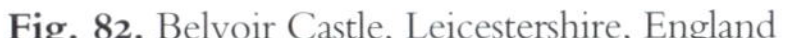

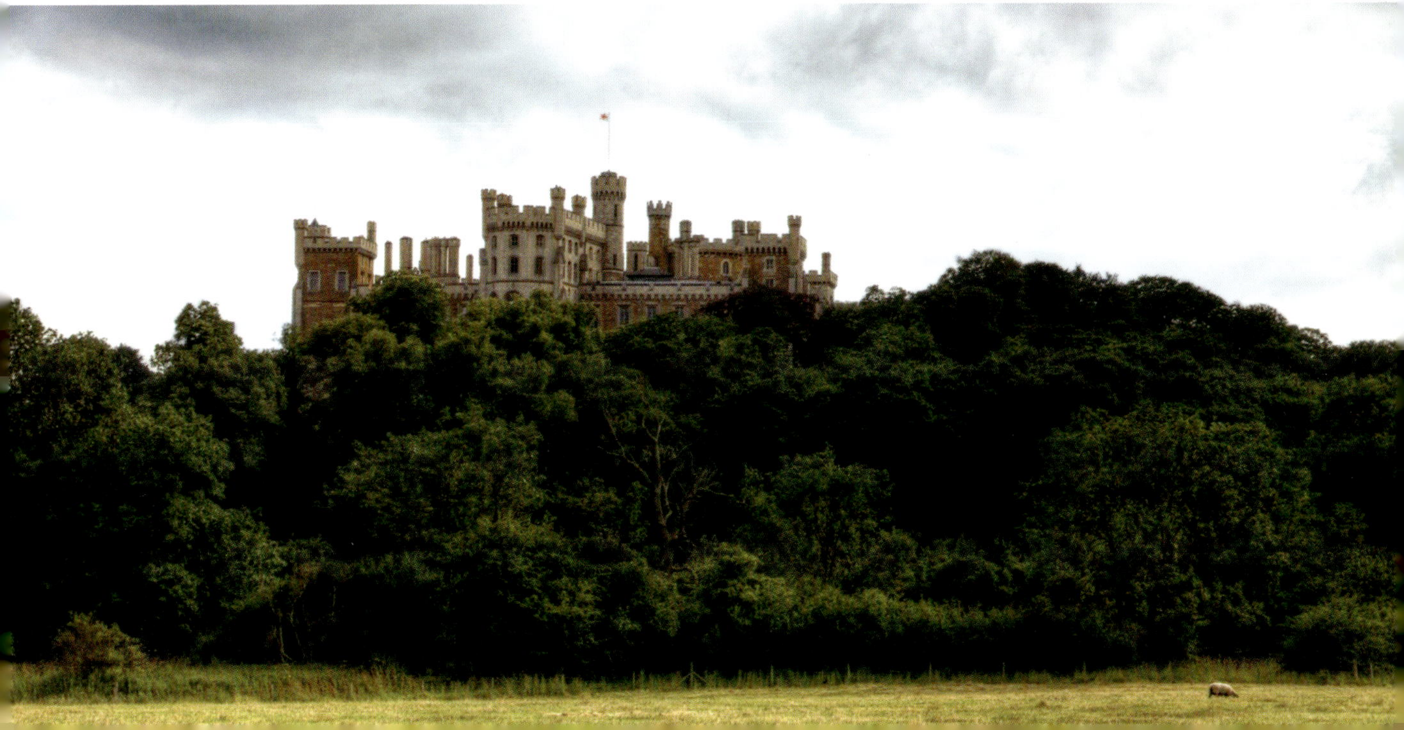

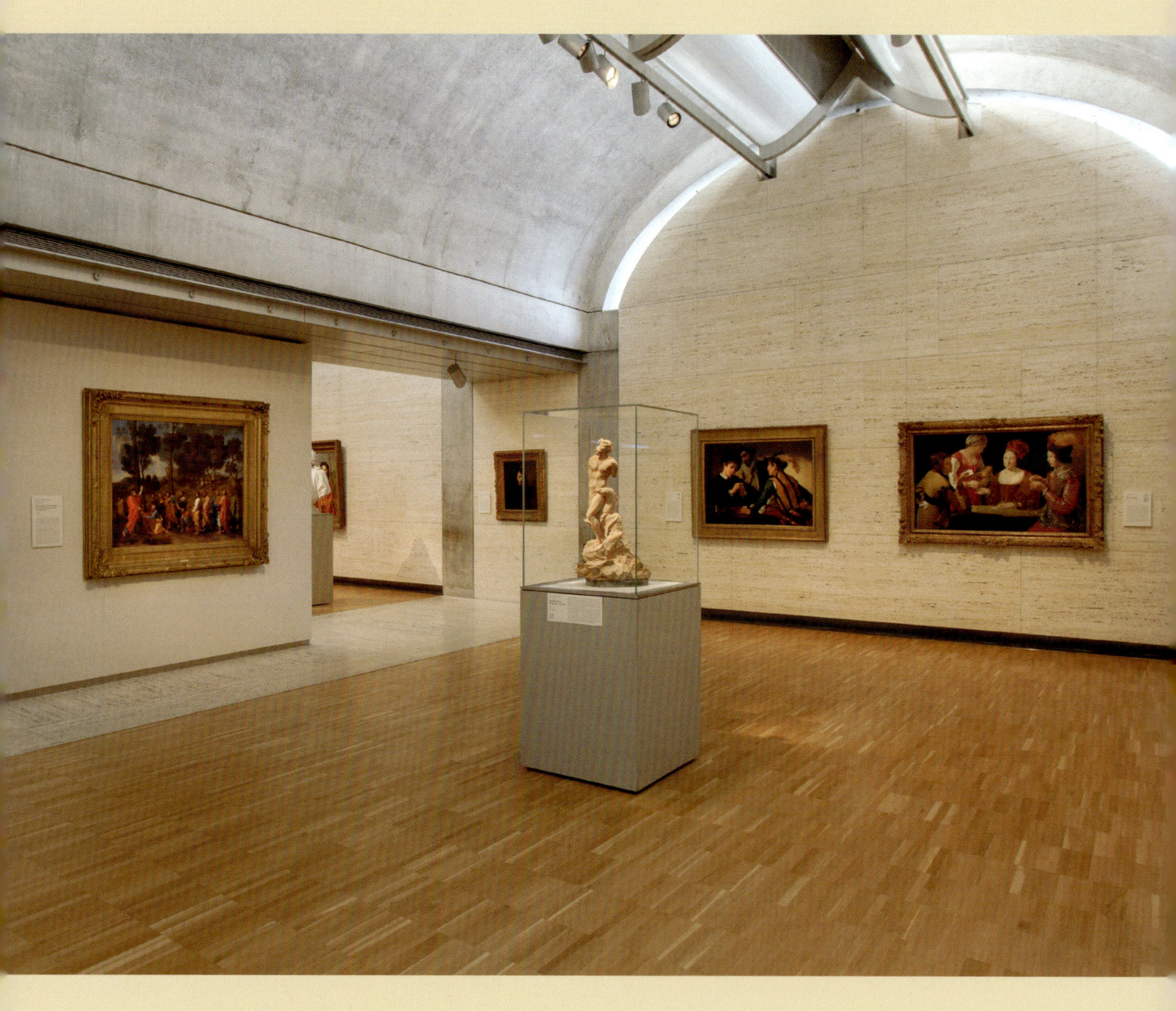

Acknowledgments

THE AUTHOR WISHES TO THANK C. D. DICKERSON, NANCY E. EDWARDS, ERIC M. LEE, AND George T. M. Shackelford of the Kimbell for inviting me to lecture about this extraordinary acquisition at the Museum in 2012 and for giving me the opportunity to probe further its beauties and mysteries through this book. I am particularly grateful to Dickerson and to Megan Smyth for the exceptional acuity, thoughtfulness, and patience with which they reviewed and helped shape this text. Thanks are due James Clifton for including me in a Renaissance Society of America conference session, "The Sacred Landscape in Raphael and French Painters of the Seventeenth Century," which gave me the chance to refine my material—and to the participants and audience on that occasion. I also wish to acknowledge my Brandeis colleagues Charles McClendon, with whom I discussed Saint Paul and early Christianity, and Jennifer Stern, who carefully read an early draft. My wife, Naoko, was a constant source of love and encouragement.

DEDICATION

To David Freedberg and David Rosand, who "ordained" me as an art historian

Fig. 83. North gallery of the Kimbell Art Museum's Louis Kahn Building with Poussin's *Sacrament of Ordination* and other works in the Kimbell's permanent collection, 2013

1. Bellori 2008 (ed.), p. 324. For further on this portrait, see Cropper and Dempsey 1996, pp. 182–96; and Bätschmann 1990, pp. 45–53.

2. Poussin 1989 (ed.), p. 67, no. 59; Jouanny 1911, pp. 134–35, no. 59.

3. Poussin is blessed with excellent contemporary biographies, whose authors knew the artist personally: see Bellori 2008 (ed.); Félibien 1981 (ed.); Passeri 1934 (ed.); and Sandrart in Thuillier 1994, pp. 185–86. A thorough modern biography is Thuillier 1988. For Poussin's artistic and intellectual context, see Blunt 1967; Cropper and Dempsey 1996; and Merot 1990. For Poussin's correspondence, see Jouanny 1911; and Poussin 1989 (ed.). Catalogues include Thuillier 1994; Rosenberg 1994; Rosenberg and Prat 1994 (for drawings); and Verdi 1995 (in English). A new paintings catalogue raisonné is in production by Pierre Rosenberg.

4. On Poussin and Marino, see Simon 1978; Cropper and Dempsey 1996, pp. 253–78; and Unglaub 2006, pp. 71–107, 133–56. On the drawings for Marino, see Costello 1955.

5. On Barberini patronage, see Haskell 1980, pp. 3–62; Beldon Scott 1991, pp. 3–18; and the studies gathered in Onori, Schütze, and Solinas 2007.

6. See Shea and Artigas 2003; Biagioli 1993, pp. 245–352; and Freedberg 2002, pp. 117–47.

7. On Marino's fortune in Barberini Rome, see Fumaroli 1989, pp. 52–62.

8. Bellori 2008 (ed.), pp. 310–12.

9. Roger de Piles, *Abrégé de la vie des peintres* (Paris, 1699), quoted in Thuillier 1994, p. 207.

10. Marino, *Adone* VIII.105–9. On the Kimbell painting, see Oberhuber 1988, pp. 79–82, cat. 6; and Unglaub 2006, pp. 103–7.

11. On the Dal Pozzo inventories that likely reference this painting, see Standring 1988, p. 618; and Sparti 1992, pp. 187, no. 276 and p. 211, no. 132.

12. Poussin 1989 (ed.), p. 35, no. 1; Jouanny 1911, pp. 1–3, no. 1; Passeri 1934 (ed.), pp. 324–25.

13. Wilberding 2000.

14. On Cassiano dal Pozzo, see Haskell 1980, pp. 98–114; Herklotz 1999, pp. 15–100; the studies gathered in Solinas 1989; Jenkins 1992; and Solinas 2000.

15. On the Republic of Letters, see Miller 2000; on Cassiano's epistolary sponsorship and engagement with scholarship, see Herklotz 1999, pp. 72–84; for the index of his vast correspondence, see Nicolò 1991. On Dal Pozzo's scientific interests, and his involvement with the Lincei, see Freedberg 2002, pp. 15–62.

16. On the Paper Museum, see Claridge, Jenkins, and Freedberg 1993; Jenkins et al. 1992; and Solinas 2000, pp. 91–168. A comprehensive multivolume catalogue is an ongoing project: McBurney, Claridge and Freedberg 1996–. On the historical context and criteria of Dal Pozzo's archaeological documentation, see Herklotz 1999, pp. 119–306.

17. Blunt 1979a, pp. 135–36; Rosenberg and Prat 1994, pp. 412–13, no. 211.

18. Bellori 2008 (ed.), p. 313. On early appreciation of Poussin's learning, see Mancini 1956–57, vol. 1, p. 261.

19. On the Dal Pozzo collections, see Haskell 1980, pp. 102–14; Standring 1988; and Solinas 2000, pp. 62–90. On the contents and arrangement of the collections in the Via Chiavari palazzo, see Sparti 1992.

20. On the *Germanicus*, see Rosenberg 1973; Verdi 1995, pp. 162–64, cat. 9; Schütze 1996b; and Dempsey 2000.

21. Tacitus, *Annales* II. 71.

22. Dempsey 2000, pp. 321–31. On the development of the independent tableau, see also Stoichita 1997.

23. On the *Saint Erasmus* commission, see Rice 1997, pp. 85–86, 225–29. On the work's contemporary reception, see Thuillier 1994, p. 185.

24. Verdi 1995, pp. 178–79, cat. 19. On the work's relationship to contemporary literary versions of the myth, see Bull 2001; and Thomas 2010.

25. Verdi 1995, pp. 159–60, cat. 7. On how this painting resonates with the ideas of Lucretius and Montaigne, see Cropper and Dempsey 1996, pp. 216–49.

26. The portrait has been excluded from the corpus by Rosenberg and Prat 1994, pp. 902–3, cat. R489. On its likely authenticity and later inscription, see Turner 1996.

27. Simon 1978; Unglaub 2006, pp. 136–56, with references to earlier studies.

28. For Poussin's "reflections" on self-identity, infirmity, art, and regeneration, see Unglaub 2004.

29. Rosenberg 1994, pp. 200–202, cat. 43. Among the recent literature on *Ashdod*, see Barker 2004; Hipp 2007; Neer 2006–7; Bonfait 1994, pp. 162–71; and Unglaub 2006, pp. 157–66.

30. Schütze 1996a; Cropper and Dempsey 1996, p. 85; Neer 2006–7, pp. 301–13.

31. Unglaub 2006, pp. 158–65; Hipp 2007, pp. 188–91. On the legacy of Raphael and Serlio for history painting, see Hénin 2003, pp. 225–48, 279–307. For the Aristotelian reading of the *Fire in the Borgo*, see Badt 1959.

32. On *Ashdod*, the 1630 outbreak of the plague, and tragic catharsis, see Barker 2004, pp. 667–71; Hipp 2007, pp. 206–15; and Bonfait 1994, pp. 164–68. On the 1630

epidemic and plague imagery in general, see Bailey et al. 2005.

33. Unglaub 2006, pp. 165–72.

34. On Poussin, Dal Pozzo, and Leonardo's *Treatise*, see Cropper and Dempsey 1996, pp. 156–69; Sparti 2003; Maguire Robinson 2008; Maguire Robinson 2009; and Barone 2009. For the preparatory drawings, see Rosenberg and Prat 1994, pp. 240–51, cats. 129.2–129.20. The final publication: *Traitté de la peinture de Léonard de Vinci, donné au public et traduit d'italien en françois par R[oland] F[réart] S[ieur] D[e] C[hambray]*. Paris: J. Langlois, 1651.

35. On the two versions, see Arikha 1983; and Arasse 2000.

36. For a rich examination of Richelieu's cultural patronage, see Goldfarb 2002.

37. On the Bacchanals, see Blunt 1967, pp. 135–48; Brigstocke 1981, pp. 35–58, cats. 15–27; Keazor 1998, pp. 81–88; Wine 2001, pp. 350–65; and Goldfarb 2002, pp. 291–304, cats. 125–32.

38. In particular, Cassiano oversaw the pendants of the *Adoration of the Golden Calf* and the *Israelites Crossing the Red Sea* for the Moses cycle commissioned by his cousin Amedeo dal Pozzo in 1634; see Wine 2001, pp. 314–23.

39. "Di alcune forme della maniera magnifica," from "Osservazioni sopra la pittura," in Bellori 2008 (ed.), p. 338; see also Blunt 1967, p. 363. In defining the grand manner, Poussin paraphrases Masacardi, *Dell'arte historica* (Rome, 1363) and Tasso, *Discorsi del poema eroica* (Naples, 1594). On the relation of these texts to Poussin's cultivation of a grand manner of narrative painting, see Cropper 1984, pp. 118–20, 153–55; Colantuono 1996; Colantuono 2000; Warwick 1999; Sohm 2001, pp. 116–30; and Unglaub 2006, pp. 12–37.

40. For a general overview of these issues, see Gray 2003, pp. 40–59.

41. Belting 1994, pp. 445–56, 458–90; Scavizzi 1992, pp. 2–61; Koerner 2004, pp. 27–152.

42. On Baronio and the *Annales Ecclesiastici*, see Pullapilly 1975, pp. 33–66, 144–77; and Scavizzi 1992, pp.176–85.

43. For a general overview of the catacombs, see Fiocchi Nicolai, Bisconti, and Mazzoleni 2009.

44. Paleotti 2012 (ed.), especially chs. 18–33 (pp. 105–43); Borromeo 2010 (ed.), book II, chs. 2–3, pp. 69–83, and ch. 12, pp. 133–7. On Borromeo and the authority of paleo-Christian image-prototypes, and his acquisition of drawings from Alonso Chacón and Giacomo Grimaldi, early documentarians of the catacombs and other early Christian sites, see Jones 1993, pp. 25–26, 173–76.

45. On theological scholarship in Cassiano's circle, see Wilberding 1997, pp. 104–10, who references Paganino Gaudenzi, *De Dogmatibus et ritibus veteris Ecclesiae haereticorum huius temporis, et praesertim Calvinianorum testimonia* (Rome 1625); George Conn (Conaeus), *Assertionum Catholicarum Libri Tres* (Rome, 1629). For Gaudenzi, see Brunelli 1999; for Conn, Solinas 1996, p. 301; and Solinas 1992, pp. 356–60.

46. On Cassiano and the production of the *Roma sotteranea*, and the correspondence of images between the Museo Cartaceo and Bosio's engravings, see Herklotz 1992, pp. 31–38; Herklotz 1999, pp. 60–62.

47. Extensively illustrated and catalogued in Osborne and Claridge 1996; see also Herklotz 1992, pp. 38–48.

48. See Severano's original Italian text "Al benigno lettore," at the opening of Bosio 1632.

49. On the Van der Weyden and other late medieval sacraments series, often part of architectural decoration and more common in Britain than elsewhere, see Nichols 1994.

50. Dati 1664, p. 41. Dati was a Florentine antiquarian and author of the *Vite dei pittori antichi* (1667). He sought Poussin's opinion on Pliny's account of monochromatic painting in antiquity; see Herklotz 1996; and Solinas 1996, pp. 303–10. The quote derives from his eulogy of Cassiano.

51. On Philips Galle's set of engravings, see Sellink and Leesberg 2001, pp. 199–208, cats. 265–72; Dolders 1987, pp. 241–48, cats. 067: 1–8; and especially Clifton 2009.

52. On the Dal Pozzo *Sacraments* in general, see Brigstocke 1981, pp. 63–84; Rosenberg 1994, pp. 240–52, cats. 63–71; Verdi 1995, pp. 221–31, cats. 39–44; and Green 2000, pp. 35–170.

53. On this painting, itself a variation of an earlier composition now in the Louvre, see Verdi 1995, pp. 208–9, cat. 32; Rosenberg 1994, pp. 220–23, cat. 53.

54. A conceit extolled in Bellori 2008 (ed.), p. 114.

55. See the entry by Maguire Robinson in Conisbee et al. 2009, pp. 379–88, cat. 83, citing Bosio 1632, book II, ch. XXI, p. 131, the catacomb of Pontianus on the Via Portuensis. For prototypes of Christ and the Baptist in Raphael's Vatican loggia fresco and for the undressing neophytes in Michelangelo's *Battle of Cascina* design, see Verdi 1995, pp. 230–31, cat. 44.

56. On the painting, see Verdi 1995, p. 228, cat. 42; on the subject, Wilberding 1997, pp. 257–64.

57. Verdi 1995, p. 227, cat. 41; Green 2000, pp. 150–59.

58. See Blunt 1939, pp. 271–75; Von Hennenberg 1987; Wilberding 1997, pp. 159–80; and Green 2000, pp. 128–39. Poussin is indebted to the Florentine painter Ludovico Cigoli's painting of this episode for Mercuriale.

59. For the drawings after Ligorio's manuscript *Delle Antichità romane*, see Vagenheim 1992.

60. Blunt 1967, pp. 199–201; Rosenberg and Prat 1994, pp. 478–79, cat. 243.

61. Blunt 1939, p. 272.

62. Verdi 1995, p. 226, cat. 40; Wilberding 1997, pp. 193–94.

63. Cropper and Demspey 1996, pp. 145–74.

64. On the installation of the *Sacraments* in the palazzo, see Sparti 1992, pp. 103–8, 186–87 (1689 inventory), 211–12 (1695 inventory), figs. 53–57.

65. On Poussin's early French reception and patrons, see Olson 2002, pp. 37–59. On Richelieu's patronage of the artist, see Goldfarb 2002, pp. 1–13, 276–78, 291–305.

66. On the summons from Louis XIII and Sublet, see Jouanny 1911, pp. 5–8, nos. 2–3. For Poussin's account of his arrival in France to Carlo Antonio dal Pozzo, see Jouanny 1911, pp. 40–46, no. 21; and Poussin 1989 (ed.), pp. 48–50, no. 21. On the Fréart brothers' voyage to Rome, see Thuillier 1988, pp. 165–85.

67. Poussin 1989 (ed.), pp. 70–76, no. 61; Jouanny 1911, pp. 139–47, no. 61. On this letter, in which Poussin distinguishes two kinds of vision, Aspect, or empirical seeing, and Prospect, or rational judgment, see Puttfarken 2000, pp. 210–14.

68. For Poussin's sojourn in Paris and service to the French Court, see Thuillier 1988, pp. 165–211.

69. Poussin 1989 (ed.), p. 59, no. 46; Jouanny 1911, pp. 46–49, 56–58, 93–99, 100–102, 105–120, 124–32, 137–39, 148–57, 159–61, 163–74, 175–79; nos. 22, 29, 45–46, 48, 51–55, 57–58, 60, 63–64, 66, 68–71, 73–74.

70. Poussin 1989 (ed.), p. 62, no. 53 (Paris, January 17, 1642); Jouanny 1911, p. 112, no. 53.

71. Jouanny 1911, pp. 125, 129, nos. 57–58; Poussin 1989 (ed.), pp. 65–66, no. 58 (Paris, April 4, 1642).

72. Jouanny 1911, pp. 214, 218, 225, 231, 239, nos. 88–89, 91, 95, 97 (Rome, August 25, 1643–January 7, 1644).

73. Jouanny 1911, pp. 245, 248, 256, 261; nos. 100–101, 104–5; Poussin 1989 (ed.), pp. 98–103; nos. 100–101, 104–5 (Rome, January 12–April 8, 1644). On the saga, see Green 2000, pp. 175–86.

74. Jouanny 1911, p. 268, no. 108; Poussin 1989 (ed.), p. 105, no. 108 (Rome, May 14, 1644).

75. One of Poussin's "Osservazioni sopra la pittura," appended to Bellori's *Life of Poussin*; see Bellori 2008 (ed.), p. 339. Poussin paraphrases Tasso's *Discorsi dell'arte poetica* (1587). On the origin of this and several other of Poussin's "Osservazioni" in Tasso, see Blunt 1967, pp. 361–66. On Poussin's appropriations from Tasso's literary theory, see Colantuono 2000; and Unglaub 2006, pp. 8–40.

76. On the context of the plagiarism case against Domenichino, see Cropper 2005, esp. pp. 135–155; on the 1639 letter from Holste (Biblioteca Nazionale dei Lincei, Archivio dal Pozzo, ms. IX (7), 149v–150r), see Unglaub 2006, pp. 45–50: Comparing Antonio Ongaro's pastoral drama *Alceo* (1582) to Tasso's *Aminta* (1573), Holste writes: "Ongaro imitates the plot part for part to such an extent that there is not a single little part in the Alceo that is not extracted from the Aminta. Nonetheless, Ongaro remains the most praiseworthy author of a most beautiful plot. I esteem the artifice of the imitation in Ongaro as much as the initial invention in Tasso."

77. See Unglaub 2006, pp. 45–55.

78. See the extensive description in Bellori 2008 (ed.), pp. 321–22; Verdi 1995, pp. 244–45, cat. 49.

79. On the series for Chantelou in general, see Brigstocke 1981, pp. 85–102; Rosenberg 1994, pp. 312–39, cats. 107–32; Verdi 1995, pp. 241–55, cats. 49–55; and Green 2000, pp. 173–364. Wilberding 1997, pp. 98–295, integrates both series in his thematic analysis.

80. Verdi 1995, pp. 248–49, cat. 51.

81. Verdi 1995, pp. 254–55, cat. 55.

82. On the phylacteries motif, see Cropper and Dempsey 1996, pp. 116–17; and especially Neer 2011, pp. 328–43.

83. On conforming to Baronio's commentary on the Last Supper (*Annales ecclesiastici* I, an. XXXIV, chs. XXII–LXV), see Powell 1985, pp. 483–84. On Christ occupying the honored position reserved for the Pontifex, according to Chacon, *De Triclinio*, see Wilberding 1997, pp. 200–201.

84. On the contemporary debate as to whether Judas received the sacrament, see Powell 1985, p. 484; and Green 2000, pp. 318–21.

85. On the privileging of what was then called "costume," see Chambray 1662, pp. 118–19; and Puttfarken 2000, pp. 231–36. On Poussin's letter responding to Chambray's praise, which includes his "definition" of painting, see Poussin 1989 (ed.), pp. 171–75, no. 210 (Rome, March 1, 1665); for translation, Blunt 1967, pp. 371–72.

86. Chambray 1662, pp. 130–32.

87. Chambray 1662, p. 127.

88. Chantelou 1985 (ed.), p. 79. On the circumstances of Bernini's visit, see Blunt's introduction, pp. xv–xxvii.

89. Luther 1959 (ed.), p. 112.

90. Calvin 1989 (ed.), p. 643 (book IV, ch. 19.28).

91. Luther 1959 (ed.), p. 117.

92. Schroeder 1978, p. 160, session 23, ch. I.

93. See Sellink and Leesberg 2001, p. 200, cat. 271; on text and image, see Clifton 2009.

94. For a refutation of the ordination of apostles at the Last Supper, see Luther 1959 (ed.), p. 111.

95. Wilberding 1997, pp. 231–33, citing treatises of Giovanni Battista Casali and Paganino Gaudenzi.

96. Bosio 1632, book III, ch. LXI, p. 565.

97. Calvin 1989 (ed.), p. 643 (book IV, chapter 19.28).

98. Powell 1985, p. 485; Wilberding 1997, pp. 234–36, citing the post-Tridentine *Catechismus Romanus*, on the authorities conferred through Ordination.

99. Wilberding 1997, pp. 236–37.

100. Jerome 2008 (ed.), p. 191.

101. Ibid., pp. 192–93.

102. Powell 1985, p. 485, referencing *Annales Ecclesiastici* I, an. XXXIII, chs. 16–18.

103. On the fresco cycles, see Ettlinger 1965; Lewine 1993; and Mejìa 2003.

104. On Perugino's fresco, see Ettlinger 1965, pp. 90–93,

111–13; Lewine 1993, pp. 69–74 (who cites it as a proto-type for Poussin's *Ordination* paintings); and Mejìa 2003, pp. 27–29.

105. On Raphael's tapestries and their full-scale cartoons, see the definitive study of Shearman 1972, as well as an updated survey in Evans, Browne, and Nesselrath 2010.

106. On the conflation of the donation of the keys and the "Feed my Sheep" episodes, see Shearman 1972, pp. 55, 62–68; and Evans, Browne, and Nesselrath 2010, p. 75.

107. On the later history of the cartoons, see Shearman 1972, pp. 143–47; and Evans, Browne, and Nesselrath 2010, pp. 57–58. After an extended period in Brussels work-shops through at least the mid-sixteenth century, they are likely recorded in Genoa before the sale to the English Crown in 1623. On the exhibition of the Vatican tapestries in the seventeenth century, and the early set woven from the cartoons and purchased by King François I before 1534, which remained in France until the revolution, see Shearman 1972, pp. 141–44.

108. Thompson 1980, pp. 8–9; Blunt 1967, p. 196: "Poussin has looked to Raphael for the disposition of his fig-ures and has done little more than transpose the tapestry design of *Feed my Sheep* into a new landscape setting."

109. Goldfarb 1989, pp. 42–44, cat. 15; Verdi 1995, p. 225, cat. 39. The sheet is rejected by Rosenberg and Prat 1994, p. 946, cat. R 663. They cite the clumsy arrange-ment of studies on the page, the disordered hatching, and the lack of hesitation in fixing poses, suggesting that the draughtsman is studying the finished painting.

110. On Raphael's fragmentary drawing of Christ (Louvre), the counterproof of the initial scheme (Windsor), and the Louvre compositional study owned by Stella, see Evans, Browne, and Nesselrath 2010, pp. 75–79; Clay-ton 1999, pp. 104–7, cat. 26; Cordellier and Py 1992, pp. 267–70, cats. 379, 381; and Shearman 1972, pp. 67–68, 96–97. Shearman suggests that the heavenward point-ing may allude to Christ's previous appearance before the apostles, when he tells them "Receive Ye the Holy Ghost" (John 20.22–23), an allusion later abandoned in favor of the conflation of John 21 with Matthew 16.

111. On the debate in the French Royale académie, occa-sioned by Sebastien Bourdon's conférence on this paint-ing, over the topographical setting of this work, see Cropper and Dempsey 1996, pp. 206–10; and Merot 1996a, pp. 123–29.

112. Blunt 1967, pp. 203–4. On the Rosa painting, see Scott 1995, p. 46.

113. As suggested by Green 2000, p. 291, citing Cornelius à Lapide, *Commentarius in quartor Evangelia* (Leiden, 1638).

114. On this figure as the embodiment of the Jewish age of the book, which parallels the spiritual myopia of the pagans, see Stanic 1996, p. 97; and Green 2000, pp. 164–65.

115. Verdi 1995, p. 225. cat. 39.

116. On Poussin studying anatomy in Sacchi's studio, see Passeri 1934 (ed.), p. 326. On the Saint Romuald altar-piece, see Harris 1997, pp. 14–15, 61–62, cat. 20. On the reduction in Cassiano's collection, see Solinas 2000, pp. 88–89, cat. 86.

117. Rosenberg and Prat 1994, pp. 192–95, cat. 105v; Keazor 1997; Goldfarb 1989, pp. 44–47, cats. 15–16; Goldfarb 1984; Blunt 1979b, pp. 124–29. The recto consolidates features of the *Death of Germanicus* (and a later draw-ing after it, Rosenberg and Prat 1994, pp. 282–83, cat. 146) and the first *Extreme Unction*. The shrouding shadows suggest a study for the nocturnal Chante-lou version (1644), though Goldfarb 1984 suggests an initial study for a Death of the Virgin, later adapted. Based on the male gender of the deceased in a copy, Keazor 1997 debunks this hypothesis. Goldfarb 1989 relates the sketch of crouching figures on the verso to one of Poussin's *Moses Striking the Rock* compositions, however Rosenberg and Prat correctly link it with the young hoarders in the *Israelites Gathering Manna* (1639), while associating the other fragmentary sketch on the verso with a late Holy Family, as does Blunt, suggesting the sheet was reused over time. Curiously, despite the exact correspondence of the head studies with the Dal Pozzo *Ordination*, Goldfarb 1989 associates them with a study after the Raphael tapestries in preparation for the Chantelou *Ordination*, while Rosenberg and Prat align the heads with those in the Dal Pozzo *Baptism*. As Blunt notes, references to "Monsieur" Sublet de Noyers in the draft letter to Chantelou must date from 1643–44, which accords with the study for this patron's first *Sacrament* picture on the recto.

118. Blunt 1979b, p. 126, followed by Keazor 1997, pp. 158–59, correctly notes the correspondences with the heads in the painting, and argues that they are prepara-tory, rather than copies after the painting, given slight deviations in the hair arrangement of Judas and Christ. Both note the exceptional nature of these detailed head studies in Poussin's surviving corpus of drawings.

119. Borromeo 2010 (ed.), pp. 73–75, quoting Nicephorus, *Historia Ecclesiastica*. On medallic portraits of Christ based on the true likeness inscribed on an emerald from Con-stantinople given by Sultan Bajezet II to Pope Innocent II, see Shearman 1972, p. 50, no. 34; and numerous examples in Hill 1920. On the importance of venerable medieval models in investing sacred art with evidentiary truth in post-tridentine writings on art and Church his-tory, see Herklotz 1985.

120. Rosenberg and Prat 1994, vol. 1, pp. 508–9, cat. 261. For an extensive account to the development of the composition through successive drawings, see Green 2000, pp. 277–93.

121. Joachim von Sandrart, *Teutsche Academie der edlen Bau-*,

Bild-, und Mahlerey-Kunste (Nuremburg, 1675); *Lettre du sieur Le Blonde de la Tour à un de ses amis, contenant quelques instructions touchant à la peinture* (Bordeaux, 1669), both in Thuillier 1994, pp. 181, 185. On this contraption, see also Arikha 1983, pp. 23–25. Both Blunt 1967, pp. 242–47; and DeGrazia and Steele 1999, pp. 64–75, create a reconstruction of the box and models, which they each relate to a sequence of drawings, for the Chantelou *Baptism* and the *Holy Family on the Steps*, respectively.

122. Rosenberg and Prat 1994, vol. 1, pp. 510–11, cat. 262.

123. Ibid., pp. 514–17, cats. 264, 265; Clayton 1995, pp. 171–74, cat. 58.

124. Verdi 1995, pp. 251–52, cat. 53.

125. Blunt 1967, pp. 189–90. On the two versions of *Confirmation*, see Verdi 1995, pp. 229–30, 246–47, cats. 43, 50.

126. Cropper and Dempsey 1996, pp. 121–44; an earlier version appeared as Charles Dempsey, "Poussin's 'Sacrament of Confirmation,' the Scholarship of 'Roma Sotterranea,' and dal Pozzo's Museo Cartaceo," in Solinas 1989, pp. 244–61.

127. Cropper and Dempsey 1996, pp. 132–34. See Bosio 1632, book III, ch. LXVI, p. 583.

128. Cropper and Dempsey 1996, pp. 123–34. On the latus clavus debate, they reference Ottavio Ferrari, *Analecta de re vestiaria* (1657); and Albert Rubens, *De re vestiaria veterum* (1655).

129. On the relation between the Chantelou *Confirmation* and the Santa Pudenziana mosaic and oratory frescoes, in the Church that marks the approximate site, see Cropper and Dempsey 1996, pp. 134–38. For the Museo Cartaceo images of Santa Pudenziana, see Osborne and Claridge 1996, pp. 306–13, cats. 142–45.

130. On the association of the Chantelou *Ordination* and the Louvre preparatory drawing with this sarcophagus type, see Blunt 1967, pp. 196–99; and Cropper and Dempsey 1996, p. 140.

131. On the Museo Cartaceo drawing after the sarcophagus excavated in 1590 (of which only fragments survive in the Vatican Museum) and the *Roma sotterranea* plate, see Osborne and Claridge 1996, vol. 2, pp.148–51, cat. 220; Herklotz 1992, pp. 34–38. Herklotz speculates that Cassiano supplied this drawing to the posthumous editors of the *Roma sotterranea*, whereas Osborne and Claridge date it earlier, suggesting that it was part of Bosio's cache of drawings engraved before his death for the project, later acquired by Cassiano. The various engravings and descriptions of "Traditio legis" sarcophagi are in Bosio 1632, book II, ch. VII, pp. 61–87 (63 corresponds to drawing).

132. On the drawing after Bosio, see Blunt 1967, pp. 199–201; Rosenberg and Prat 1994, pp. 480–81, cat. 244. For the engraving after the sarcophagus, see Bosio 1632, p. 85.

133. On the history and development of the "Traditio legis," iconography, see Rasmussen 1999; Patitucci Uggeri 2010, pp. 137–83; Jensen 2011, pp. 512–14.

134. Blunt 1967, pp. 196–99.

135. Cropper and Dempsey 1996, pp. 138–42.

136. Cropper and Dempsey 1996, pp. 142–43. Some have questioned whether this setting is specifically Roman. Blunt 1967, pp. 204–5, had compared the pyramidal tomb structure with reconstructed Appian Way tombs, or, more aptly, engravings after similarly designed cut rock tombs outside Jerusalem, such as the Tomb of Absalom. Using such antiquarian details to designate a Middle-Eastern locale, while the remaining architecture is generically Roman, was Poussin's standard procedure for designating the ancient setting the subject required, in this case Caesarea; see Wilberding 1997, pp. 248–49. Green 2000, pp. 295–96, suggests that the configuration of Christ and Peter might recall the legendary votive statue of Christ healing a hemorrhaging woman erected at Caesarea, one of the earliest alleged sculpted images of Jesus, which Eusebius, Theodosius, Baronio, and Bosio all discuss. The miracle appears in a side relief of the sarcophagus, whose background buildings Poussin copied from Bosio 1632, p. 87, on the verso of his drawing of the traditio legis motif (Rosenberg and Prat 1994, pp. 480–81, cat. 244v).

137. On the importance of the key symbolism, which Baronio, Casali, and other contemporary theological apologists for the sacrament emphasize, see Powell 1985, p. 485; and Green 2000, pp. 288–89.

138. On "Ei," see Blunt 1967, pp. 201–3, referring to Plutarch, *Moralia*; Stanic 1996, pp. 97–99; and Green 2000, pp. 302–10. For "Ecclesia," see Cropper and Dempsey 1996, pp. 142–43.

139. Green, 2000, pp. 297–98, assumes Paul's presence in the *traditio legis* drawing.

140. For background on Paul and his conversion, see Acts 7.58–9.30; 22.1–30; and Porter 2011.

141. Blunt 1967, p. 203, fn. 72: "At first sight this figure might be taken to be an apostle, but in fact there are twelve in the main group."

142. On the *Paul Preaching in Athens* tapestry as the culmination of the Apostle's ministry to the gentiles and his attempts to reconcile Christianity and pagan Platonism, exemplified in the conversion of Dionysius the Areopagite, see Shearman 1972, pp. 70–73; and Kleinbub 2010, pp. 81–89.

143. On this sheet, with recto and verso assembling motifs from the catacombs of Saint Domitilla and Saints Peter and Marcellinus, including a banqueting scene and the caspa, see Blunt 1967, pp. 199–201; and Rosenberg and Prat 1994, pp. 478–79, cat. 243.

144. On the standard physiognomy of Paul and his early portrait in the sepulcher of the *fossor* Diogenes in the catacombs of Saint Domitilla, see Jensen 2011, pp. 509–10; Wilpert 1903, vol. 1, pp. 106–7, 229, 498, vol. 2, pls. 180–82; Bisconti 2009, pp. 172–75; and Patitucci Uggeri 2010, pp. 29–40. See also the entries by Barbara

Mazzei in Utro 2009, pp. 181–84, cats. 53–55, who notes that this example was first illustrated in M. A. Boldetti in 1720, at approximately the same time the central bust of Christ was destroyed during a botched attempt at removal. Though this example is not illustrated, a similar image of Paul from the catacombs of Sant'Agnese on the Via Nomentana is engraved in Bosio 1632, book III, ch. L, p. 475. Another early portrait of Paul is in the catacomb of Saint Priscilla on the Via Salaria. See Bosio 1632, book III, ch. LXI, p. 519.

145. For the original of the frescoes in Poussin's sketch, see Fiocchi Nicolai, Bisconti, and Mazzoleni 2009, pp. 86–87, 111, figs. 95, 126; Patitucci Uggeri 2010, pp. 114, 120–22; and Wilpert 1903, vol. 1, pp. 227–28, vol. 2, pls. 157, 193; On the engravings Poussin likely consulted from the catacombs discovered in 1567 and 1594, see Bosio 1632, book III, ch. XXIII, p. 221, and ch. XXXVII, p. 391.

146. Fiocchi Nicolai, Bisconti, and Mazzoleni 2009, pp. 129–31, fig. 144; Wilpert 1903, vol. 2, pls. 252–54; entries by Barbara Mazzei in Utro 2009, pp. 184–85, cats. 56–57. The vault fresco is reproduced on the plan of the catacombs of Santi Marcellino e Pietro in Bosio 1632, book III, ch. LXI, p. 591.

147. Paolo Zander in Urto 2009, pp. 247–49, cat. 87. The composition of the original fresco was preserved in documentary drawings by Domenico Tasselli and Giacomo Grimaldi. The detached fresco heads entered the collection of Poussin's Giustiniani patrons. On the Giustiniani and their antiquarian interests, see Cropper and Dempsey 1996, pp. 64–81.

148. Patitucci Uggeri 2010, pp. 53–55; on the Santa Maria Maggiore mosaics more generally, see Brandenburg 2004, pp. 180–89; and Poeschke 2010, pp. 70–93. Green 2000, pp. 164–66, notes the intriguing compositional and thematic parallels between the Dal Pozzo *Ordination* and the Santa Maria Maggiore nave mosaic of Moses distributing the law to the twelve tribes of Israel of the same period.

149. On the origins of Paul iconic types in busts of Plotinus, see Jensen 2011, pp. 509–10; Bisconti 2009, pp. 163–66; Utro 2009, pp. 179–81, cats. 51–52; and Utro 2011, pp. 27–29. On the larger phenomenon of assimilating the philosopher portrait type to early Christian iconography, see Zanker 1995, pp. 289–307.

150. Bosio 1632, book II, ch. VII, p. 75. Also noted in Wilberding 1997, pp. 241–42. On the contemporary Barberini restorations of ancient images of Leo III and Peter on the Lateran Tricilinium arch to reinforce claims of Papal authority, see Herklotz 1995.

151. On the Santa Costanza mosaic, see Deckers 2007, pp. 94–96; entries by Barbara Mazzei in Utro 2009, pp. 185–86, cat. 58; and Brandenburg 2005, pp. 85–86. On the shrine in general, see Brandenburg 2005, pp. 73–86.

On the mosaic and the "tradition legis" formula, see Rasmussen 1999, pp. 21–30; Patitucci Uggeri 2010, pp. 137–48; and Jensen 2011, pp. 512–13, who notes that this may be the earliest image of the type.

152. On the Santa Pudeniziana apse mosaic building on the formula of Christ enthroned flanked by seated Peter and Paul and assembled apostles first seen in the Saint Domitilla cubiculum niche, see Patitucci Uggeri 2010, pp. 109–14, 120; Brandenburg 2005, pp. 140–42.

153. On the Santa Pudenziana oratory, see Osborne and Claridge 1996, pp. 308–13, cats. 143, 145; Cropper and Dempsey 1996, pp. 135–38.

154. On the Saints Cosma and Damiano apse mosaic (c. 527), see Brandenbrug 2005, pp. 223–24; and Poeschke 2010, pp. 94–107. For an insightful survey of the iconography, symbolism, and theological purpose of mosaic Church decoration throughout the Mediterranean in the fifth and sixth centuries, see Kessler 2007.

155. Herklotz 1992, pp. 38–45; Osborne and Claridge 1996, vol. 1, pp. 47–68. On Eclissi's drawings after Santa Pudenziana and Santi Cosma and Damiano, see Osborne and Claridge 1996, vol. 1, pp. 94–96, 306–13; cats. 14, 142–45.

156. On the copies after the apse mosaic of Sant'Agata dei Goti, which collapsed in 1589 but was recorded in drawings by the Dominican antiquarian Alonso Chacón (1530–99), see Osborne and Claridge 1996, vol. 2, pp. 48–53, cats. 163–66.

157. Osborne and Claridge 1996, vol. 1, pp. 119–21, cat. 27.

158. Osborne and Claridge 1996, vol. 1, pp. 81, 322–24, cats. 6, 150. On watercolors after the apse mosaic of Old Saint Peters, reconstructed c. 1200 and destroyed in 1592, of which several documentary copies were made at the time, see ibid, vol. 2, p. 76, cat. 177.

159. The apse fresco was destroyed in the remodeling of 1650 and the Eclissi drawing is the unique record. See Osborne and Claridge 1996, vol. 1, pp. 190–91, cat. 71.

160. Calvin 1995 (ed.), pp. 188–89. On the seminal importance of Paul's teaching for the formulation of Justification by Faith alone and other Protestant doctrines, see Mattox 2011; Lane 2011; and Westerholm 2004. On Cesare Baronio, and the issue of the Roman primacy of Peter and Paul, see Cropper and Dempsey 1996, pp. 134–40.

161. Cropper and Dempsey 1996, pp. 140–42.

162. Poussin 1989 (ed.), pp. 134–35, no. 156; Jouanny 1911, p. 372, no. 156.

163. On Poussin paraphrasing the reconstruction of the Modes in Gioseffo Zarlino's *Istituzioni harmoniche* (1553), see Blunt 1967, pp. 225–27; Hammond 1996. On the possible origins of these ideas in Poussin's Roman milieu, his patron Giulio Rospigliosi, and its operatic culture fostered by the Barberini, see Unglaub 2011.

164. Poussin 1989 (ed.), pp. 135–36, no. 156; Jouanny 1911, pp. 373–74, no. 156; transl. in Blunt 1967, pp. 369–70.

On the importance of the Modes letter for Poussin's theory and practice of painting, and its later codification in French Academic doctrine, see Montagu 1992; Puttfarken 2000, pp. 214–21; and Sohm 2001, pp. 124–43.

165. Letter to Chantelou of April 28, 1639, in Poussin 1989 (ed.), p. 45, no. 11; Jouanny 1911, p. 21, no. 11.

166. This narrative approach was further explicated in terms of a unified plot in Le Brun's 1666 conférence before the Académie royale de peinture et de sculpture; see Mérot 1996a, pp. 98–112. The fundamental study on these issues is Thuillier 1967; for a comprehensive account of poetic unity in both the conception and reception of the *Manna*, with references to extensive earlier literature, see Unglaub 2006, pp. 157–97.

167. On the Barberini landscape in the Museo Cartaceo, see Claridge, Jenkins, and Freedberg 1993, pp. 113–14, cat. 68; Whitehouse 2001, pp. 202–8, cat. 48. On the *Manna* and Holste's allegory, see McTighe 1996, pp. 107–11. The *Manna* foreshadows Poussin's eventual use of the landscape to create a unified stage in the *Birth of Bacchus* (1657), wherein Porphyry's allegory links not the unfolding of a single narrative, but distinct myths from Ovid and Philostratus; see ibid., pp. 163–71. On the mythographic rather than allegorical resonance of the landscape accounting for the juxtapositions, see Cropper and Demsey 1996, pp. 295–302.

168. The analogy of the Manna and the Eucharist originates in John 6.31–59, where Christ contrasts the Manna with the Son of Man as the Bread of Life, anticipating the Eucharist ritual. On the exhaustive elaboration of this association in relation to an engraving of the Manna that has some affinity with Poussin's painting, see Richeome 1601, pp. 160–222; an engraving of the Last Supper in this text was a clear source for Poussin's *Sacrament of the Eucharist*; see ibid., pp. 440–518; and Vanuxem 1960.

169. Bosio 1632, book IV, ch. XXXII, p. 630. Bosio cites Augustine's *Exposition of Psalm 72*, which digresses on the grafting imagery in Romans 11. See Augustine 2001 (ed.), pp. 471–72.

170. Bosio 1632, book IV, ch. XXXII, p. 630.

171. Rosenberg and Christiansen 2008, pp. 192–99, cats. 27–29; Wine 2001, pp. 342–49.

172. Several Poussin landscapes seem to have been exhibited together; see Dal Pozzo inventories of 1689 and 1695 in Sparti 1992, pp. 187, 209.

173. These sketching trips are recorded by their companion and biographer Joachim Sandrart, reprinted in Thuillier 1994, pp. 185–86. On affinities and differences between Poussin and Claude, see Kitson 1961; and Lagerlöf 1990, pp. 53–94.

174. For these drawings, see Whiteley 1998, pp. 87–89, cat. 40v; and Rosenberg and Christiansen 2008, pp. 318–21, cats. 78–79. For a recent account of Claude's nature drawings, see Rand 2006, pp. 22–92.

175. On the Buen Retiro commission, see Úbeda de los Cobos 2005, pp. 241–84. On the *Jerome*, see Rosenberg and Christiansen 2008, pp. 200–201, cat. 30.

176. On the Italian Renaissance attitude towards landscape, as determined by its decorative and pastoral functions, see Gombrich 1985; and Lagerlöf 1990, pp. 23–36.

177. On Carracci's landscape mode, see Lagerlöf 1990, pp. 40–53.

178. On Agucchi's and Mancini's elevation of landscape and emphasis on its literary basis, see Lagerlöf, 1990, pp. 27–41.

179. Rosenberg and Christiansen 2008, pp. 210–13, cats. 35–36. Painted for for Gian Maria Roscioli, Pope Urban VIII's secretary.

180. Poussin 1989 (ed.), pp. 141–42, no. 162; Jouanny 1911, p. 384, no. 162 (June 22, 1648).

181. On Poussin's Stoicism, see Blunt 1967, pp. 160–76; and McTighe 1996, pp. 23–31, who associates Poussin with the libertine sect of this movement.

182. On Charron's *De la Sagesse* and his political and meteorological hierarchies, see McTighe 1996, pp. 18–23; and Verdi 1982, pp. 681–82.

183. On the landscape paintings that might relate to a Fortune cycle, or at least visualize the "tempests" of Fortune, see Verdi 1982; and McTighe 1996, pp. 18–52.

184. On Fortune and reversal in the *Orpheus and Eurydice* (Paris, Musée du Louvre), see McTighe 1996, pp. 53–78. On *Pyramus and Thisbe* (Frankfurt, Städelishes Kunstinstitut), see Bätschmann 1990, pp. 93–110.

185. On *Diogenes* and the Fortune series, see Verdi 1982, pp. 682–83. The later dating of the *Diogenes* to the mid to late 1650s need not extricate the picture from relating to the Fortune themes. See Mahon 1995; Verdi 1995, pp. 281–82, cat. 70; and Rosenberg and Christiansen 2008, pp. 280–83, cat. 62.

186. Poussin 1989 (ed.), pp. 103, no. 105; Jouanny 1911, pp. 261–62, no. 105 (April 8, 1644).

187. On Poussin's hostility toward Mazarin, documented in his correspondence with Sublet's cousin Chantelou, see Olson 2002, pp. 74–131.

188. See Blunt 1967, pp. 160–76. On Poussin's daily routine, see Bellori 2008 (ed.), pp. 322–25.

189. Verdi 1995, pp. 289–90, cat. 75; Rosenberg and Christiansen 2008, pp. 264–67, cat. 57; Bätschmann 1990, pp. 93–110.

190. Blunt 1967, pp. 313–56; Cropper and Dempsey 1996, pp. 295–312; McTighe 1996, pp. 31–52, 152–81; Rosenberg and Christiansen 2008, pp. 269–305.

191. On Poussin and the French Academy, see Puttfarken 1985, pp. 4–29; and Duro 1997, pp. 63–155; as well as the original texts gathered in Mérot 1996a.

192. On the dispersal of the Museo Cartaceo, see the essay by Haskell and McBurney in Osborne and Claridge 1996, pp. 9–26; on the collection, see Sparti 1992, pp. 145–62.

193. For an overview of the Grand Tour phenomenon, see Chaney 1998 and Wilton and Bignamini 1996.

194. See Clark and Bowron 1985, p. 228, no. 62; Bowron and Kerber 2007, p. 26. In other Poussin-inspired compositions, Batoni explicitly resolves the conceptual ambiguities of his models; see Clark and Bowron 1985, pp. 215, 219, cats. 22, 38; and Unglaub 2003, p. 127.

195. See Byres 1894 (ed.). On Byres, see Ford 1974. On the copies by André de Mujnck, see Bruno Contardi's entry in Solinas 2000, pp. 187–91, cats. 213–19.

196. Reynolds 2000 (ed.), p. 142, no. 136 (July 5, 1785).

197. Ibid., p. 151, no. 143 (September 26, 1785).

198. Ibid., p. 169, no. 160.

199. Ibid., pp. 172–73, no. 162 (October 4, 1786). The post-cleaning appearance of the *Sacraments* deflated a rival collector, Wellbore Agar, who had passed up chance to land them at a much lower price years earlier because of their evident grime.

200. Ibid., p. 170, no. 160.

201. Ibid., pp. 173, no. 162.

202. Ibid., pp. 175–76, no. 164 (December 2, 1786).

203. See the exhibition proposal and report to the duke of the royal visit in ibid., pp. 180–81, no. 171 (February 13, 1787); p. 183, no. 172 (May 3, 1787).

204. On Poussin and Cézanne, see Reff 1960 and Verdi 1990.

Bibliography

Arasse 2000
Daniel Arasse. "Rome, Poussin, et les Sabines." In *L'Europa e l'arte italiana: Per i cento anni dalla fondazione del Kunsthistorisches Institut in Florenz*, edited by Max Seidel, pp. 337–51. Venice, 2000.

Arikha 1983
Avigdor Arikha. *Nicolas Poussin: The Rape of the Sabines.* Exh. cat., Museum of Fine Arts, Houston, 1983.

Augustine 2001 (ed.)
Augustine. "Expositions of the Psalms, 51–72." *The Works of Saint Augustine.* Vol. III/17, translated by Maria Boulding. Hyde Park, New York, 2001.

Badt 1959
Kurt Badt. "Raphael's 'Incendio del Borgo.' " *Journal of the Warburg and Courtauld Institutes* 22 (1959), pp. 35–59.

Bailey et al. 2005
Gauvin A. Bailey et al. *Hope and Healing: Painting in Italy in a Time of Plague, 1500–1800.* Exh. cat., Worcester Art Museum, Massachusetts. Chicago, 2005.

Barker 2004
Sheila Barker. "Poussin, Plague, and Early Modern Medicine." *The Art Bulletin* 86 (2004), pp. 659–89.

Barone 2009
Juliana Barone. "Poussin as Engineer of the Human Figure: The Illustrations for Leonardo's *Trattato.*" In *Re-Reading Leonardo: The "Treatise on Painting" across Europe, 1550–1900*, edited by Claire Farago, pp. 197–235. Farnham, United Kingdom, and Burlington, Vermont, 2009.

Bätschmann 1990
Oskar Bätschmann. *Nicolas Poussin: Dialectics of Painting.* London, 1990.

Beldon Scott 1991
John Beldon Scott. *Images of Nepotism: The Painted Ceilings of Palazzo Barberini.* Princeton, 1991.

Bellori 2008 (ed.)
Giovanni Pietro Bellori. *The Lives of the Modern Painters, Sculptors, and Architects.* [*Le Vite de'pittori, scultori et architetti moderni*, Rome, 1672.] Translated by Alice Sedgwick Wohl. Cambridge and New York, 2008.

Belting 1994
Hans Belting. *Likeness and Presence: A History of the Image before the Era of Art.* Translated by Edmund Jephcott. Chicago and London, 1994.

Biagioli 1993
Mario Biagioli. *Galileo, Courtier: The Practice of Science in the Culture of Absolutism.* Chicago, 1993.

Bisconti 2009
Fabrizio Bisconti. "La Sapienza, la concordia, il martirio: La figura di Paolo nell'immaginario iconografico della tarda antichità." In *San Paolo in Vaticano: La figura e la parola dell'apostolo delle genti nelle raccolte pontificie*, edited by Umberto Utro, pp. 163–76. Todi, Italy, 2009.

Blunt 1939
Anthony Blunt. "The Triclinium in Religious Art." *Journal of the Warburg and Courtauld Institutes* 2 (1939), pp. 271–76.

Blunt 1967
Anthony Blunt. *Nicolas Poussin.* The Andrew W. Mellon Lectures on the Fine Arts 7. Princeton, 1967.

Blunt 1979a
Anthony Blunt. *The Drawings of Poussin.* New Haven and London, 1979.

Blunt 1979b
Anthony Blunt. "Further Newly Identified Drawings by Poussin and His Followers." *Master Drawings* 17, no. 2 (summer 1979), pp. 119–46; 173–90.

Bonfait 1994
Olivier Bonfait. *Roma 1630: Il trionfo del pennello.* Exh. cat., Villa Medici, Rome. Milan, 1994.

Bonfait et al. 1996
Olivier Bonfait et al., eds. *Poussin et Rome: Actes du colloque à l'Académie de France à Rome et à la Bibliotheca Hertziana 16–18 novembre 1994.* Paris, 1996.

Borromeo 2010 (ed.)
Federico Borromeo. *Sacred Painting.* [*De Pictura sacra*, 1624.] Edited and translated by Kenneth Rothwell Jr. Cambridge, Massachusetts, and London, 2010.

Bosio 1632
Antonio Bosio. *Roma sotterranea nella quale si tratta de'sacri cimiterii di Roma.* Edited by Giovanni Severano. Rome, 1632.

Bowron and Kerber 2007
Edgar Peters Bowron and Peter Björn Kerber. *Pompeo Batoni: Prince of Painters in Eighteenth-Century Rome.* Exh. cat. Museum of Fine Arts, Houston. New Haven and London, 2007.

Brandenburg 2005
Hugo Brandenburg. *Ancient Churches of Rome from the Fourth to the Seventh Century: The Dawn of Christian Architecture in the West.* Turnhout, Belgium, 2005.

Brigstocke 1981
Hugh Brigstocke, ed. *Poussin: Sacraments and Bacchanals.* Exh. cat., National Galleries of Scotland. Edinburgh, 1981.

Brunelli 1999
Giampiero Brunelli. "Paganino Gaudenzi." *Dizionario biografico degli Italiani* 52 (1999), pp. 676–78.

Bucarelli and Morales 2011
Ottavio Bucarelli and Martín María Morales, eds. *Paulo apostolo martyri: L'apostolo San Paolo nella storia, nell'arte e nell'archeologia.* Miscellanea historiae pontificae 69. Rome, 2011.

Bull 2001
Malcolm Bull. "Poussin's Loves of the Goddesses." *Gazette des Beaux Arts* 137 (2001), pp. 61–70.

Byres 1894 (ed.)
James Byres. "Letters." In *The Manuscripts of His Grace the Duke of Rutland, G.C.B. preserved at Belvoir Castle.* 14th Annual Report (1894), appendix 1.

Calvin 1989 (ed.)
John Calvin. *Institutes of the Christian Religion* [1536, 1559.] Translated by Henry Beveridge. Grand Rapids, 1989.

Calvin 1995 (ed.)
John Calvin. *Harmony of the Gospels: Matthew, Mark, and Luke* [1584]. Calvin's New Testament Commentaries 2. Translated by T. H. L. Parker. Grand Rapids, 1995.

Chambray 1662
Roland Fréart, sieur de Chambray. *L'Idée de la perfection de la peinture.* Les Mans, 1662.

Chaney 1998
Edward Chaney. *The Evolution of the Grand Tour: Anglo-Italian Cultural Relations Since the Renaissance.* London and Portland, 1998.

Chantelou 1985 (ed.)
Paul Fréart de Chantelou. *Diary of the Cavaliere Bernini's Visit to France.* Edited by Anthony Blunt and translated by Margery Corbett. Princeton, 1985.

Claridge, Jenkins, and Freedberg 1993
Amanda Claridge, Ian Jenkins, and David Freedberg, eds. *The Paper Museum of Cassiano dal Pozzo.* Quaderni Puteani 4. Exh. cat., British Museum, London. Ivrea, Italy, 1993.

Clark and Bowron 1985
Anthony M. Clark and Edgar Peters Bowron. *Pompeo Batoni: A Complete Catalogue of His Works with an Introductory Text.* Oxford, 1985.

Clayton 1995
Martin Clayton. *Poussin Works on Paper: Drawings from the Collection of Her Majesty Queen Elizabeth II.* Exh. cat., Museum of Fine Arts, Houston. London and New York, 1995.

Clayton 1999
Martin Clayton. *Raphael and His Circle: Drawings from Windsor Castle.* Exh. cat., Queen's Gallery. London, 1999.

Clifton 2009
James Clifton. "Appositis Exemplis, ac Sententiis illustrata: Philips Galle's Series of the Sacraments and the Works of Mercy." In *Infant Milk or Hardy Nourishment? The Bible for Lay People and Theologians in the Early Modern Period,* edited by W. François and A. A. Den Hollander, pp. 297–335. Louvain, Belgium, 2009.

Colantuono 1996
Anthony Colantuno. "Interpréter Poussin: Métaphore, similarité et 'maniera magnifica.' " In Mérot 1996b, pp. 647–65.

Colantuono 2000
Anthony Colantuono. "Poussin's 'Osservazioni sopra la pittura': Notes or Aphorisms?" *Studi Secenteschi* 41 (2000), pp. 285–309.

Conisbee et al. 2009
Philip Conisbee et al. *French Paintings of the Fifteenth through the Eighteenth Century in the National Gallery of Art, Washington.* Princeton, 2009.

Cordellier and Py 1992
Dominique Cordellier and Bernadette Py. *Raphaël, son atelier, ses copistes.* Inventaire general des dessins italiens 5. Paris, 1992.

Costello 1955
Jane Costello. "Poussin's Drawings for Marino and the New Classicism: I—Ovid's *Metamorphoses.*" *Journal of the Warburg and Courtauld Institutes* 18 (1955), pp. 296–317.

Cropper 1984
Elizabeth Cropper. *The Ideal of Painting: Pietro Testa's Düsseldorf Notebook.* Princeton, 1984.

Cropper 2005
Elizabeth Cropper. *The Domenichino Affair: Novelty, Imitation, and Theft in Seventeenth-Century Rome.* New Haven and London, 2005.

Cropper and Dempsey 1996
Elizabeth Cropper and Charles Dempsey. *Nicolas Poussin: Friendship and the Love of Painting.* Princeton, 1996.

Dati 1664
Carlo Roberto Dati. *Delle lodi del commendatore Cassiano dal Pozzo: Orazione.* Florence, 1664.

Deckers 2007
Johannes G. Deckers. "Constantine the Great and Early Christian Art." In Spier 2007, pp. 87–109.

DeGrazia and Steele 1999
Diane DeGrazia and Marcia Steele. "The 'Grande Machine.' " In *A Painting in Focus: Nicolas Poussin's "Holy Family on the Steps."* Exh. cat., Cleveland Museum of Art. *Cleveland Studies in the History of Art* 4 (1999), pp. 64–75.

Dempsey 1966
Charles Dempsey. "The Classical Perception of Nature in Poussin's Earlier Works." *Journal of the Warburg and Courtauld Institutes* 29 (1966), pp. 219–49.

Dempsey 2000
Charles Dempsey. "Nicolas Poussin between Italy and France: Poussin's *Death of Germanicus* and the Invention of the Tableau." In *L'Europa e l'arte italiana: Per cento anni dalla fondazione del Kunsthistorisches Institut in Florenz,* edited by Max Siedel, pp. 321–35. Venice, 2000.

Dolders 1987
Arno Dolders. *Netherlandish Artists: Philips Galle.* The Illustrated Bartsch 56. New York, 1987.

Donati 2000
Angela Donati, ed. *Pietro e Paolo: La storia, il culto, la memoria nei primi secoli.* Milan, 2000.

Duro 1997
Paul Duro. *The Academy and the Limits of Painting in Seventeenth-Century France.* Cambridge and New York, 1997.

Ettlinger 1965
Leopold D. Ettlinger. *The Sistine Chapel before Michelangelo: Religious Imagery and Papal Primacy.* Oxford, 1965.

Evans, Browne, and Nesselrath 2010
Mark Evans, Clare Browne, and Arnold Nesselrath, eds. *Raphael: Cartoons and Tapestries for the Sistine Chapel.* Exh. cat., Victoria and Albert Museum. London, 2010.

Félibien 1981 (ed.)
André Félibien. *Entretiens sur les vies et sur les ouvrages des plus excellens peintres anciens et modernes: Huitième entretien* [Paris, 1685.] In *Félibien's Life of Poussin,* by Claire Pace, pp. 109–149. London, 1981.

Fiocchi Nicolai, Bisconti, and Mazzoleni 2009
Vincenzo Fiocchi Nicolai, Fabrizio Bisconti, and Danilo Mazzoleni. *The Christian Catacombs of Rome: History, Decoration, Inscriptions.* Translated by Cristina Carlo Stella and Lori-Ann Touchette. Regensburg, 2009.

Ford 1974
Brinsley Ford. "James Byres, Principal Antiquarian to the English Visitors to Rome." *Apollo* 99 (1974), pp. 446–61.

Freedberg 2002
David Freedberg. *The Eye of the Lynx: Galileo, His Friends, and the Beginnings of Modern Natural History.* Chicago, 2002.

Fumaroli 1989
Marc Fumaroli. *L'Inspiration du poète de Poussin: Essai sur l'allégorie du Parnasse.* Paris, 1989.

Goldfarb 1984
Hilliard T. Goldfarb. "A Highly Important Poussin Acquisition and Chantelou's *Seven Sacraments* Series." *The Bulletin of the Cleveland Museum of Art* 71, no. 8 (Oct. 1984), pp. 290–99.

Goldfarb 1989
Hilliard T. Goldfarb. *From Fontainebleau to the Louvre: French Drawing from the Seventeenth Century.* Exh. cat., Cleveland Museum of Art. Bloomington, Indiana, 1989.

Goldfarb 2002
Hilliard T. Goldfarb, ed. *Richelieu: Art and Power.* Exh. cat., Montreal Museum of Fine Arts. Ghent, Belgium, 2002.

Gombrich 1985
Ernst H. Gombrich. "The Renaissance Theory of Art and the Rise of Landscape." In *Norm and Form,* pp. 107–121. 4th ed. London, 1985.

Gray 2003
Madeleine Gray. *The Protestant Reformation: Belief, Practice, and Tradition.* Brighton and Portland, Oregon, 2003.

Green 2000
Tony Green. *Nicolas Poussin Paints the Seven Sacraments Twice.* Somerset, 2000.

Hammond 1996
Frederick Hammond. "Poussin et les modes: Le point de vue d'un musicien." In Bonfait et al. 1996, pp. 75–91.

Harris 1977
Ann Sutherland Harris. *Andrea Sacchi: Complete Edition of the Paintings with a Critical Catalogue.* Oxford, 1977.

Haskell 1980
Francis Haskell. *Patrons and Painters: A Study in the Relations between Italian Art and Society in the Age of the Baroque.* New Haven and London, 1980.

Hénin 2003
Emmanuelle Hénin. *Ut pictura theatrum: Théâtre et peinture de la Renaissance italienne au classicisme français.* Geneva, 2003.

Henneberg 1987
Josephine von Henneberg. "Poussin's Penance: A New Reading." *Storia dell'arte* 61 (1987), pp. 229–42.

Herklotz 1985
Ingo Herklotz. "Historia sacra und mittelalterliche Kunst während der zweiten Hälfte des 16. Jahrhunderts in Rom." In *Baronio e l'arte: Atti del convegno internazionale di studi, Sora, 10–13 ottobre 1984*, edited by Romeo de Maio, pp. 21–74. Sora, Italy, 1985.

Herklotz 1992
Ingo Herklotz. "Cassiano and the Christian Tradition." In Jenkins et al. 1992, pp. 31–48.

Herklotz 1995
Ingo Herklotz. "Francesco Barberini, Nicolò Alemanni, and the Lateran Triclinium of Leo III: An Episode in Restoration and Seicento Medieval Studies." *Memoirs of the American Academy in Rome* 40 (1995), pp. 175–96.

Herklotz 1996
Ingo Herklotz. "Poussin et Pline L'Ancien: À propos des monocromata." In Bonfait et al. 1996, pp. 13–29.

Herklotz 1999
Ingo Herklotz. *Cassiano dal Pozzo und die Archäologie des 17. Jahrhunderts.* Römische Forschungen der Biblioteca Hertziana 28. Munich, 1999.

Hill 1920
George F. Hill. *The Medallic Portraits of Christ.* Oxford, 1920.

Hipp 2007
Elizabeth Hipp. "Poussin's *Plague at Ashdod*: A Work of Art in Multiple Contexts." In *Piety and Plague: From Byzantium to the Baroque*, edited by Franco Mormando and Thomas Worcester, pp. 177–223. Kirksville, Missouri, 2007.

Jenkins et al. 1992
Ian Jenkins et al. *Cassiano dal Pozzo's Paper Museum.* Quaderni Putenai 2–3. 2 vols. Ivrea, Italy, 1992.

Jensen 2011
Robin Jensen. "The Legacy of Paul: Art." In Westerholm 2011, pp. 507–30.

Jerome 2008 (ed.)
Saint Jerome. *Commentary on Saint Matthew.* Edited and translated by Thomas P. Scheck. Washington, DC, 2008.

Jones 1993
Pamela M. Jones. *Federico Borromeo and the Ambrosiana: Art Patronage and Reform in Seventeenth-Century Milan.* Cambridge and New York, 1993.

Jouanny 1911
Charles Jouanny, ed. *Correspondance de Nicolas Poussin.* Archives de l'art francaise 5. Paris, 1911.

Keazor 1997
Henry Keazor. "Nicolas Poussin: Strides, Reverses and Backlogs—Some Notes on the Cleveland Drawing." *Konsthistorisk tidskrift* 66 (1997), pp. 155–65.

Keazor 1998
Henry Keazor. *Poussins Parerga: Quellen, Entwicklung und Bedeutung der Kleinkompositionen in den Gemälden Nicolas Poussins.* Regensburg, Germany, 1998.

Kessler 1987
Herbert L. Kessler. "The Meeting of Peter and Paul in Rome: An Emblematic Narrative of Spiritual Brotherhood." *Dumbarton Oaks Papers* 41 (1987), pp. 265–75.

Kessler 2007
Herbert L. Kessler. "Bright Gardens of Paradise." In Spier 2007, pp. 111–39.

Kitson 1961
Michael Kitson. "The Relationship between Claude and Poussin in Landscape." *Zeitschrift für Kunstgeschichte* 24 (1961), pp. 142–62.

Kleinbub 2010
Christian K. Kleinbub. *Vision and the Visionary in Raphael.* University Park, Pennsylvania, 2010.

Koerner 2004
Joseph Leo Koerner. *The Reformation of the Image.* Chicago, 2004.

Lagerlöf 1990
Margaretha Rossholm Lagerlöf. *Ideal Landscape: Annibale Carracci, Nicolas Poussin, and Claude Lorrain.* New Haven and London, 1990.

Lane 2011
Anthony N. S. Lane. "Readers of Paul: Calvin." In Westerholm 2011, pp. 391–405.

Lewine 1993
Carol Lewine. *The Sistine Chapel Walls and the Roman Liturgy*. University Park, Pennsylvania, 1993.

Luther 1959 (ed.)
Martin Luther. "The Babylonian Captivity of the Church" [1520], translated by A. T. W Steinhäuser. In *Luther's Works*, edited by Abdel Ross Wentz, vol. 36, pp. 11–126. Philadelphia, 1959.

Maguire Robinson 2008
Pauline Maguire Robinson. "Leonardo's *Trattato della Pittura*, Nicolas Poussin, and the Pursuit of Eloquence in Seventeenth-Century France." In *Leonardo da Vinci and the Ethics of Style*, edited by Claire Farago, pp. 189–236. Manchester and New York, 2008.

Maguire Robinson 2009
Pauline Maguire Robinson. "Leonardo's Theory of Aerial Perspective in the Writings of André Félibien and the Paintings of Nicolas Poussin." In *Re-Reading Leonardo: The Treatise on Painting across Europe, 1550–1900*, edited by Claire Farago. Farnham, United Kingdom, and Burlington, Vermont, 2009, pp. 265–97.

Mahon 1995
Denis Mahon. "The Written Sources for Poussin's Landscapes, with Special Reference to His Two Landscapes with Diogenes." *The Burlington Magazine* 137 (1995), pp. 176–82.

Mancini 1956–57 (ed.)
Giulio Mancini. *Considerazioni sulla pittura*. Edited by Adriana Marucchi and Luigi Salerno. 2 vols. Rome, 1956–57.

Mattox 2011
Mickey L. Mattox. "Readers of Paul: Luther." In Westerholm 2011, pp. 375–90.

McBurney, Claridge, and Freedberg 1996–
Henrietta McBurney, Amanda Claridge, and David Freedberg, eds. *The Paper Museum of Cassiano dal Pozzo: A Catalogue Raisonné*, series A, "Antiquities"; series B, "Natural History" (London: Harvey Miller, 1996–).

McTighe 1996
Sheila McTighe. *Nicolas Poussin's Landscape Allegories*. Cambridge and New York, 1996.

Mejía 2003
Cardinal Jorge María Mejía. "Biblical Reading of the Frescoes on the Walls of Sistine Chapel." In *The Fifteenth-Century Frescoes in the Sistine Chapel*, edited by Francesco Buranelli and Allen Duston, pp. 9–37. Recent Restorations of the Vatican Museums 4. Vatican City, 2003.

Mérot 1990
Alain Mérot. *Nicolas Poussin*. New York, 1990.

Mérot 1996a
Alain Mérot, ed. *Les Conférences de l'Académie royale de peinture et de sculpture au XVIIe siècle*. Paris, 1996.

Mérot 1996b
Alain Mérot, ed. *Nicolas Poussin (1594–1665): Actes du colloque organisé au Musée du Louvre par le service culturel du 19 au 21 octobre 1994*. Paris, 1996.

Miller 2000
Peter N. Miller. *Peiresc's Europe: Learning and Virtue in the Seventeenth Century*. New Haven and London, 2000.

Montagu 1992
Jennifer Montagu. "The Theory of the Musical Modes in the Académie Royale de Peinture at de Sculpture." *Journal of the Warburg and Courtauld Institutes* 55 (1992), pp. 233–48.

Neer 2006–7
Richard T. Neer. "Poussin and the Ethics of Imitation." *Memoirs of the American Academy in Rome* 51/52 (2006–7), pp. 297–344.

Neer 2011
Richard T. Neer. "Poussin's Useless Treasures." In *Judaism and Christian Art: Aesthetic Anxieties from the Catacombs to Colonialism*, edited by Herbert L. Kessler and David Nirenberg, pp. 328–58. Philadelphia, 2011.

Nichols 1994
Ann Eljenholm Nichols. *Seeable Signs: The Iconography of the Seven Sacraments, 1350–1544*. Woodbridge, 1994.

Nicolò 1991
Anna Nicolò. *Il carteggio di Cassiano dal Pozzo: Catalogo*. Quaderni del Rinascimento 11. Florence, 1991.

Oberhuber 1988
Konrad Oberhuber. *Poussin, the Early Years in Rome: The Origins of French Classicism*. Exh. cat., Kimbell Art Museum, Fort Worth. New York, 1988.

Olson 2002
Todd Olson. *Poussin and France: Painting, Humanism, and the Politics of Style*. New Haven and London, 2002.

Onori, Schütze, and Solinas 2007
Lorenza Mochi Onori, Sebastian Schütze, and Francesco Solinas, eds. *I Barberini e la cultura Europea del seicento: Atti del convego internazionale Palazzo Barberini alle Quattro Fontane, 7–11 dicembre 2004*. Rome, 2007.

Osborne and Claridge 1996
John Osborne and Amanda Claridge, eds. *Early Christian and Medieval Antiquities. The Paper Museum of Cassiano dal Pozzo: A Catalogue Raisonné*, series A, "Antiquities and Architecture," part 2. 2 vols. London, 1996.

Paleotti 2012 (ed.)
Gabriele Paleotti. *Discourse on Sacred and Profane Images*. [*Discorsi intorno alle imagini sacre et profane ed il abuso loro*, Bologna, 1582.] Translated by William McCuaig. Los Angeles, 2012.

Passeri 1934 (ed.)
Giovanni Battista Passeri. *Vite de'pittori, scultori, ed architetti*. In *Die Künstlerbiographien von Giovanni Battista Passaeri nach den Handschriften des Autors*, edited by Jacob Hess. Leipzig, 1934.

Patitucci Uggeri 2010
Stella Patitucci Uggeri. *San Paolo nell'arte paleocristiana*. Vatican City, 2010.

Poeschke 2010
Joachim Poeschke. *Italian Mosaics, 300–1300*. Translated by Russell Stockman. New York, 2010.

Porter 2011
Stanley E. Porter. "The Portrait of Paul in Acts." In Westerholm 2011, pp. 124–38.

Poussin 1989 (ed.)
Nicolas Poussin. *Lettres et propos sur l'art*. Edited by Anthony Blunt. Paris, 1989.

Powell 1985
Veronique Gerard Powell. "Les *Annales* de Baronius et l'iconographie religieuse du XVIIe siècle." In *Baronio e l'arte: Atti del convegno internazionale di studi, Sora, 10–13 ottobre 1984*, edited by Romeo de Maio, pp. 473–87. Sora, Italy, 1985.

Pullapilly 1975
Cyriac Pullapilly. *Caesar Baronius: Counter-Reformation Historian*. South Bend, Indiana, 1975.

Puttfarken 2000
Thomas Puttfarken. *The Discovery of Pictorial Composition: Theories of Visual Order in Painting, 1400–1800*. New Haven and London, 2000.

Rand 2006
Richard Rand. *Claude Lorrain—The Painter as Draftsman: Drawings from the British Museum*. Exh. cat., Clark Art Institute, Williamstown, Massachusetts. New Haven and London, 2006.

Rasmussen 1999
K. B. Rasmussen. "Traditio Legis." *Cahiers archéologiques* 47 (1999), pp. 5–37.

Reff 1960
Theodore Reff. "Cézanne and Poussin." *Journal of the Warburg and Courtauld Institutes* 23 (1960), pp. 150–74.

Reynolds 2000 (ed.)
Sir Joshua Reynolds. *The Letters of Sir Joshua Reynolds*. Edited by John Ingamells and John Edgcumbe. New Haven and London, 2000.

Rice 1997
Louise Rice. *The Altars and Altarpieces of New St. Peter's: Outfitting the Basilica, 1621–1666*. Cambridge and New York, 1997.

Richeome 1601
Louis Richeome. *Tableaux sacréz des figures mystiques du trés auguste sacrifice et Sacrement de l'Eucharistie*. Paris, 1601.

Rosenberg 1973
Pierre Rosenberg. *La "Mort de Germanicus" de Poussin, du Musée de Minneapolis*. Exh. cat., Musée du Louvre. Paris, 1973.

Rosenberg 1994
Pierre Rosenberg, ed. *Nicolas Poussin 1594–1665*. Exh. cat., Grand Palais. Paris, 1994.

Rosenberg and Christiansen 2008
Pierre Rosenberg and Keith Christiansen, eds. *Poussin and Nature: Arcadian Visions*. Exh. cat., The Metropolitan Museum of Art, New York. New Haven and London, 2008.

Rosenberg and Prat 1994
Pierre Rosenberg and Louis-Antoine Prat. *Nicolas Poussin 1594–1665: Catalogue raisonné des dessins*. 2 vols. Milan, 1994.

Scavizzi 1992
Giuseppe Scavizzi. *The Controversy on Images from Calvin to Baronius*. New York, 1992.

Schroeder 1978
Henry J. Schroeder, ed. and trans. *Canons and Decrees of the Council of Trent*. [1563.] Rockford, Illinois, 1978.

Schütze 1996a
Sebastian Schütze. "Aristide de Thèbes, Raphael et Poussin: La représentation des affetti dans les grands tableaux d'histoire de Poussin des années 1620–30." In Mérot 1996b, pp. 571–601.

Schütze 1996b
Sebastian Schütze. "Poussin interpretiert Tacitus 'le plus grand peintre de l'antiquité' – Der 'Tod des Germanicus' und sein historischer Kontext." In *Ars naturam adiuvans: Festschrift für Matthias Winner zum 11. März 1996*, edited by Victoria von Flemming and Sebastian Schütze, pp. 485–504. Mainz, 1996.

Scott 1995
Jonathan Scott. *Salvator Rosa: His Life and Times.* New
Haven and London, 1995.

Sellink and Leesberg 2001
Manfred Sellink and Marjolein Leesberg, eds. *Philips Galle.*
The New Hollstein Dutch & Flemish Etchings, Engravings,
and Woodcuts 1450–1700. Vol. 10. Rotterdam, 2001.

Shea and Artigas 2003
William R. Shea and Mariano Artigas. *Galileo in Rome: The
Rise and Fall of a Troublesome Genius.* Oxford, 2003.

Shearman 1972
John Shearman. *Raphael's Cartoons in the Collection of Her
Majesty the Queen and the Tapestries for the Sistine Chapel.*
London, 1972.

Simon 1978
Robert B. Simon. "Poussin, Marino, and Interpretation of
Mythology." *The Art Bulletin* 60, no. 1 (Mar. 1978), pp. 56–68.

Sohm 2001
Philip Sohm. *Style in the Art Theory of Early Modern Italy.*
Cambridge and New York, 2001.

Solinas 1989
Francesco Solinas, ed. *Cassiano dal Pozzo: Atti del seminario
internazionale di studi.* Rome, 1989.

Solinas 1992
Francesco Solinas. " 'Portare Roma a Parigi': Mecenati,
artisti ed eruditi nella migrazione culturale." In *Documentary
Culture: Florence and Rome from Grand-Duke Ferdinand I to
Pope Alexander VII,* edited by Elizabeth Cropper, Giovanna
Perini, and Francesco Solinas, pp. 227–61. Villa Spelman
Colloquia 3. Bologna, 1992.

Solinas 1996
Francesco Solinas. "Poussin et Cassiano dal Pozzo. Notes et
documents sur une collaboration amicale." In Mérot 1996b,
pp. 287–336.

Solinas 2000
Francesco Solinas, ed. *I segreti di un collezionista: Le
straordinarie raccolte di Cassiano dal Pozzo 1588–1657.* Exh. cat.,
Galleria Nazionale d'Arte Antica, Palazzo Barberini. Rome,
2000.

Sparti 1992
Donatella L. Sparti. *Le collezioni Dal Pozzo: Storia di una
famiglia e del suo museo nella Roma seicentesca.* Modena, 1992.

Sparti 2003
Donatella L. Sparti. "Cassiano dal Pozzo, Poussin, and the
Making and Publication of Leonardo's *Trattato.*" *Journal of
the Warburg and Courtauld Institutes* 66 (2003), pp. 143–88.

Spier 2007
Jeffrey Spier, ed. *Picturing the Bible: The Earliest Christian Art.*
Exh. cat., Kimbell Art Museum, Fort Worth. New Haven
and London, 2007.

Standring 1988
Timothy J. Standring. "Some Pictures by Poussin in the Dal
Pozzo Collection: Three New Inventories." *The Burlington
Magazine* 130 (Aug. 1988), pp. 608–26.

Stanic 1996
Milovan Stanic. "Le mode énigmatique dans l'art de
Poussin." In Bonfait et al. 1996, pp. 93–117.

Stoichita 1997
Victor I. Stoichita. *The Self-Aware Image: An Insight into Early
Modern Meta-Painting.* Translated by Anne-Marie Glasheen.
Cambridge and New York, 1997.

Thomas 2010
Troy Thomas. "Poussin, Gombauld, and the Creation
of *Diana and Endymion.*" *Art History* 33 (Sept. 2010), pp.
620–41.

Thompson 1980
Colin Thompson. *Poussin's Seven Sacraments in Edinburgh.*
Glasgow, 1980.

Thuillier 1967
Jacques Thuillier. "Temps et tableau: La théorie des
péripéties." In *Stil und Überlieferung in der Kunst des
Abendlandes: Akten der 21 Internationalen Kongresses für
Kunstgeschichte in Bonn.* Vol. 3, pp. 191–206. Berlin, 1967.

Thuillier 1988
Jacques Thuillier. *Nicolas Poussin.* Paris, 1988.

Thuillier 1994
Jacques Thuillier. *Nicolas Poussin.* Paris and New York, 1994.

Turner 1996
Nicholas Turner. "L'Autoportrait dessiné de Poussin au
British Museum." In Mérot 1996b, pp. 79–97.

Úbeda de los Cobos 2005
Andrés Úbeda de los Cobos, ed. *Paintings for the Planet King:
Philip IV and the Buen Retiro Palace.* Exh. cat., Museo del
Prado, Madrid. London, 2005.

Unglaub 2003
Jonathan Unglaub. "Poussin's *Esther before Ahasuerus*:
Beauty, Majesty, Bondage." *Art Bulletin* 85 (March 2003),
pp. 114–36.

Unglaub 2004
Jonathan Unglaub. "Poussin's Reflection." *The Art Bulletin*
86 (September 2004), pp. 505–28.

Unglaub 2006
Jonathan Unglaub. *Poussin and the Poetics of Painting: Pictorial Narrative and the Legacy of Tasso.* New York and Cambridge, 2006.

Unglaub 2011
Jonathan Unglaub. "Poussin and Rospigliosi: Novità, Copies, and Modes." In *"Novità": Neuheitskonzepte in den Bildkünsten um 1600,* edited by Ulrich Pfisterer and Gabriele Wimböck, pp. 447–70. Berlin, 2011.

Utro 2009
Umberto Utro, ed. *San Paolo in Vaticano: La figura e la parola dell'apostolo delle genti nelle raccolte pontificie.* Todi, Italy, 2009.

Utro 2011
Umberto Utro. "Alle origini dell'iconografia paolina." In *Paulo apostolo martyri: L'apostolo San Paolo nella storia, nell'arte e nell'archeologia,* edited by Ottavio Bucarelli and Martín María Morales, pp. 27–44. Rome, 2011.

Vagenheim 1992
Ginette Vagenheim. "Des inscriptions Ligoriennes dans le Museo Cartaceo pour une étude de la tradition des dessins d'apres l'antique." In Jenkins et al. 1992, vol. 1, pp. 79–104.

Vanuxem 1960
Jacques Vanuxem. "Les 'tableaux sacrés' de Richeome et l'iconographie de l'Eurcharistie chez Poussin." In *Nicolas Poussin,* edited by André Chastel, pp. 151–62. Paris, 1960.

Verdi 1982
Richard Verdi. "Poussin and the 'Tricks of Fortune.'" *The Burlington Magazine* 124 (Nov. 1982), pp. 681–85.

Verdi 1990
Richard Verdi. *Cézanne and Poussin: The Classical Vision of Landscape.* Exh. cat. National Gallery of Scotland, Edinburgh. London, 1990.

Verdi 1995
Richard Verdi. *Nicolas Poussin 1594–1665.* Exh. cat., Royal Academy of Arts. London, 1995.

Warwick 1999
Genevieve Warwick. "Poussin and the Arts of History." In *Commemorating Poussin: Reception and Interpretation of the Artist,* edited by Katie Scott and Genevieve Warwick, pp. 134–54. Cambridge and New York, 1999.

Westerholm 2004
Stephen Westerholm. *Perspectives Old and New on Paul: The "Lutheran" Paul and His Critics.* Grand Rapids, Michigan, 2004.

Westerholm 2011
Stephen Westerholm, ed. *The Blackwell Companion to Paul.* Oxford and Malden, Massachusetts, 2011.

Whitehouse 2001
Helen Whitehouse. *Ancient Mosaics and Wall Paintings. The Paper Museum of Cassiano dal Pozzo: A Catalogue Raisonné,* series A, "Antiquities and Architecture," part one. London, 2001.

Whiteley 1998
J. J. L. Whiteley. *Claude Lorrain: Drawings from the Collections of the British Museum and the Ashmolean Museum.* London, 1998.

Wilberding 1997
Erick Wilberding. "History and Prophecy: Selected Problems in the Religious Paintings of Nicolas Poussin." Ph.D. dissertation, Institute of Fine Arts, New York University, 1997.

Wilberding 2000
Erick Wilberding. "Poussin's Illness in 1629." *The Burlington Magazine* 142 (Sept. 2000), p. 561.

Wilpert 1903
Josef Wilpert. *Roma sotterranea: Le pitture delle catacombe romane.* 2 vols. Rome, 1903.

Wilton and Bignamini 1996
Andrew Wilton and Ilaria Bignamini, eds. *The Grand Tour: The Lure of Italy in the Eighteenth-Century.* Exh. cat., Tate Gallery. London, 1996.

Wine 2001
Humphrey Wine. *National Gallery Catalogues: The Seventeenth-Century French Paintings.* London, 2001.

Zanker 1995
Paul Zanker. *The Mask of Socrates: The Image of the Intellectual in Antiquity.* Translated by Alan Shapiro. Berkeley and Oxford, 1995.

Kimbell Art Museum, photograph by Robert LaPrelle (front cover; frontispiece; figs. 1, 3, 73, 83; pp. 4, 54, 64)